Russia's Oil Barons and Metal Magnates

Russia's Oil Barons and Metal Magnates

Oligarchs and the State in Transition

Stephen Fortescue

Associate Professor
School of Politics and International Relations
University of New South Wales, Australia

First published 2006 by
PALGRAVE MACMILLAN
Houndmills, Basingstoke, Hampshire RG21 6XS and
175 Fifth Avenue, New York, N.Y. 10010
Companies and representatives throughout the world.

PALGRAVE MACMILLAN is the global academic imprint of the Palgrave Macmillan division of St. Martin's Press, LLC and of Palgrave Macmillan Ltd. Macmillan® is a registered trademark in the United States, United Kingdom and other countries. Palgrave is a registered trademark in the European Union and other countries.

ISBN-13: 978–1–4039–8617–7
ISBN-10: 1–4039–8617–7

This book is printed on paper suitable for recycling and made from fully managed and sustained forest sources.

A catalogue record for this book is available from the British Library.

Library of Congress Cataloging-in-Publication Data
Fortescue, Stephen.
   Russia's oil barons and metal magnates : oligarchs and the state in transition / Stephen Fortescue.
      p. cm.
   Includes bibliographical references and index.
   ISBN 1–4039–8617–7 (hardback)
   1. Business people—Russia (Federation) 2. Privatization—Russia (Federation) 3. Wealth—Russia (Federation) 4. Russia (Federation)—Economic conditions—1991- I. Title.
HC340.12.F673 2006
338.092'247—dc22   2006045752

10 9 8 7 6 5 4 3 2 1
15 14 13 12 11 10 09 08 07 06

Printed and bound in Great Britain by
Antony Rowe Ltd, Chippenham and Eastbourne

In memory of Oleg

Contents

List of Tables   ix

Preface   xi

1 Introduction   1

A comparative historical perspective   2
Historical overview of the Russian oligarchs   8
Enemies of all   9
Western investors   17
Review of the evidence   18

2 Who are the Barons and Magnates?   21

The samples   21
The possibilities   24
The 'Gang of Seven'   25
The 'new oligarchs'   30
Conclusions   35

3 How Did They Get Rich?   40

The financial sector   41
Privatization   43
    Spontaneous privatization   44
    Mass privatization   45
Corporate governance   52
Shares-for-credit   54
The second *peredel*   60
Use of the courts, civil and criminal   65
The use of criminal 'authorities'   67
Corporate governance 'enlightenment'   71
Socially responsible business   73
Conclusions   75

**4   The Economic Performance of the Barons
     and Magnates**   **77**

Are oligarch companies worse off than they were before?   81
Norilsk Nickel   86
Apatit   87
North Urals Bauxite Mine (SUBR)   88
Yukos   89
Extraction of excessive returns   92
Investment   93
Conclusions   98

5   Oligarchy and Political Power   **99**

1991–95   100
1996–98   101
1998–2000   107
2000–03   108

6   Taxation in the Resource Sector   **112**

Tax in the mid-1990s   112
Tax in the late 1990s and beyond   117

7   The Yukos Affair   **121**

The arrest of Lebedov   121
The arrest of Khodorkovsky   123
The threat to Yukos   126
The sale of Yuganskneftegaz   130
What was it all about?   136

8   The Aftermath of Yukos   **149**

The Yukos effect: good or bad?   149
Investment and growth   152
Increased tax burden   155
Was justice done?   157
New concepts in tax law   163
Yukos, tax and democracy   168

9   Conclusion   **173**

Notes   180

Bibliography   220

Index   226

List of Tables

3.1	Results of shares-for-credit auctions	56
4.1	Russian oil production and exports, 1988–98, million tonnes	89
6.1	Profits and profits tax paid by the metals sector, billion rubles	114
6.2	Whole economy and metals sector as a percentage of gross domestic product	115
6.3	Tax takes as a percentage of sales	115
6.4	Tax payments by the metals sector into the federal budget, billion new rubles	116

Preface

The word 'oligarch' was deliberately avoided in the title of this book, and at various times during its writing consideration was given to avoiding its use wherever possible. As Hans-Henning Schröder has written:

> The term is overly used in political polemics and is employed so vaguely that the public associates completely heterogeneous ideas with it.[1]

Not only is it overused and heterogeneously so. It is also the case that Russia's oil barons and metal magnates have never closely resembled or even wanted to be an oligarchy in the strictest sense of the word. They never ran the country in the way the suffix '-archy', with its ancient Greek meaning of supreme power or rule, suggests they ought. With a small number of brief exceptions none of them has ever sought or held formal political office, and they have shown no inclination or capacity to determine policy in a whole range of areas that are fundamental to the running of the country.

Another reason to avoid the word is that for many who use it or witness its use by others it has strongly pejorative overtones. It is a concept which in its original usage by Plato and Aristotle was not seen as the ideal form of government and, least of all in our democratically informed times, it does not have a naturally positive ring to it. The particular circumstances in which the objects of our interest in this book came to prominence did nothing to attenuate the negative connotations of the word. After the arrests of Platon Lebedev and Mikhail Khodorkovsky in 2003, Arkadii Volsky, the head of the Russian Union of Industrialists and Entrepreneurs, the industrial association of which the oligarchs had become such prominent members, implored journalists, 'I beg you, don't call us the oligarchs' trade union, or even worse their club, any more.'[2]

These are all good reasons to avoid the word – too vague, inappropriate to the extent that it is precise, and value laden. In the end, though, it proved simpler to use it, rather than go to elaborate and at times awkward lengths to avoid it. It is so widely used that it would indeed seem almost perverse not to use it here. And although in day-to-day usage it might be unclear who is or is not included in the category of oligarch, the same could be said of the various alternatives – business elite, big business, economic bourgeoisie and so on. The title of the book probably describes best of all who is being written of here – the oil barons and metal magnates. But that is too much of a mouthful to use on a regular basis. And it is not actually totally accurate in describing those included in the category of oligarch for the purposes of the book, since a few of them are not primarily involved in oil or metals. But it does convey the major importance in both the Russian political economy and this book of the owners of Russia's privately held resource wealth

It is the private ownership of wealth that is part of the definition of oligarch used in this book, some might say arbitrarily so. However it is the author's belief that the political and economic behaviour of private owners and state-employed managers, no matter how narrowly self-interested the latter might be, is sufficiently different to warrant keeping the two separate. And over the last decade the activities of the private owners have been more important than those of the state-employed managers.

One of the key foci of the book is how the oligarchs run their businesses, in the economic and commercial sense. Are they efficient owners or not? But the author is after all a political scientist, and it is hard to devote much attention to the oil barons and metal magnates without coming across the political aspect of their activities. And so even if the oligarchs never made up an oligarchy, the word is useful in that it conveys consistently the political significance, and complexity, of the oligarch story.

While not denying Schröder's statement that the word is understood in many different ways, among specialists it has come to take on a reasonably consistent, if not strictly correct, meaning. In the opening paragraph of the introductory chapter President Putin's working definition of an oligarch is quoted: 'These people who fuse power and capital.' He has in mind the willingness and capacity to use economic power to influence politics and policy, in a way that greatly outstrips the capacity of other sectors of society to do so. It is not a purpose of this book to determine whether the oligarchs fused power and capital to the degree needed to justify the term 'oligarchy'. Having said that, how much political power the oligarchs have had and how they have used it, regardless of the definitional implications of the findings, will be an important part of the book.

As for the value-laden nature of the word, the reader will quickly learn that the purpose of this book is to evaluate, as objectively as possible, the oligarchs' contribution, whether it be good or bad, to the political and economic development of Russia. The approach of Guriev and Rachinsky is adopted here:

> We do not use the word to imply a legal, economic or moral judgement on Russia's richest businessmen, but merely as the conventional and convenient term for referring to Russian industrial tycoons.[3]

Like them, if the author has any subjective preconceptions regarding the oligarchs, it is more positive than negative.

So oligarchs, *aka* oil barons and metal magnates, they are. As already suggested the purpose of the book is to evaluate their contribution to Russia's development in the transition years. In economic terms it is a simple matter – simple in the statement if not the execution – of measuring whether their business activities, beginning with how they obtained their assets through to what they subsequently did with them, have been of net gain or loss to the Russian economy. In terms of politics the approach cannot be so straightforward, since at least as big a part of the story as the oligarchs' political activities is the political attitude of the state towards them, whether it be collaboration, capitulation or confrontation. Certainly there will be an evaluation of the good or ill that the oligarchs have brought to Russian political development. But no less important is the good or ill wrought by the state in its dealings with them.

The book has grown out of a project that in its conception was limited to the study of the Russian metals industry. There is therefore more on the metals industry than might be typical of a book on the oligarchs. The author would like to think that that is an important aspect of the book's contribution.

In the first chapter the arguments of those for and against the oligarchs are set out. In doing so many of the issues to be examined in more detail in the following chapters are identified. Chapter 2 is devoted to an analysis of the biographies of two samples of oligarch, the financial oligarchy that reached the peak of its influence in the mid-1990s, and the 'new' oligarchs, a group based in the 'real' economy from the beginning and which came to prominence somewhat later. The chapter undertakes to determine the extent to which the oligarchs shared a common background and to what extent background might have played a role in their subsequent careers. The next chapter follows their careers from their origins through to gaining 'oligarch' status. Attention is paid to the role of the state in promoting their careers, and why it might have done so. Chapter 4 examines their economic performance, essentially in terms of whether they have been the asset strippers their critics claim. In this chapter their management style is described, including changes over time. Chapter 5 outlines the political relationship of the oligarchs to the state, up to the arrest of Platon Lebedev, Mikhail Khodorkovsky's second-in-command, in July 2003. The story of subsequent developments in what has become known as the Yukos affair is held back until Chapter 7, with the intervening chapter briefly setting out the tax arrangements employed by the oligarchs, from the tax arrears of the mid-1990s through to the domestic offshore zones of the early years of the new decade. This is essential background for the detailed account in Chapter 7 of the Yukos affair, given the prominence of tax in it. Many other factors that might have played a role are also described. In the following, penultimate chapter those issues arising out of the Yukos affair with possible long-term ramifications are examined, including its effect on investment, the rule of law and the movement towards democracy. The final chapter, the Conclusion, very briefly summarizes the evidence for and against the oligarchs, before offering some speculative comment on future developments, in terms both of the transformation of the oligarchy into something with less concentrated economic power, and of the political consequences of such a development.

A quick word on transliteration. In the text I have used a 'user friendly' transliteration system, based on what I think looks least awkward for an English-speaking reader. In the footnotes I have used a stricter system, which means that there are often differences in the spelling of names in the text and the footnotes.

The funding for the project which grew into this book, called 'The Russian metals industry in transition', was provided by an Australian Research Council Large Grant (Number A79800192). I have gained much from my participation in three international research projects while working on the metals industry. For the invitation to participate in the project 'Transformation and Globalization – driving actors and factors of post-Soviet change' in Berlin, my thanks to Karl Segbers. Heiko Pleines was responsible for my involvement in the project 'The role of economic culture in Russia's tax system', based at the University of Bremen. I am currently involved in the project 'Does the geography of Russian peripheries really change?' at the University of Joensuu. My thanks to Markku Tykkylainen and in particular Vesa Rautio for being such steadfast friends and colleagues. I enjoyed the intellectual stimulation and hospitality of the Swedish Institute of Transition Economics during a sabbatical in Stockholm in the first three months of 2002. My thanks to Erik Berglof and the rest of the staff. Splendid accommodation was provided by the Wenner-Gren Foundation. During the following three months I was fortunate to be provided with facilities and intellectual engagement at the Centre for Economic and Financial Research at the New Economic School in Moscow. For many years I have enjoyed and gained much from visits to the Swedish National Defence Research Agency in Stockholm, and acknowledge my gratitude to Per-Olov Nilsson, Lars Wallin and Jan Leijonhielm. Many individuals have contributed in small and large ways to my work, and I will make no attempt to mention them all. But in addition to those already named I would like to say thanks in particular to Graeme Gill, Yakov Pappe, Sergei Peregudov, Kyle Wilson and Aleksei Zudin. And to Elena Fortescue, thanks for the research assistance and much more besides.

STEPHEN FORTESCUE

1
Introduction

There is a small group of immensely wealthy people in Russia who have inspired a richly lurid collection of book titles, such as *Godfather of the Kremlin. Boris Berezovsky and the looting of Russia; Sale of the Century. Russia's wild ride from communism to capitalism;* and *Casino Moscow. A tale of greed and adventure on capitalism's wildest frontier.*[1] They have also inspired their head of state, Vladimir Putin, to use language most unstatesmanlike in its brutality:

> These people who fuse power and capital: there will be no oligarchs of this kind as a class.[2]

And

> The state has a club, the kind that you only need to use once. Over the head. We haven't used the club yet. But when we get seriously angry, we will use this club without hesitation.[3]

The second statement speaks for itself. The first has strong Stalinist overtones, Stalin having notoriously spoken of the need to destroy the kulaks as a class through collectivization.[4]

Who are these people who have attracted such abuse and what have they done to deserve it? Those are the questions that will be answered in this book. Who they are in definitional terms is answered with admirable concision by Putin in the shorter statement immediately above: 'these people who fuse power and capital'. While a little strict for our purposes, it is nevertheless a good definition of 'oligarch', the word which, with all its shortcomings, has become the one most widely used to describe the people who are the centre of our attention. It is a word which in its collective form has been much used and abused as a political concept since first given currency by Plato and Aristotle over 2000 years ago.[5] In Russian usage the word often refers to anyone with power and privilege, the post-Soviet synonym of *nomenklatura* or Mafia, and sometimes interchangeably both.[6] But here we use Putin's definition, and deal with that very small group who have capital and have at least attempted to parlay it into political power, under both Yeltsin and Putin.

Part of our examination of the oligarchs' attempts to gain and use political power will be a discussion of whether in Russian circumstances the word 'oligarchy', as a collective noun, has any practical meaning. Some commentators doubt that the rich business people of whom we are speaking were ever even potentially able to overcome serious collective action problems so as to justify the application to them of a collective noun. 'Oligarch', as a singular noun, might be inherently meaningless. Nevertheless it is the common usage, meaning no more than a rich and influential individual. Whether that is the sum total of the concept, a group of individuals with no collective identity and consequently with no collective and ultimately little individual power, will be part of the discussion in this book.

We are not only interested in the political aspects of the oligarchs' presence in the Russian transition. We are also interested in the specifically economic use they have made of their capital. They have been subjected to just as much criticism for their abuse of economic power as political power. We will examine whether their commercial activities have been as catastrophic for the economy as is so often suggested.

We will also look at how both political and economic power is changing, in the short and long term. The short term involves close examination of what President Putin might be up to, politically and economically. In the longer term the question is whether and how the oligarchs can be transformed into what might be called more benignly a business elite.

Membership of the oligarchy has been by no means constant. Individuals have moved in and out as their political and economic fortunes have waxed and waned. Indeed, in the next chapter, in which the oligarchs are described in biographical terms, two 'longitudinal' examples are analysed. Even as one writes, the second, later sample is changing its composition.

A comparative historical perspective

Before moving on to concentrate on the oligarchy of the Russian transition, we will place the Russian oligarchs into some sort of historical perspective. Much of the existing analysis of the Russian oligarchy suggests – usually implicitly rather than explicitly – that the Russian experience is unique. One sees the occasional reference to the 'Robber Barons', but the reference is usually brief and journalistic. While the historically comparative approach in this volume will be cursory and far from fully developed, a sense of how business elites have formed and operated in the early stages of capitalist development in other places and at other times could well be useful, particularly when we attempt to outline some possible future paths of development in Russia. That attempt will be as speculative as this 'general theory of oligarchy' is crude.[7]

Oligarchies – small groups of people with economic power who use that power to make significant claims on political power – are most likely to appear when politico-economic systems are going through rapid and challenging change. In particular the state is challenged by the growing complexity and breadth of the demands on a ruler resulting from economic and technological change. The challenge might be such that the state – or at least the state system of rule – collapses altogether and new political arrangements have to be made. The change might be a matter of the sudden opening of new markets or even new domains, including the opening of new territories and acquisition of colonies. This radically shifts the balance of economic power and makes new demands on political governance in what has suddenly become, where colonies have been acquired, a metropolitan power. In most historical examples, the shift from the relationship of the state with traditional land-owning elites to a relationship with new commercial elites is the key factor.[8] Even strong states are likely to find new economic power-holders pushing for political power as those states suddenly find themselves facing radical new commercial opportunities or being transformed into imperial powers. In the new domains it is probable that brand new economic opportunities will arise, and the opportunity for brand new local politics as well. Indeed non-metropolitan oligarchies are likely to appear in the colonies of the imperial powers, particularly if the latter choose or are forced to 'rule at a distance'.

Highly violent revolutionary change probably makes it hard for economic power to coalesce around small groups of individuals, since it takes time to assert 'ownership' of economic assets in the requisite way. This suggests that oligarchs are likely to have some sort of roots in the past, which have given them privileged access to or claims on economic assets. This is certainly the view of those who see the Russian oligarchs as *nomenklatura*-based. That having been said, change has to be radical enough to challenge severely and compromise access to or claims on economic assets by existing elites. Regardless of where they come from the members of the oligarchy will be a self-consciously perceived, small and new group of claimants on power (which is not to say that they will not face serious collective action problems between themselves).

Initially oligarchies are likely to be based in the financial sector. States that are being challenged by new demands and opportunities need funding to meet those challenges. An important part of the challenge is that the state can no longer adequately fund its activities from its own immediate sources. To use the language of tax state theory, we are talking of the shift from a demesne state, in which rulers fund their activities from sources within their own possession, to a tax and fiscal state, in which rulers obtain funding through tax and borrowings.[9] How oligarchs are part of that shift specifically in terms of tax will be examined in more detail in a later chapter.

If new economic opportunities are to be taken advantage of by private operators, they also need to have funds. Who has the funds, whether they be for funding the state or private endeavours, but the bankers? Thus we find the bankers of the city states of the Italian Renaissance, the financiers of the Dutch and British empires, the High Finance of nineteenth-century French and German industrialization, and the financial oligarchs of early US capitalism.

But few nations are able to exist for long on the basis of finance alone, and therefore financial elites are not usually able for long to dominate the economy to the degree that would enable them to parlay economic power into exclusive political power. Financiers reproduce their money by giving it to others at interest. If they are prospering in such an activity, presumably so are those they are funding, who will then use their prosperity as the basis for claims on political power.

What happens at this stage is crucial. If financial elites are unable to maintain their dominance, what takes their place? Is it possible that a new group based on some other sector of the economy will lay claim to domination, or might economic power become so diffused that oligarchy would become an irrelevant term?

What happens depends to a considerable extent on the nature of the economy and the new economic opportunities that set off the whole process. For some, especially those in the Marxist tradition, the broad-based movement of capitalism beyond the financial-merchant state leaves the capitalists, as a class, in control. For others, a small elite within business dominates the capitalist class, but that elite sees it as its role in the political arena to defend the interests of the capitalist class as a whole rather than pursue its own particular interests.[10] Given that, oligarchy becomes an inappropriate word, particularly as once 'business' as a whole becomes the unit of analysis, most business and politics analysts would consider the interests of business to be so broad and internally contradictory as to leave plenty of room for other claimants to political power to have a realistic chance.

Oligarchy – a subset of business which does pursue its own interests in the political arena – is most likely to arise where economic activity and opportunities are narrow and focused. As examples we can mention the plantation economies of the New World, the railways of the late nineteenth century and, for our purposes most topically, resource economies.

Russia today, in terms of the outline presented so far, is the outcome of a state system, the Soviet Union, trying to maintain all aspects of economic activity within its domain but being unable to cope with the technological demands being made of it and as a consequence collapsing. The state system which replaced it did not wish to repeat the experiment of a state-owned and controlled economy, and so was strongly committed to private enterprise. The state needed money, and a financial oligarchy arose to provide it. But as the true opportunity for making money and dominating the economy was in the resource sector, that is to where the oligarchs gravitated. That process will be a major part of the story described in this book.

At the end of the book we will consider what might happen to the Russian oligarchs in the future. To inform that part of the book, what in general can we say about the survival prospects of oligarchies? To maintain themselves they need three things: continued dominance of the economy; a procedure for succession among their membership; and realistic claims on political power.

Continued dominance of the economy

An oligarchy generally needs to dominate a sector which dominates the rest of the economy. As economies change, however, once dominant sectors decline, leaving the oligarchy without an economic base for a privileged claim on political power. For example, in the United States the railways quite quickly ceased to be the dominant economic sector and centre of economic-based political power. This was partly a consequence of the railway industry ceasing, through saturation, to be a growth industry, and also because it was upstaged by other transport forms, particularly the car and its related oil industry. But the real story of the US economy is that it became too broadly based to support an oligarchy in any particular sector.

The New World plantation economies, and the oligarchies they nurtured, lasted longer. But in different ways, over a long period of time they were unable to retain their economic effectiveness. Often their plantation- and estate-owning oligarchs diversified into other areas – the big families of the Philippines representing a good example. But diversification always brings with it the risk of an oligarchy-undermining disintegration of common interests. A number of the Russian oligarchs have become engaged in a wide range of businesses outside their primary resource focus in recent years, and the effect on them as an oligarchy will receive some attention later in the book.

The resource issue is one of the biggest in contemporary development economics. The 'resource curse' is a popular concept to describe, on the one hand, the economic, political and social difficulties faced by nations that are heavily reliant on commodity resources and, on the other hand, the barriers they face as they try to diversify away from a resource reliance.[11] The debate over the resource curse, although in its detail outside the scope of this study, is fundamental to any consideration of the future of the Russian resource oligarchy. The continued dominance of the resource sector within the Russian economy would not guarantee the oligarchs their own continued dominance. But it would certainly be a better basis for long-term survival as an oligarchy than a more balanced economy.

Succession procedures

Oligarchs tend to be aggressively entrepreneurial individuals, for whom succession is likely to be a deeply personal matter, not something to be handled in terms of retirement packages, executive search agencies and so on. The most enduring oligarchies have been family-based. There have been famous banking dynasties from the time of the Italian city states through to modern times. The landowning elites of Latin America and the Philippines have been made up of a small number of powerful families.[12]

Families have the advantage of providing a basis for commonality of interests beyond the purely economic, indeed in forms that should be both durable and flexible. Nevertheless families are on the whole an inefficient form of economic management and succession. It is precisely the emotional aspect of family life which, when it is not providing bonding and commitment, acts as the source of conflict, passion and jealousy. Inheritance laws and practices can be particularly problematic. A primogeniture approach maintains the unity of the economic assets, but often at the cost of intense sibling rivalries. Family firms notoriously suffer from a lack of commitment and competence in the second and later generations.

In Russia the oligarchs are generally too young for succession to be an immediate issue, and the prospects for such succession to be family-based are as yet unclear. At this stage the betting would appear to be against it. There is an element of the Russian oligarchy which is unusual and of more immediate relevance than family-based succession. Most of the individual oligarchs have around them 'teams', a small group of colleagues who had often studied together and begun their businesses together. A topic of great current interest among analysts of Russian business is the immediate future of these teams, and how it relates to the increasing reliance on professional managers in oligarch firms. One would expect professional management to be not supportive of oligarchy.

Claims on political power

Oligarchies and oligarchs generally seem unwilling or unable to take official political office. The exception appears to be in Latin America and the Philippines (and some banking families in Renaissance Italy). In those cases the formally ruling oligarch sometimes appears able and willing to represent the interests of the rest of the oligarchy. At other times he or she is accused by other members of the oligarchy of pursuing personal or family interests, or the economic magnate turned ruler finds it impossible to ignore the interests and claims of social forces outside the economic elite. This suggests that oligarchs tend not to pursue formal political power, because to possess it would exaggerate the collective action problems that are rife within oligarchies. Not only are there clear temptations for the one with formal power to cheat on the rest. There are also the competing claims from outside the oligarchy that a formal leader cannot completely ignore. As well as that, there is no referee, no higher political leader, to whom feuding oligarchs can appeal, since the ruler-referee is one of their own.

Because oligarchs are by definition small in number and perhaps by inclination greedy, they always have a lot of potential opponents, making it difficult for them to achieve power and to keep it, particularly if their opponents are able to form alliances. And oligarchs are vulnerable in the sense that their economic power, although great, tends to be highly concentrated. This makes it relatively accessible to expropriation if a political opposition successfully mobilizes.

All this suggests that oligarchies are inherently unstable. They will probably break up of their own accord, as the economic basis of their power shifts and as they struggle with succession issues. And if they do not break up of their own accord, political opposition is likely to form against them.

How they break up is important for the long-term development of society. There are considerable risks involved in a political challenge, particularly if it is one that is not contemporaneous with or subsequent to shifts in the economic balance of power. Political attacks on oligarchs that retain their dominant position in the economy have to be based on expropriation, and are likely to have a populist element to them – the mobilization of the masses against the rich in a programme of 'dispossession'. It is probably better if economic shifts and succession can be allowed to run their course. That is something that can be considered further in the Russian context. There, economic shifts and succession are both problematic – the resource dominance of the economy is hard to shake off, and in most cases succession is some years off. Perhaps that is one reason why the oligarchs have been subjected to a political challenge, and indeed a challenge that bears many of the signs of being of the authoritarian populist variety. Whether that is in fact the case, and whether it has to be, will make up the discussion in the final pages of this book.

Historical overview of the Russian oligarchs

We will now shift from a very broad and generalized account of the rise and fall of oligarchies in capitalist societies to a brief overview of relevant events in Russia over the last 15 or so years.

In the late Soviet Union opportunities began to open up for vigorous entrepreneurial activity. The illegal blackmarket activities that had become so widespread in the late Brezhnev period were semi-legalized under Gorbachev. Many thousands of Russians took advantage of the new opportunities. Some were small-time blackmarketeers; some were operating out of middle-level bureaucratic and scientific research positions. The most prominent found themselves, as the Soviet Union collapsed and in the early years of transition, focusing ever more strongly on the financial sphere. By the mid-1990s, as bankers this small group had become sufficiently wealthy, and occupied such strategic positions in the economy, that they were able to exercise considerable political influence, most spectacularly in their funding of Yeltsin's re-election campaign in 1996.

Another less prominent group of entrepreneurially minded individuals eschewed the financial sector and in the first half of the 1990s was building up its presence in the so-called 'real economy', most particularly in the oil and metals industries. Some of the financial magnates were also interested in the real economy, buying into it in the mass privatization programme of the early 1990s and most controversially in the shares-for-credit deals of 1995.

That began the transformation of the oligarchs into the resource owners who are the primary focus of interest in this book, a transformation that was given added force by the financial crisis of August 1998. In the immediate aftermath of August 1998 many commentators proclaimed 'the death of the oligarchs'. While it might have marked the death of the oligarchs as primarily bankers, in more general terms the obituaries were premature.[13] Those oligarchs who had strong positions in the real economy survived the crisis and, although in a significant number of cases they retained financial interests, their primary commitment was now in the resource sector.

The focus of commentators' attention has been on the oligarch presence in the oil sector. It is the dominant sector of the economy in private hands and deservedly attracts the most attention. However there are oligarchs and oligarchical behaviour in the metals sector as well. While not quite a primary resource in the way that crude oil is, Russian metals in the transition period are primarily commodity metals sold on the global market. The economics of the metals sector is therefore similar to that of the oil sector and consequently its ownership, governance and political characteristics are also similar. As reflected by the title, in which metal magnates join the better-known oil barons, the metals sector will receive considerable attention in this book.

Although the 1998 financial crisis was a very testing time, the coming to power of Vladimir Putin in 2000 proved even more problematic for the oligarchs. Two prominent members of the group, Vladimir Gusinsky and Boris Berezovsky, were quickly forced into exile under threat of arrest. Then in 2003 Mikhail Khodorkovsky, one of the biggest of the resource oligarchs, was imprisoned. While the true significance of that drama is still unfolding, it appears unlikely that it was directed purely against Khodorkovsky, without any implications for the others. But whether that means that their days are inevitably numbered remains to be seen. Or will they be allowed to maintain their positions under new rules of the game, and if so will they be able to continue to influence the setting of the new rules? Those are questions to which we will return later in the book.

Enemies of all

Throughout the waxing and waning of their political and economic fortunes, there have been consistently negative attitudes towards the oligarchs from a number of important sources of opinion, including senior Russian political leaders, the Russian people, Western and Russian academic commentators and international agencies.

The political leadership

Even under Yeltsin the official attitude towards the oligarchs was not consistently positive. The liberals who drove economic policy had at best an ambivalent and essentially instrumental attitude towards them. They might have been tolerated as part of the transition to capitalism and even welcomed as an instrument in the destruction of the final remnants of Soviet socialism but their style of 'oligarchic capitalism' was far from the reformers' ideal, and at some point steps to reduce their role would be required. The more ideologically pure of the liberals were particularly nervous about them, but their free market ideology made it difficult for them to put in place controls on the oligarchs' activities. There was another group of liberals, of a more pragmatic and instrumental approach, who arrived at a strategic commitment to fostering big business. But even Anatolii Chubais, one of the most instrumental of the reformers, alluded to the tension in the relationship in a November 2003 interview:

> So in 1996, using the newly created Russian big business, we resolved the problem of 'communism in Russia'. But then that very big business decided that at last everything was in place and now it will begin to run the country.

According to Chubais, the government then had to work hard to get the message across to business that it was not its job to run the country and, he claimed, had had some success in doing so.[14]

The greatest governmental opposition to the oligarchs during the Yeltsin presidency came from the Kirienko government, briefly in power in 1998. He and others in his government, particularly Boris Nemtsov and Boris Fedorov, were harshly critical of the oligarchs. The following quotation is not from Putin in 2003, but Fedorov, as Minister of Finance, in mid-1998: 'You guys are not paying taxes. We'll arrest you, we'll take your property, we'll make your companies bankrupt.'[15] Nemtsov, as deputy prime minister, described 'oligarchic capitalism' in the most negative terms:

> The reason for this crisis is that after seven years of trying to build a market economy, we've ended up with oligarchic capitalism ... It is

characterized by the fact that a few FIGs [financial-industrial groups], which, incidentally, work very inefficiently and are managed by greedy managers whose aim is to pump money out of their enterprises and stockpile it abroad, produce the lion's share of GDP.[16]

Yeltsin himself said in his 1999 presidential address:

> The Bank of Russia and the government have begun work on the restoration of the banking system. But if it is restored in its previous form, then we will end up with nothing other than new 'oligarchs'.[17]

The oligarchs were able, on the whole, to withstand the attacks on them from the reformers. But as the quotations that opened this chapter indicate, it was when Vladimir Putin came to power that the oligarchs found themselves firmly on the wrong side of the rhetoric at the top levels of Russian political power. This is not the place to describe and analyse Putin's attitudes towards the oligarchs in detail – that will come in a later chapter. Suffice it to say at this stage that, while his attitudes and behaviour have in fact been more ambiguous and inconsistent than the quotations above might suggest, nevertheless the net effect of his ascension to the presidency has been a significant diminution in the oligarchs' power and status.

Despite his *silovik* origins and orientations,[18] as a politician Putin is strongly committed to maintaining a high degree of popularity among the general voting population,[19] not least because he does not want to find himself in the situation in which Yeltsin found himself, of having to surrender to the oligarchs because he had no support anywhere else. Putin bases his appeal to the population on a combined promise to provide stability and to deal toughly with those who threaten that stability. The element of contradiction within that dual promise is strongly evident in the area of domestic security, most particularly the Chechnya issue. But it is also evident in his relations with the oligarchs. They are presented as a threat to political stability through their manipulation of the media and over-vigorous lobbying, and to economic stability through their theft of the nation's rent. But in order to deal with them as sternly as required, there is a threat to the very economic growth which is such a strong component of his high poll ratings. Putin has stated things in precisely these terms in comments on resource sector tax rates. In a TV address in December 2003 he described the oil sector as 'the goose that lays the golden eggs', and assured the audience that killing it would be 'stupid and impermissible' and 'won't happen'.[20]

Whether he wants to or will be able to keep his word on that score will be a key theme of this book.[21]

Popular opinion

While Putin is aware of the need not to kill the golden goose, strong anti-oligarch popular sentiment allows him to get away with subjecting it to considerable pain. Polls conducted in recent years, while Putin's anti-oligarch campaigns have been in full swing, show that something like 60–75 per cent of the population believe that the oligarchs play a negative role in society.[22] In a poll taken at the time of the arrest of Platon Lebedev, 88 per cent believed that wealth could only be gained illegally and 77 per cent disapproved of the way the oligarchs used the assets they had gained through privatization.[23] When Khodorkovsky himself was arrested a few months later only 11 per cent of respondents viewed the measures taken against him negatively. It is claimed that even in towns to which Yukos, by all reports, had brought a degree of prosperity, attitudes towards Khodorkovsky are negative.[24] A poll in early 2005 found that 43 per cent of respondents wanted the government to continue to 'settle accounts' with big business, with only 16 per cent opposed. When asked whether the energy sector should be nationalized, 45 per cent responded positively, although the percentage opposed was a substantial 33 per cent. Only 5 per cent thought that energy companies should be sold to foreigners.[25] As Igor Bunin puts it: 'Social support for business is therefore too small for business to be able to count on successfully competing with the state.'[26]

In later chapters the relationship between Putin and popular attitudes towards the oligarchs will be analysed in more detail.

Western commentators

A sense of the attitude of Western commentators towards the oligarchs can be gained from the titles of recently published books cited in the first sentence of this chapter. In what is now a large literature, ranging from the journalistic to the academic, Western writers find grounds for condemnation in the very origins of the oligarchs as individuals, the origins of their wealth, their ongoing activities, and their effect on the political, economic and social well-being of Russia and the transition. If they do not derive from the Soviet Union's *nomenklatura*, its petty blackmarket, or the *tolkach* or professional criminal class, then they are representatives of an entirely new and no less disreputable social category, the 'new Russians'.[27]

The oligarchs used illicit means of various kinds, including corruption and extreme violence, to build up their start-up capital. They then used their newly acquired capital to further pervert the political and bureaucratic process in order to seize the most lucrative and strategic economic assets, particularly in the media and resource sectors. Since they gained their most lucrative assets through privatization they are accused of not being genuine entrepreneurs, because they have not created anything new. Marshall Goldman, for example, makes it clear that this shortcoming applies to both those who made their fortunes in the dubious circumstances of the late Soviet and early transition financial and consumer services sectors, and those who throughout concentrated on the 'real economy'.[28] Joseph Stiglitz writes that 'America's robber barons created wealth, even as they accumulated fortunes. They left a country much richer, even if they got a big slice of the larger pie. Russia's oligarchs stole assets, stripped them, leaving their country much poorer.'[29]

Western commentators further claim they are guilty of gross misdeeds in the areas of corporate and financial governance, engaging on a massive scale in asset stripping, skimming and looting, capital flight and tax evasion. Andrew Barnes, in his comparative study of the transitional political economies of Poland, the Czech Republic and Russia, sees Russia as deserving the generic label 'asset destruction', as against Hungary's 'asset development' and the Czech Republic's 'asset limbo'.[30] Black, Kraakman and Tarassova, in one of the most detailed academic critiques of privatization and corporate governance, persistently describe the big Russian business owners, including most specifically Mikhail Khodorkovsky, as kleptocrats, who appropriated to themselves the value in their dubiously obtained assets and hid it overseas.[31] They are seen as responsible for most of the problems of Russia, including gross social inequality, the crowding out of less well-connected local business people, a forbidding investment climate for outside investors, and the total loss of legitimacy of both political and economic reform in the eyes of both the state and the population.[32] Black, Kraakman and Tarassova call in strong terms for the dispossession of the kleptocrats, including the use of some 'exemplary justice'.[33]

Some of the best-known names among pro-reform analysts have also been critical of the oligarchs. Anders Åslund, for example, blames the 1998 crash on, among others, 'the so-called oligarchs, big businessmen who thrived on high interest rates carried by the government bonds'. He praises Putin's tax reforms for ending the 'special privileges in the form of negotiated taxes' that the oligarch companies had enjoyed (although he is unenthusiastic about the Yukos affair). However he also notes that 'Russia's economic growth has been generated by the large competitive private companies that controlled the resource sector'. While he appears to be more approving of the 'new oligarchs', where he draws the line between the old and the new is not entirely clear.[34] Åslund's more positive views will be described a little later. Another high-profile Western reformer, Jeffrey Sachs, is quoted in 1999 as conceding to having been 'overly optimistic about . . . mass privatization' and admitting that all too often the result was 'corrupt asset grabs, managerial plunder of enterprises, and paralysis of firms'.[35]

Russian academic commentators speak of the oligarchs in similar terms. Dzarasov and Novozhenov claim that mass privatization drove out of enterprises the 'last effective Soviet managers – people who were genuinely interested in the success of their enterprises'. Their place was taken by 'those representatives of the *nomenklatura* and criminal world who earlier than everyone else rejected communist values and who were least fussy in their methods'. Their interest is in short-term gains, rather than long-term investment and growth. 'The typical big Russian businessman more closely resembles an adventurist and feudal baron than a rational entrepreneur.' Because he has bought his assets at below market value, asset stripping is profitable for him, and he extracts insider rent through the exploitation of his employees, reduced investment, expropriation of minority shareholders, the breaking of contracts, and non-payment of taxes.[36] However like Åslund, Dzarasov and Novozhenov, in a way to be described in more detail later, see some positive management benefits that oligarchs have brought to large-scale Russian industry.

International agencies

Less strident, but no less telling, has been criticism of the oligarchs from international agencies. The main focus of the criticisms of the Russian economy coming out of the World Bank and European Bank for Reconstruction and Development in recent years has been excessive levels of concentration, particularly the proportion of total economic activity that is derived from a small number of very large industrial groups. Usually it is noted that these groups are based in the resource sector, meaning not just that the economy is over-concentrated, but that it is over-dependent on resource exports.

The problem is usually described in relatively restrained and technical terms: that there is no evidence that big firms perform better than small firms; that there is evidence that small firms are starved of investment.[37] But the subtext is usually clear, and occasionally surfaces in the form of statements on the political implications of the concentration of economic power. A World Bank report carefully claims:

> The data confirm that ownership rights in Russia are highly concentrated, although this concentration is subject to wide variation across sectors. The data also show the ambivalent role of large owners in economic development. Such owners can use their investment resources for new capital formation and for the acceleration of growth. However, they may also often become large not because of economic merit but because they operate in an environment characterized by weak market institutions and inadequate enforcement of rules. This environment rewards size because it allows more effective lobbying and influence peddling. Thus the large owners can just as well become a brake on growth by subverting resources and by colluding with state structures or with each other.[38]

The European Bank for Reconstruction and Development stated that big companies systematically destroyed entrepreneurial initiative, and saw the main economic reform task as reducing dependence on the energy sector.[39] Willem Buiter, the then chief economist of the EBRD, albeit with a 'personal view' disclaimer, in 2000 referred to the 'widespread predation', which together with insecure property rights, had 'depressed capital formation in all its dimensions'.[40]

Raghuram Rajan, appointed chief economist of the IMF in October 2003, had earlier that year co-authored a book very critical of the oligarchs. There it was stated that the oligarchs'

> primary competence was contacts rather than business acumen. It is little wonder that these 'businessmen' came to be known as oligarchs, reminiscent of the reactionary feudal lords who stood in the way of capitalism. Not only do these oligarchs oppose the development of free markets and free access to finance, but they also offer little countervailing force to a powerful state. Since their empires are not built on competence, they can be taken away as easily as they were acquired.[41]

The international agencies have been almost as careful in their comments on Putin's most recent anti-oligarch actions, specifically the hounding of Khodorkovsky and Yukos, as they were in their criticism of big business. In the World Bank report just quoted there is very restrained approval of Putin's efforts to extract more tax from big business. In recalculating Russia's national accounts to adjust for transfer pricing – a process which greatly increases the oil and gas sector's share of the economy – the authors of the study state:

> [R]ecalculating the national accounts raises the particular issue of tax loopholes for the oil and gas sectors . . . [T]he high profitability of the firms in question provides a strong economic rationale for enforcing full tax payments.[42]

Khodorkovsky and Yukos are not specifically mentioned in the report. An earlier, November 2004 report from the World Bank's Moscow office had been even more careful in referring to tax issues within the sector:

> [I]ncentives in the oil sector currently suffer from an overall high degree of uncertainty over future tax and regulatory conditions. The investment climate would certainly profit from a clarification of stable conditions for the future division of profits between oil companies and the government.
>
> . . . While high rates of taxation on this sector of the economy make sense in general, it is important that tax and other regulatory conditions remain consistent with strong incentives and financial opportunities for the healthy development of the industry. Some analysts claim that marginal taxation in this industry has become excessive from this point of view, and this question requires careful attention.[43]

The EBRD has spoken positively of Putin's tax reform, including 'a general shift of the tax base towards the extractive industries'.[44] However in recent reports it has also referred specifically to the Yukos affair (although coyly refusing to refer to Khodorkovsky by name) in very carefully critical terms. While noting that a strengthening of the judiciary is necessary to prevent corporate governance abuses, one report states:

> The current administration's efforts to rein in big business may address this problem, but in doing so could raise another concern: the perception that the law is being applied selectively to those who disagree with the authorities. The merits of the case against the oil company Yukos and its founder for tax-related offences will be decided by the courts. While these charges against Yukos are in conformity with Russian law, critics have noted several instances in which due process and compliance with Russian legal procedures and statutes have been

exceeded. Further, the decision to prosecute this business group and not others who are believed to have committed similar offences has given rise to questions of arbitrary use of the judicial system.[45]

The report also suggests:

> More clarity will be needed on the part of the Government with regard to the role of the state in the economy. Establishing transparent, pre-dictable and fair rules of the game for all market participants is another key challenge. An early, transparent and market-oriented resolution of the Yukos affair would be an important step in this direction.[46]

It is not clear what a market-oriented resolution might entail.

In practice the World Bank, through its International Finance Corporation, is prepared to work with those oligarchs who, in the words of an executive vice-president of the IFC, are prepared to 'make a real contribution to the development of Russia, who return capital to the country, who strive to make their companies transparent (even if that is not immediately achieved in full)'. The IFC, in some cases in partnership with EBRD, has given money to Severstal, SUAL and Lukoil, three oligarch controlled companies.[47]

Western investors

While the international agencies have been extremely careful and ambiguous in their commentary, Western investors are blunter in the expression of their feelings. Many of them have been badly bruised in their dealings with the oligarchs.

When in 2004 the Russian parliament was considering government-sponsored amendments to the corporations act, to allow shareholders with holdings over 90 per cent to buy out other shareholders on an involuntary basis, one prominent Western banker involved in the Russian market, William Browder of Hermitage, protested:

> We are sure that President Putin will not allow the oligarchs, the main shareholders of big Russian companies, to sow panic in the Russian financial market, by bringing such amendments into force.[48]

Hoffman comments that Westerners, especially those active in the financial markets, were pleased with Putin's attacks on the oligarchs; Pappe concurs that international business does not like 'oligarchical behaviour'.[49] When Oleg Deripaska claimed in early 2004 that Russia was not a good place to invest, foreign financial advisors retorted that he was talking that way just to discourage outsiders from providing competition. Russia, in fact, has the highest rates of return in the world, 'because there is insufficient competition. And that is because of the likes of Deripaska.'[50]

Review of the evidence

The condemnation of the oligarchs is vigorous and wide-ranging. Essentially they are blamed for all the ills of political and economic transition. They are seen as the visible tip of the Mafia or old *nomenklatura* icebergs. They misuse relational capital and corrupt and bully both elected and appointed officials. They expropriated state assets through rigged privatization deals and dispossessed minority shareholders through corporate governance abuses. They then stripped the assets they had so dubiously obtained through transfer pricing, capital flight and tax evasion on a monumental scale. They ensure that the Russian economy remains highly dependent on low value-added commodity resource exports, but keep the lion's share of the profits to themselves, indeed to the degree not just that the state and society are deprived of a just return, but that the assets themselves are run down and depleted.

The charges are serious, and often supported with convincing evidence. The oligarchs, nevertheless, do have their defenders. Åslund, who we have already cited as a critic, is nevertheless able to describe them as

> economically highly useful. They are a natural product of large economies of scale and little legal security, and very large enterprises can hardly develop without them . . . It is difficult to see how a market economy could be introduced under these conditions without generating super-rich businessmen. The emergence of oligarchs is a natural consequence of the prevailing conditions.[51]

The oligarchs' supporters, rather than focusing on their criminal or *nomenklatura* origins, believe them to have shown themselves, often from the very beginnings of their adult life in the late Soviet Union, to be people with highly developed entrepreneurial instincts and the determination to use them. They took advantage of the opportunities provided them by a reforming government to build new businesses from scratch. That gave them the start-up capital to displace Soviet-era managers and bureaucrats with no entrepreneurial instincts or capabilities from existing run-down Soviet-era assets. They very quickly improved the management of the enterprises they moved into and brought them back to life. As Shleifer and Treisman claim:

> Oligarch-controlled companies have performed extremely well, and far better than many comparable companies that remained controlled by the state or by their Soviet-era managers. They are responsible for much of the dramatic increase in output in recent years, as well as the amazing stock market book.[52]

While the methods they used were necessarily rough and ready, the concentration of corporate control they eventually won for themselves encouraged the oligarchs to adopt a long-term view of corporate development that was reflected in an increased willingness to invest. They even began to recognize that their own capacity to develop their businesses was limited, and so turned to outsiders, including foreign investors and managers. They undertook the reforms of corporate governance and financial accounting needed to attract such outsiders. The concentration of economic power in their hands is typical of the global economy and essential to be competitive within it. The dominance of the resource export sector is the natural reflection of comparative advantage, and anyway the resource oligarchs have shown a willingness to invest in non-resource sectors of the Russian economy. Rather than rapacious asset strippers, from the beginning they have been effective creators and reproducers of wealth. With time they have become ever more 'civilized' in their approach.

Politically, while they might have at times misused the political system to protect their own interests to an excessive degree, nevertheless the oligarchs served a useful function in destroying the last remnants of Soviet socialist corporate control and management. They are needed to continue to serve as a counterweight to bureaucratic and authoritarian forces. In the words of Guriev and Rachinsky:

> Some consider the oligarchs to be the engine of Russia's economic recovery and institutional reform since 1999. As oligarchs are the only currently feasible counterweight to the predatory and corrupt Russian bureaucracy, they are a unique constituency that is both willing and able to lobby for development of market institutions. They are also the only Russian owners who can afford to invest and restructure Russian industries in a very hostile environment.[53]

We have vigorously presented charges against the oligarchs, as well as a defence. Given the situation in which Russia finds itself at the moment, a very cool-headed and objective examination of both the charges and the defence is called for. It is a time when Russia has been enjoying its first period of reasonably sustained growth since the beginning of transition. Is that growth because of or in spite of the oligarchs' domination of the economy and perhaps of policy making also? Is it a brief window of opportunity to put Russia on the path to truly sustained prosperity which can be seized only by dispossessing the oligarchs and freeing up Russia's resource wealth for genuine development? Or is to attack the oligarchs to destroy what progress has been made, just at the time when they have been showing serious signs of adopting an approach to corporate governance and management that would earn Russian business a secure place in the global economy?

We will begin the task of answering those questions by examining the origins – social and entrepreneurial – of the oligarchs. Were their origins as shady as often claimed? Does it matter? Those questions will be posed in the next chapter.

2
Who are the Barons and Magnates?

Particularly among those who are ill-disposed towards the oligarchs it is often implied or explicitly stated that their malevolent behaviour and pernicious effect on Russian society derive from some particular aspect of their Soviet backgrounds. Those who view them in more benign terms are likely to be impressed by market-oriented entrepreneurial skills that they came to possess in unpromising Soviet circumstances but which could be put to good use only after the collapse of communism.

The purpose of this chapter is to outline the backgrounds of the oligarchs and the ways, if at all, those backgrounds played a role in their rise to wealth. As Bunin suggests, in noting their varied backgrounds, a high degree of consistency in origin would allow for stronger conclusions on the role of background in their emergence:

> It is clear that the new class is formed from various sources – from proto-entrepreneurs from the time of stagnation, mainly operating in the structures of the shadow market; from representatives of the *nomenklatura* who, undergoing social conversion, have found themselves a place in a new economic space; 'Red Directors' who have successfully changed colour; and, finally, from new people ('new Russians', to use the phrase made popular by the newspaper *Kommersant*). It is important to determine which group dominates quantitatively and in a psychological and ideological sense.[1]

The samples

The first task that faces us is to identify who we have in mind when we refer to the oligarchs. Two important events in the transition period – the financial collapse of August 1998 and the replacement of Yeltsin as

21

president by Putin – produced such changes in the membership of the oligarchy that two samples are required.[2] As one writes, changes in the second sample are taking place.

The first sample is of a very small group of bankers who were seen by some commentators as totally dominating the Russian political economy, particularly in the second half of Yeltsin's term as president. Around 1996 the Russian word *semibankirshchina* ('the time of the seven bankers') came into circulation.[3] The notorious 'Gang of Seven' (G7) were: Berezovsky, Vinogradov, Gusinsky, Potanin, Smolensky, Fridman and Khodorkovsky.[4] Many of these individuals began their entrepreneurial careers with friends and acquaintances, often fellow students, who continue even now to play a major role in their corporate activities.

Because of events from 1998 through into the Putin presidency, the G7 is not a very useful sample for analysis of the situation today. Two of the seven, Smolensky and Vinogradov, either chose not to or were unable to take advantage of the shares-for-credit deals of the mid-1990s, and paid the price in the August 1998 crisis by not having a resource base to fall back on when their financial empires crumbled.[5] Two more, Gusinsky and Berezovsky, failed to survive the early days of Putin. Since their falls from grace were related to their media activities, not to any resource issues, their situation was different from that in which Khodorkovsky later found himself. Nevertheless, the imprisonment of Khodorkovsky leaves only two of the G7 still on the scene, Potanin and Fridman. As we will see later in the book, both have had their moments of extreme insecurity in recent times.

With only those two remaining, we clearly need a new sample. As recognized by Anders Åslund, there is indeed a number of 'new oligarchs' who can be used to make a new list. It is a list which is much more resource-oriented than the first 'bankers' list. These are 'a group of new young entrepreneurs ... that has consolidated ownership of each large-scale mature industry (such as oil, steel, aluminium, nonferrous metals, and coal) into a handful of large companies'.[6] The resource orientation is appropriate, given that since the move of the more prescient bankers into the resource sector the main focus of the oligarch debate has shifted from financial to resource rents. This process was greatly accelerated by the financial crisis of 1998.

The second sample is bigger than the first, and is made up of names less familiar to casual observers of the Russian scene. Some of those on it had quietly established themselves in the resource sector early in transition, without taking the banking route of the G7. Others are more recent arrivals. A good number of them are based in the metals sector, resembling their oil-sector colleagues in that their wealth is based on the export of non-manufactured commodities.[7] The names on the list are: Abramov, of the steel and coal producer Evrazkholding; Abramovich, until recently of the oil producer Sibneft; Alekperov, of the oil producer Lukoil; Bogdanov, of the oil producer Surgutneftegaz; Vekselberg, of the aluminium producer SUAL and the oil firm TNK; Deripaska, of the aluminium producer Rusal; Lisin, of the Novolipetsk Metal Combine, a steel producer; Makhmudov, of the Urals Mining-Metals Corporation, primarily involved in copper; Melnichenko, of the financial conglomerate MDM; Mordashov, of the steel producer Severstal; and Rashnikov, of the Magnitogorsk Metal Combine, another steel producer.[8]

The ownership structures of the Russian resource sector, and therefore the make-up of the 'new' oligarch sample, are not fully settled. Most noticeably Roman Abramovich has over the last couple of years sold all his Russian resource assets. He sold his half share in the dominant aluminium producer, Rusal, to its founder Oleg Deripaska, in two tranches in 2003 and 2004, and then in 2005 sold Sibneft to Gazprom.[9] In mid 2006 it was unexpectedly announced that he was buying a 41 percent holding in Abramovis Evrazkholding, the steel and coal producer. The beneficiary of the dismemberment of Yukos, Sergei Bogdanchikov of Rosneft, has moved into the list of the most important Russian business people. However, because Rosneft is a state-owned company, Bogdanchikov, like Miller of Gazprom, does not fit the criteria for inclusion in our sample.

In the ferrous metals sector private newcomers, who might some time soon justify inclusion in the sample, are becoming more prominent. Alisher Usmanov is attracting the most attention. Born in Uzbekistan in 1953, he has a classic middle-level *nomenklatura* background. After graduating from the elite Moscow State Institute of International Relations in 1976, he worked in the apparatus of the Uzbek Komsomol Central Committee and then as general director of the Foreign Economic Assistance Association of the Soviet Peace Committee. After working in various financial companies in the 1990s, including the 'pocket' bank of the aircraft manufacturer MAPO, in 1998 he began work at Gazprom. Described as a close friend of former Gazprom head Rem Vyakhirev, he was put in charge of the gas monopolist's metals industry arm Gazprominvestkholding, a position he still holds. But he has worked harder on his private activities, forming a partnership with Vasilii Anisimov, once a middle-ranking figure in the aluminium industry, to build up a major group based on Russia's European iron ore producers, as well as the Oskol Electrometal Combine and Mechel. He now controls over

50 per cent of Russian iron ore output and 12 per cent of steel. That puts him in the same league as the other steel magnates in our sample, Lisin, Mordashov, Rashnikov and Abramov.[11]

The possibilities

Having devised our samples, our task now is to record the origins and early career paths of the identified oligarchs. To provide a basis for analysis and comparison, we will take as a start the four types identified by Bunin: blackmarketeers, members of the *nomenklatura* (*nomenklaturshchiki*), Red Directors and new Russians. Without being too precise in our definitions, each type needs some explanation. Blackmarketeer refers to more than the day-to-day under-the-counter dealings that nearly every Soviet citizen engaged in. But neither does it necessarily mean the large-scale underground production operations of some of the biggest participants in the Soviet black market. Nevertheless we are referring to the unofficial buying and selling of goods and services at a level that would have been seen by the individual involved as a 'business' meant to bring a financial return. As the scope for such activities became ever wider under Gorbachev, and might even have been legalized under cooperative legislation, it could have become a business profitable enough to provide the start-up capital for a serious entrepreneurial career in new post-Soviet circumstances.

Members of the *nomenklatura* for our purposes are those making careers in the party, Komsomol (Young Communist League) or non-industrial state hierarchies. This is a somewhat narrower meaning of the word than when it is used to denote elite, privileged status regardless of area of activity. As with any elite-based concept there is the question of how far down the hierarchy we go. Here we include officials some way below the highest levels of the party–state hierarchy.

One reason that we have limited the hierarchies to which the *nomenklatura* category is applied to the party, Komsomol or non-industrial hierarchies is that, like Bunin, we want to separate *nomenklaturshchiki* and Red Directors. Strictly speaking Soviet enterprise directors were part of the *nomenklatura*. But for an analysis which is directed at those who became the owners of very large privatized enterprises, it is useful to separate those who began their careers in Soviet times in enterprise management and those who worked in other hierarchies. Red Directors are those who worked in Soviet enterprise management. As with the *nomenklaturshchiki*, so with the Red Directors we will be liberal with the level of the management hierarchy at which they were placed. They do not have to have been general directors of a Soviet enterprise to be included in the Red Director category.

'New Russians' here has a more specific meaning than its usual one of someone who has made a lot of money in the transition and adopted a corresponding life style. Here the term means rather someone who made their start purely in the post-Soviet period, without relying on either wealth or connections made in the Soviet period.

For those who don't like the oligarchs, all of these possible origins have negative behavioural implications, whether it be the readiness to cut legal corners and be 'slick operators' of the blackmarketeers, the reliance on 'relational capital' and elitist disregard for social welfare of the *nomenklaturshchiki*, the addiction to subsidies and technocratic solutions of the Red Directors, or the absence of any moral responsibility or taste of the 'new Russians'.

The 'Gang of Seven'

Our G7 ranged in age during the year of the Soviet collapse, 1991, from 45 (Berezovsky) to 27 (Fridman), with a fair spread of ages in between. Clearly we are dealing with a young generation, although one old enough to have had sufficient post-education experience in the late Soviet Union to allow us to fit them into Soviet-era categories.

Muscovites are in a strong majority, with only two provincials. (Vinogradov was born in Ufa, and Fridman in Lvov. They both came to Moscow to study.) We are short of information on parentage and social origins, although the information we have suggests a mixed bag. The parents of Fridman and Khodorkovsky were engineers in industrial plants. It is noted in one source that Khodorkovsky's parents were not well off.[12] Potanin, born in 1961, is the son of a mid-level official in the Ministry of Foreign Trade.[13] Berezovsky is the son of a Jewish construction engineer, resident in Moscow since the 1930s, and a paediatric nurse.[14] Some sources stress his 'intellectual' and 'educated' background.[15] Gusinsky was born into a poor working-class Moscow family with some very direct experiences of Stalinist repression. Smolensky was born in Moscow in 1954 of an Austrian Jewish mother (her father had been a member of the Bund).

The black market is certainly represented in the sample. Gusinsky, Smolensky and Fridman were classic *fartsovshchiki* (involved in theatre tickets, underground printing of bibles, and again theatre tickets, respectively). Gusinsky and Smolensky had both faced criminal charges for their activities.

Gusinsky claims to have endured anti-semitic prejudices, including being denied entry to the prestigious Moscow Physics-Technical

Institute. He instead studied at the Moscow Gubkin Oil and Gas Institute and then gained a second degree in theatrical production at GITIS, the prestigious Moscow theatre school. He had an indifferent career as a theatrical producer, and was reduced to working as an event organizer, including some of the events associated with the Goodwill Games in 1986. Throughout, it is said, he drove a gypsy taxi and operated as a small-time *fartsovshchik*. When the cooperative movement was legalised, he began with a metal-working business, making everything from bracelets to garages. It appears to have been while he had this business that he faced criminal charges in December 1986. In 1988 he set up a financial and real estate consulting firm, which the following year became the joint venture 'MOST' (the Russian word for 'bridge') with the US legal firm Arnold & Porter. In 1990 Gusinskii bought out his American partners.[16]

Smolensky claims that the considerable discrimination to which he was subjected in Soviet times, including the inability to gain entry to any tertiary educational institution, was based on his 'foreignness' as much as his Jewishness. According to Hoffman he had been involved in the underground printing of business cards and bibles since his army service days. It was this activity that in 1981 earned him a two-year term of enforced labour on construction sites. That experience was enough to get him legal work in the construction industry. That work could well have been of a *tolkach* nature, making him the one possible example of a *tolkach* in our sample. In 1987 he set up a cooperative for the recycling of construction materials. A cooperative bank followed in 1988, after he had had trouble getting credit from the state construction bank Promstroibank. His bank was registered in 1989 as Stolichnyi Bank.[17]

It is Fridman who has been the subject of some of the most colourful accounts of Soviet-era blackmarket activities. He came to Moscow from Lvov to study at the Moscow Institute of Steel and Alloys in the early 1980s. Like Gusinsky, he claims to have been unable to get into the Moscow Physics-Technical Institute because of his Jewish nationality.[18] He combined his studies with the standard student occupation of working as a storeman and, most famously, dealer in Bolshoi Theatre tickets.[19]

He claims that his ability to supply theatre tickets enabled him after graduation to arrange a convenient work allocation to the Elektrostal plant outside Moscow. As a provincial a Moscow residence permit would have been very difficult to obtain, but Elektrostal was close enough for him to be able to continue running the theatre ticket business. From 1988 he operated a private business involved in a wide range of trading and service activities.[20] He registered Alfa-Bank in 1991.

Three blackmarketeers out of our sample of seven is, clearly, a significant proportion.[21] But four are left, and we will attempt to apply to them the category that appears most often in commentary on the origins of the oligarchs, that of *nomenklaturshchik*. That is the category which seems to suit Khodorkovsky best of all. Although not as senior a Komsomol official as is sometimes suggested, he was deputy secretary of the Komsomol committee while studying at the Mendeleev Chemistry-Technical Institute between 1981 and 1986.[22]

As deputy secretary of the institute committee he took advantage of a 1986 Gorbachev decree, legalizing clubs and amateur associations to open an (unsuccessful) student café.[23] With time and new Gorbachev decrees the business became a Centre for the Scientific-Technical Creativity of Youth (NTTM, to use the Russian acronym), and Khodorkovsky became involved in commercial R&D contracting. At this stage in his career he received the support of Aleksandr Sheindlin, the director of the prestigious Institute of High Temperatures. Sheindlin records that he was excited by the enthusiasm and youthful vigour of the new entrepreneurs and wanted to give them a hand. He had no expectations of any sort of return.[24] In the eyes of some the NTTMs were a Gorbachev-inspired effort to nurture an 'official entrepreneurialism' among the up-and-coming generation. For others they were created by senior members of the *nomenklatura* as structures through which party funds could be laundered before the increasingly evident and inevitable collapse came.[25] Khodorkovsky implies that his bank was never asked to hold party funds, but also states that he would have seen nothing wrong in doing so, since the party was a legal organization at the time.[26]

There is little doubt that the main function of his NTTM was to provide a structure for the transformation of enterprises' *beznalichnye* funds into fully negotiable cash. *Beznalichnye* money refers to the funds held by enterprises which were used for transactions between state-owned entities. It was held purely as an accounting entry. State-owned enterprises had not been able to turn such funds into cash. But the NTTMs could, and Khodorkovsky earned some good start-up capital doing so.[27]

The NTTM business was threatened when a decree was issued forbidding enterprises to grant credits to such structures. Payment could only be made for completed work. This meant that Khodorkovsky needed bank credit. He turned to the state-owned Zhilsotsbank. To quote Khodorkovsky, 'they turned us down: it's not allowed. But if we were a bank ...'. This was the time of the first commercial banks, so Khodorkovsky and his colleagues put up 2.5 million rubles and set up Menatep Bank in 1988. 'We met with virtually no resistance from state structures – a rare combination of circumstances.'[28] It is generally considered that Khodorkovsky is guilty of considerable understatement here. His new bank was in fact strongly supported by senior officials. Indeed Menatep was not just state sponsored, but very quickly, still in the Soviet period, became an agency bank for the government, with state credits to enterprises passing through it.[29]

Khodorkovsky's inclusion in the *nomenklatura* category seems appropriate, not just because he had been a junior Komsomol official, but also because it was through officially sponsored structures, whatever their real purpose, that he got his start. Potanin and Vinogradov are also clearly *nomenklaturshchiki*, in that their positions in the official Soviet hierarchy were highly strategic as far as their future careers were concerned. Although trained as a space and nuclear power engineer at the Moscow Aviation Institute Vinogradov was sent by his employer, the giant nuclear plant builder Atommash, to study economics at the Plekhanov Economics Institute. He moved from there into late Soviet banking. When he moved into the private sphere he did so with strong official backing. His Inkombank was set up in October 1988 with the support of the rector of the Plekhanov Economics Institute and the Science and Technology Administration of the Moscow city government.[30]

While not labelled in the same way as Khodorkovsky as a 'Komsomol leader', Vinogradov had also taken on what was known as 'social work' in his early days. He was the deputy chair for ideology of his dormitory student council while an undergraduate and is described as the secretary of the Komsomol committee of, variously in different sources, Atommash and the Ministry of Power Industry's Special Design Bureau from 1983 to 1985.[31] This was the sort of activity that did not necessarily indicate an interest in a party apparatus career, but was rather a test of one's general administrative skills. Nevertheless it is hard to see the likes of Gusinsky, Smolensky and Fridman being involved in such activities.

Potanin studied economics at the prestigious Moscow State Institute of International Relations (the position of his father almost certainly playing a role in his admission). During his studies he worked as an instructor for the institute's Komsomol committee. After graduation in 1983 he worked in various Soviet foreign trade organizations, including the division of Soyuzpromeksport dealing in the minerals trade.[32] In 1990 he moved to the International Bank of Economic Cooperation, the official bank of the CMEA, the communist world's economic cooperation organization. The same year he formed the private trading association Interros. In 1992–3 he was vice-president and then president of the International Finance Company (MFK), which worked very closely with his best-known financial vehicle ONEKSIMbank, formed in 1993. The founding shareholders of ONEKSIMbank were a group of former Soviet foreign trade organizations, which needed something to replace Vneshekonombank, the Soviet Union's foreign trade bank whose operations had been frozen by the foreign creditors of the former Soviet Union. According to Kryukov and Moe, the Ministry of Finance and the Central Bank were also very involved in the establishment of Potanin's bank.[33]

Neither Khodorkovsky, Vinogradov or Potanin could be described in any way as members of the top elite. They were not *synki* (the 'little sons', the children of the top elite who were given cushy jobs usually far removed from the hard-core party and industrial management jobs of their fathers), and they occupied relatively modest positions in their hierarchies. Nevertheless it was those positions in those hierarchies that provided them with the original opportunity for their private entrepreneurial careers. That justifies placing them in the *nomenklatura* category.[34]

We so far have an uncomfortable 3:3 split between blackmarketeers and *nomenklaturshchiki*, with Berezovsky, seen by many as the most shady and controversial of them all, as yet unclassified. There are scurrilous sources which place him, as a dealer in carpets, in the blackmarket category.[35] However both better documented and more important is his research career. A graduate of the electronics and computing faculty of the Moscow Timber Technology Institute,[36] he had a number of applied research positions before moving to the Academy of Science's Institute of Control Problems in the early 1970s. He worked his way up to laboratory head.[37] In Soviet times, and seemingly in an entirely legal way, he had close commercial links with the giant VAZ car plant, with his laboratory providing VAZ with computer-controlled automation technology under contract.[38] When cooperatives were legalized, he continued the technology transfer through such structures, and then used his VAZ contacts to move into car dealing.

To the extent that it was Berezovsky's official position that provided him with entry into private entrepreneurialism, he is like the *nomenklaturshchiki*. There is no reason to see career-oriented researchers as any less part of the Soviet *nomenklatura* than Komsomol activists, bankers or trade officials. Nevertheless the 'researcher' as a career type was sufficiently well developed in the Soviet Union to include it in our classification as a separate category. A research career was seen as one in which status and even a modicum of wealth and influence could be gained, without being fully subordinate to the strictures of the party or state hierarchies. In transition circumstances the *zavlab* (*zaveduiushchii laboratoriei*, laboratory head) became a well-identified category, featuring heavily among leaders of the reform movement and those hanging on to their coat-tails. The term, often in a derogatory way, was applied to the likes of Gaidar, Fedorov and Chubais. But under them were many others moving out of their institutes into new careers. Berezovsky might not be typical of the category, and he is lonely within it among the G7. But as we move on to our next sample, we might find some company for him.

To conclude on the G7. We have an even split between blackmarketeers and *nomenklaturshchiki*, with one *zavlab*. If one accepts that a *zavlab* is closer to a *nomenklaturshchik* than to a blackmarketeer, the *nomenklaturshchiki* have a small majority. The even division between the legal and illegal operators is striking, unless one subscribes to the view that in the late Soviet period the distinction between legal and illegal was an entirely unreal and irrelevant one.[39] Nevertheless the fact that some of our sample had to get their start on the streets, and others could do it from their offices, is a distinction worth noting, even if in the end they ended up equally rich. To add to the sense of an evenly divided sample, of the two survivors of the G7, one (Fridman) was a blackmarketeer and the other (Potanin) a *nomenklaturshchik*. The final point to note about the G7 is the complete absence of Red Directors and new Russians. The early shift into banking, which was so much a part of the G7, presumably was not an attractive or feasible option for enterprise managers. We can also surmise that the G7 consists of people who gained oligarch status early enough in the transition that they would not have had time to build up their wealth without a headstart in the Soviet period.

The 'new oligarchs'

If we had to summarize in a few words the biographies of the G7, we would probably arrive at something like 'young Muscovites, some of whom had blackmarket backgrounds, some strategic middle-level bureaucratic positions'. How do they compare to the 'new oligarchs', those who came to wealth other than through early 1990s banking and shares-for-credit? In making this comparison we will try to retain the categories used to classify the G7. The first thing to note about the 'new oligarchs' is that, despite the appellation 'new', they are in fact older than the G7. If the average age of the G7 in 1991 was 34.6 years, for the new oligarchs the figure was 41.5. Admittedly this is an average that derives from a very wide range – the oldest is Rashnikov, born in 1948, the youngest Melnichenko, born in 1972. The other noticeable feature of the new oligarchs is that there is not a Muscovite among them, in strong contrast to the G7. They were born in a wide range of provincial places, both in Russia and the other republics of the Soviet Union.

As with the G7, so here we do not have full details on family background. But again the evidence suggests a mixed bunch of origins. In this sample, however, there is definitely a stronger representation of those of 'proletarian' background. Mordashov and Rashnikov are the children of steel mill workers,[40] Bogdanov was born in a Siberian village, Abramovich and Alekperov were orphaned at an early age, Derispaska did not have the connections to avoid military service. Only Makhmudov and Melnichenko can be positively identified as of middle-class background, both being born into a family of provincial university lecturers.

Beyond these basic biographical data, how do the new oligarchs compare to the G7 in terms of the categories set out at the beginning of the chapter? A category which was strongly represented in the G7 was the blackmarketeer. In this new sample there are none who can be unequivocally included in that category. There are claims that Andrei Melnichenko was engaged in kerbside foreign currency dealing at the very end of the Soviet period, while a student in the Physics Faculty of Moscow State University.[41] Even if true, these activities could be seen as part of the death throes of the system rather than of its sclerosis, as the activities of Fridman, Gusinsky and Smolensky could be better described. Once given the opportunity in 1991, Melnichenko gave up his studies and began work in a registered exchange kiosk, and quickly built that business into a financial empire. We will return to his biography later in the chapter.

If we cannot find a single blackmarketeer in the new oligarch sample, we can find no *nomenklaturshchik* either, in the sense that the word is being used here. Makhmudov, whose career will be described later, could possibly be fitted into the category, in that he worked in the Soviet import agency Uzbekintorg in his native Tashkent before moving to Moscow to begin his private entrepreneurial career. But there is no evidence that that work provided him with anything more than some early training in commercial procedures.

What of the third of Bunin's categories, the Red Director? There were no Red Directors among the G7. The situation in the case of the new oligarchs is very different. There are a number in this sample who made enterprise management careers in the late Soviet period, and indeed did so in classic 'proletarian' style. Rashnikov, for example, was born in 1948 into the family of a Magnitogorsk worker. He went straight from school to work as a fitter and turner at the Magnitogorsk Metal Combine, studied at the Magnitogorsk Mining-Metallurgical Institute, and proceeded to work his way up the managerial hierarchy of the combine, reaching chief engineer/first deputy general director in 1991.[42] He gained control of the company only after a bruising ownership struggle through the second half of the 1990s.[43] Bogdanov, born in a Tiumen village in 1951, studied oil drilling at the Tiumen Industrial Institute and then worked his way up the hierarchy in the Tiumen oil industry. By 1984 he was already general director of Surgutneftegaz, the position he still holds in its privatized form.[44] Alekperov, the son of a Baku bureaucrat who died soon after his birth in 1950, followed a similar route in the Azerbaidzhan oil industry. In 1979 he moved to the West Siberian oil fields, making a major name for himself there, before being appointed Deputy Minister for the Oil and Gas Industry in 1990.[45] One could genuinely describe these three as Red Directors, both in the sense of holding senior management positions in the Soviet period and following the classic 'proletarian' career path to get there.

Lisin, born in 1956 and so a little younger than these three, was not as far advanced but was well on the way on a similar career path in the steel industry. (He was unusual only in being more peripatetic than was typical, a point noted in a 2000 interview in the business weekly *Kompaniia*).[46] Born in 1956 in Ivanovo, hardly a steel town, he began work as a fitter and turner in the South Kuzbass Coal Combine and then studied metallurgy at the Siberian Metal Institute. On graduation in 1979 he worked at the pig iron producer Tulachermet and then the Karaganda Metal Combine in Kazakhstan, where he became a favourite of the powerful general director Oleg Soskovets. By 1991 he was deputy general director of that giant combine. The following year he became a general trouble shooter for the infamous British-based metals trader, TWG, being on the board of many of their Russian enterprises.

Mordashov, born in 1965, also largely fits the pattern: from a respectable working-class background and pursuing a career in his home-town Cherepovets Metal Combine, now known as Severstal. He differed slightly in having gained his education in a metropolitan institute, the Leningrad Engineering-Economics Institute, and in having an economics rather than engineering specialisation. (This is the institute in which Chubais studied and taught. Although there is some overlap in the years they were there, the author has seen no reports that they knew each other.) On completing his studies in 1988 Mordashov returned to Cherepovets as a senior economist in the plant and had worked his way up to financial director by 1992.

Both Lisin and Mordashov, even if too young to have made the ranks of the Red Directors before it was too late, nevertheless had strong Red Director patrons. Lisin worked under Oleg Soskovets at the Karaganda Metal Combine and Mordashov was a favourite of the last Soviet general director of the Cherepovets plant, Lipukhin.[47] With the exception of Lisin, who had no 'home' enterprise, all those in our Red Director category worked hard in the 1990s to gain control as private owners of the plants in which they had 'grown up'.

In our analysis of the G7 we created a new category, of researcher or *zavlab*, just for Berezovsky. It is a category which finds two representatives in the new oligarch sample. Abramov, born in 1959, came from Krasnodar to study at the Moscow Physics-Technical Institute (the institute Gusinsky and Fridman were unable to enter because of their Jewishness). He then took up a research career in the Academy of Science's Institute of High Temperatures. This is the institute run by Aleksandr Sheindlin, the senior academician who had provided Khodorkovsky with early financing. The author has seen no evidence of links between Khodorkovsky and Abramov, who was nevertheless *commercial* director of the institute before beginning his private entrepreneurial career.[48]

Vekselberg, born in the Lvov region in 1957, graduated from the less illustrious Moscow Institute of Transport Engineers in 1979. He completed postgraduate work in the Computing Centre of the Academy of Sciences, and went on to head a laboratory in a design bureau. When Gorbachev created the opportunity he became involved in a standard 'official' R&D cooperative.[49] In 1989 he met up with his friend from student days, now US-based businessman Lev Blavatnik, and began running for him an investment business called 'Renova'. During privatization they bought into the oil and aluminium sectors. Renova has worked together with Fridman's Alfa Bank on many projects, most importantly the TNK oil company. But to treat them as a single entity, as for example Barnes does, is almost certainly an exaggeration.[50] Vekselberg's aluminium company, SUAL, in particular appears to be an independent operation.

We still have four new oligarchs unaccounted for: Abramovich, Makhmudov, Melnichenko and Deripaska. Abramovich was born in Saratov in 1966, seemingly there because his mother returned home to give birth. The family, however, lived in Syktyvkar, in the far northern Komi Republic. Both his parents died before he was four and he grew up with relatives in the Komi Republic and then Moscow.[51] After army service he graduated from the Moscow Gubkin Oil and Gas Institute and began his entrepreneurial activity running a toy-making cooperative during the Gorbachev period. It is unclear whether this was a lucrative enough activity to provide the start-up capital for his post-Soviet career. It seems more likely that he started more or less from scratch with his early post-Soviet trading activities. He faced criminal charges – which seemingly never made it to court – in 1992 for a typical commodity trading offence of the time.[52] In 1993 he became head of the Moscow office of the Swiss-registered trading company Runicom. From there he made good use of his connections with Berezovsky and the Yeltsin family to build up a major fortune. Above all, with Berezovsky he bought into the oil producer Sibneft in 1995. Berezovsky hurriedly sold his Sibneft shares to Abramovich in 2000, when under the new Putin regime criminal charges were brought against him. He remains to this day unhappy about the price that he got.[53]

Makhmudov is the son of Tashkent university lecturers. He studied Arabic at university in that city, and then worked as an interpreter for Soviet organizations in Libya and Iraq.[54] When he returned home, well into the perestroika period, he worked for the state import agency Uzbekintorg. He moved from there to Moscow and began commodity trading on his own account, primarily in copper, initially in partnership with the subsequently notorious Mikhail Chernoi. He bought copper enterprises during privatization and from there built up a major copper empire through the 1990s. Many commentators describe him as the central figure in a tightly if informally controlled conglomerate bringing together the businesses of a number of the new oligarchs. Yakov Pappe has coined the acronym 'the Big MADAM' to describe the grouping, made up of Makhmudov, Abramov, Deripaska, Abramovich and Melnichenko.[55]

The final M of the MADAM, Andrei Melnichenko, has already been mentioned as not truly fitting the category of Soviet blackmarketeer. Born in Gomel (Belorussia) in 1972, into the family of a physics lecturer, he completed his schooling at Moscow State University's elite boarding school in Moscow and then studied physics as an undergraduate from 1989. Some sources claim that he began his entrepreneurial career running a legal tourist bureau and office equipment company while still a student; others that he sold foreign currency from the kerbside.[56] Either way, at the end of 1992 he began working at a foreign exchange kiosk, a business which he built into a substantial financial empire, based around his MDM-Bank. He has remained much more a banker than the others in our samples.

The last new oligarch is Deripaska, the aluminium magnate. Although born in Dzerzhinsk, near Nizhnii Novgorod, in 1968, he grew up in the Kuban.[57] He came to Moscow to study in the Physics Faculty of

Moscow State University. He overlapped with Melnichenko in that faculty, something which apparently later played a role when Melnichenko's MDM-Bank first came to prominence raising finance for Deripaska at the Sayanogorsk Aluminium Factory.[58] Seemingly Deripaska began his entrepreneurial career while at university, and went straight from there in 1993 into aluminium trading and then the next year into enterprise management, running the Sayanogorsk plant for the infamous British-based aluminium trader TWG. It is said that Deripaska, like Lisin, was a protégé of Oleg Soskovets.[59]

In these last four cases there is no indication that their Soviet lives had a great role to play in their subsequent careers. Certainly Abramovich had taken advantage of the opportunities given him by Gorbachev's cooperative legislation to discover his entrepreneurial skills, and Makhmudov gained similar experience within official Soviet structures. While the two might have thus shown their inclinations, there is not enough here to suggest that Soviet experience was instrumental in creating post-Soviet opportunities for them. Deripaska and Melnichenko did not have time to make use of any Soviet opportunities. In terms of our original definitions these four could be classified as new Russians.

In summary the new oligarchs have quite different origins from the G7, with Red Directors, totally absent in the first contingent, making up the biggest group. There is also a significant group of new Russians, also totally absent in the G7. On the other hand, the blackmarketeers and *nomenklaturshchiki*, who were so important in the G7, are poorly represented in the later sample.[60]

Conclusions

The origins of the oligarchs in both samples are quite scattered, with all the categories identified by Bunin represented, plus our own *zavlab* category. On that basis it would be hard to conclude that Bunin's desire 'to determine which group dominates quantitatively and in a psycho-logical and ideological sense' has been fulfilled.[61]

To the extent that new Russians, that is, people who appear to have made no use of Soviet experiences or connections in their rise to wealth, are entirely absent in the G7 and in a minority among the new oligarchs (and in those cases new Russian status being largely a consequence of youth), we could say that the majority of the oligarchs owe their position to some extent to their Soviet backgrounds. Indeed if we take out the small group of blackmarketeers, most made good early use of 'official' positions.

Is this a finding that provides support for those who believe that post-Soviet Russia is no more than a continuation in power and wealth of the old *nomenklatura*? I would submit that it does so only in a small and unremarkable sense. It was the nature of the transition that a strategic position in the Soviet system could be parlayed into a position of wealth and power in the new system. This was not a revolution in which membership or even potential membership of an old elite was grounds for exclusion from power or wealth under the new regime. But those strategic positions did not have to be, and indeed were not, at the top levels of the old *nomenklatura*. While outside the scope of this study, it appears that senior members of the regional Soviet *nomenklatura* were well able to retain their positions (as were those in the union republican *nomenklatury* in newly independent states). But at the central level they had far less success, particularly through the entrepreneurial route. Much was made in the early transition period of ministers and other top bureaucrats setting up private or semi-private structures that would allow them to retain their positions.[62] With the exception of Gazprom, those structures never counted for much. Certainly no former top bureaucrats, with the partial exception of Alekperov, are in the ranks of the oligarchy.[63] He had a brief, albeit strategically important, period as deputy Minister of the Oil and Gas Industry.

If Klebnikov is right, and younger and more dynamic occupants of middle positions of the *nomenklatura* were given the task by their superiors of being the front men for their continued power and influence,[64] then it would appear that the front men did the dirty on their patrons and sponsors. One suspects that the early patrons and sponsors of the likes of Khodorkovsky, Potanin and Vinogradov are far from destitute. But there is no evidence that they have or ever had real power behind the scenes. Bunin puts it persuasively:

> The *nomenklatura* is not some Masonic lodge. Its unity could be ensured only by the 'socialist state' and the system of universal principles possessed by its members. It was able to create no more than 'survival zones' in some branches (for example, the gas industry) or the regions. Every commercialized part of the *nomenklatura* quite quickly acquired independent and often conflicting interests. In practice it was not so much that the *nomenklatura* used commercial structures, as new entrepreneurs were able to avail themselves of party money.[65]

The same can be said for the Red Directors in our sample. While we undoubtedly have people in our samples who parlayed positions in the

Soviet management hierarchy into positions of personal ownership, there is no evidence that they did so as representatives of a 'class' endeavouring to retain its position. Further discussion of this point will be required when we look in more detail at privatization, which some commentators claim was in practice precisely a policy which allowed the managerial class to retain its position. At least as far as the oligarch Red Directors are concerned, and based on the limited evidence so far, a personal motivation appears far more likely. There is not much about the Red Directors in our sample, Bogdanov perhaps aside, that reminds us of the 'Old Guard'. Alekperov is apparently driven by a more-or-less patriotic desire to maintain the Russian oil industry as a leading player in the global economy, which might or might not be a stronger motivation than personal enrichment. But the pursuit of that goal entailed for him, from an early stage, the rejection of the 'corporatization' of *nomenklatura* power through pseudo-market institutions, not their creation.[66]

It is perhaps not a very profound conclusion that a good number of our sample made use of their positions in official Soviet hierarchies to gain power and wealth, even if their motivation was not to ensure the continuity of those hierarchies. It is perhaps even less profound to note that essentially everyone in the samples showed very early interest in and aptitude for entrepreneurial activity. The opportunities to display that interest and aptitude came in different ways, but they all took advantage as early as possible of the opportunities, whether it be black-market opportunities provided by Soviet shortages or the legal and semi-legal opportunities provided by Gorbachev's reforming legislation.

A more profound issue is to what extent was it entrepreneurial talent or relational capital that brought them success. The question is an important one not just for normative reasons, talent being more admirable than connections. It is also important because one of the big debates about the oligarchs is their level of competence. Were they capable of running a business without relying on the state to protect them? The oligarchs themselves, not surprisingly, place the emphasis on qualities other than the ability to make contacts. Gusinsky is quoted by Hoffman as saying, 'Back then, the will, the desire, the drive solved absolutely everything.'[67] Be that as it may, certainly a capacity to create and make use of contacts appears to have been vital, whether it be the ingratiating style of Berezovsky, the charm of Khodorkovsky, or the professional patronage enjoyed by Lisin and Mordashov. But it could be argued that the capacity to cultivate contacts is an essential feature of entrepreneurship in any circumstances, whether the contacts be with patrons, partners or customers. In a later chapter we will analyse the performance of the oligarchs as corporate managers, and we will be in a better position to judge whether talent counted for more than connections after the evidence there has been presented.

In considering the personal qualities of the oligarchs, it is interesting to look in a comparative way at the life stories of entrepreneurs who have created successful businesses, usually also with contacts playing a major role, but who have not become oligarchs. There the drive in the quote from Gusinsky, the sense that all is possible, and even that all is permissible, is missing. Let us take two from Igor Bunin's excellent series of interviews with middle-level business people: Vladimir Gusarov, of the bank 'Derzhava', and Sergei Shapiguzov, of the auditing-consulting company FBK. We see the same sorts of backgrounds as the oligarchs, as well as a strong desire to be independent. But we also see a willingness to be satisfied with a niche, and a desire to minimize risks, both economic and political. Gusarov says that 'from the beginning we chose a "careful" strategy. It consisted of a refusal to chase after the oligarchs and those close to them, regardless of the fact that they have lots of money. That's not for us.' When Shapiguzov was asked whether he had ever wanted to become an oligarch, he replied that 'generally there was no desire to play risky games, connected with violations of the rules of heaven and the Criminal Code'.[68] Some might argue that the oligarchs minimized risk by using relational capital. But relational capital, particularly of the Russian variety, is a poor form of insurance. What distinguishes the oligarchs from Gusarov and Shapiguzov is their willingness to take on risk, not their relational capital.

A useful aspect of our analysis is that we have two samples. One, the G7, essentially fell by the wayside. The new oligarchs who replaced them are still in place. Given the uncertainties of the Russian political economy one hesitates to suggest that the latter sample is more 'successful' than the former – their fall might be just around the corner. Nevertheless is there a difference between the samples of analytical significance? The fact that the G7 made itself into essentially a financial elite while the new oligarchs were from the beginning much more oriented towards the 'real' economy is to a large extent a reflection of the nature of the economy at the time they rose to prominence. In the first half of the 1990s it was in the financial sector that the serious money was to be made. Nevertheless the new oligarchs, with the exception of Melnichenko, made very early choices – in some cases, we could say, from birth – to make their careers and fortunes in the real economy. Even when there was money to be made in the financial sector, they looked towards the real economy. One suspects that that was an important choice. They had the background that pushed them towards the real economy and the skills to operate effectively within it. A number of the G7 oligarchs made the move into the real economy as well, but for varying reasons with less success than the new oligarchs. Rather speculatively, one could suggest that the more 'traditional' working-class background that we have detected in at least part of the new oligarch sample not only pushed them into the real economy rather than the more 'flashy' world of finance, but also better equipped them temperamentally for dealing with the retro-political realities of Putin's state.

It will take examination of the oligarchs in operation to explore these matters further. And in doing so we will attempt to determine whether the skills that they applied, whether in the financial or real economy sectors, were asset-stripping and rent-seeking skills or business-building and wealth-creating skills. Essentially we will be testing the words of Willen Buiter:

> The talents that make a good productive, wealth-creating entrepreneur are not that different from the talents that make an efficient predator.
>
> When the returns to productive activity are low and the return to predation high, talented individuals will tend to choose the latter career over the former.[69]

In the next chapter we describe how, after the early starts to their careers described in this chapter, the oligarchs went on to build huge business empires and enormous wealth.

3
How Did They Get Rich?

One might argue – and indeed the author has some sympathy for the view – that today it is not how the oligarchs gained their wealth and power that is important, but what they did with them once gained. If overall they have made good use of their assets, and if one sees the oligarch phenomenon as a normal stage on the road to 'normal' capitalism, then we might forgive them any sins in the past. Even if they have misused their assets, to dispossess them of those assets might raise such difficult problems that it could well not be worth it.

There is an alternative view, that holds that until such time as the sins of the past are faced fairly and squarely, and the sinners if not punished then at least relieved of their ill-gotten gains, then private property an capitalism in Russia will never have legitimacy in the eyes of the population and so will never develop normally either politically or economically. Until the issue is faced up to, in the background of all politics will always be the politics of dispossession. At best politicians will be tempted to appeal to that type of politics, and at worst a government will be able to enjoy genuine popular support only to the extent that it appears committed to dispossession. While recognising the dangers of trying to reverse the process that brought the oligarchs such wealth, Willem Buiter is nevertheless of the opinion:

> The legitimacy of any distribution of property rights, and therefore the security of these rights, cannot be independent of the manner in which these property rights were acquired or assigned. The fact that the redistribution of state property in Russia since 1988 is unlikely to be viewed as legitimate by the vast majority of Russians who did not share in the free-for-all (or rather the free-for-some) is bound to be an obstacle to the efficient utilization of these assets in productive enterprise.[1]

Further, a capitalism that is dominated by a small group of excessively large and powerful companies will not provide the room for the broad-scale entrepreneurialism which capitalism and liberal democracy need to thrive.

If, of course, the popular perception of the legitimacy or otherwise of the oligarchs' rise to wealth and power has such a political effect, then it does not necessarily matter whether the perception is right or wrong. All the indications are that the general population believes the oligarchs to have stolen both the assets that they own and the returns from those assets with a conviction that is unlikely to be shaken by even the most persuasive revisionist history.[2] It is a popular view which is echoed by much specialist commentary. At the end of the book we will return to the question of how, if at all, the oligarchs' wealth might be made legitimate in the eyes of the Russian population. But here we will examine as objectively as possible what actually happened.

The financial sector

As we have already seen, one group of future oligarchs, mostly those in the G7 sample but also a good number from among the 'new oligarchs', began their entrepreneurial careers in trade, whether in blackmarket goods or the more official commodity trading of those coming from the middle ranks of the late Soviet bureaucracy. But even before the collapse of the Soviet Union they were moving into the financial sector, in a number of cases to help fund their trading activities, often using funds provided by partner state banks. They also presumably provided credit to other traders, and in some cases were able to give themselves free credit by using state subsidy money passing through their accounts on the way to enterprises. As mentioned in the previous chapter, Khodorkovsky had a particularly lucrative business helping enterprises convert their *beznalichnye* money into cash and then converting that cash into foreign currency. It is hard to imagine that they did not take the nearly limitless advantage of the considerable gap between the official and blackmarket ruble exchange rates at the time.[3] The arrangements by which imported items could be paid for with official rubles and sold privately at blackmarket rates were particularly lucrative. In these circumstances the oligarchs' financial activities quickly displaced their trading activities.[4]

Despite the regular accusations made against the oligarchs that they have never built a business of their own, not only their original start-ups but also their banks were built from scratch. It is not even entirely true that they were all built only with the patronage and assistance of state officials and agencies. There is no evidence that Fridman, Smolensky or Melnichenko obtained start-up capital from official structures. As noted in the previous chapter there is conflicting evidence on the origins of Vinogradov's Inkombank. Kryukov and Moe claim that Menatep, Inkombank, Alfa and other oligarch banks were established not so much with the support and participation of state agencies and officials, but rather business groups, especially trading companies.[5] The banks that became true oligarch banks were those that quickly outgrew their founding partners (*uchrediteli*), whoever they might have been. Banks that remained beholden to their founding partners did not flourish. These were mainly the so-called 'pocket' banks of industrial sectors and enterprises.

After the banks were created, official patronage and assistance was lucratively important, particularly through the 'agency' bank phenomenon. Private bankers would use their contacts in state agencies to arrange to handle the financial transactions of those agencies. ONEKSIMbank handled customs payments, Gusinsky's MOST the accounts of the Moscow city government, Menatep the Federal Pension Fund, and so on.[6] Credits from the state to subsidised enterprises, of which there were a vast number in the first half of the 1990s, also passed through the banks, as did the repayments of the credits when and if they were made. The banks were adept at hanging on to the money for as long as possible. The Audit Chamber estimated that in 1995–6 alone banks earned $1.32 billion through agency agreements, although Tompson provides an estimate of a significantly lower figure of $25 million per annum from the management of state budget funds.[7] The practice was ended by presidential decree in May 1997.[8]

The banks used the money sitting in their accounts to finance foreign currency speculation. As Hans-Henning Schröder explains, in the years of very high inflation from 1992 to 1994 it was very profitable to borrow rubles or change into foreign currency ruble deposits on which negative real interest rates were paid and invest them at positive real interest rates. Inexpensive ruble credits were obtained from the Central Bank as it pursued an expansionary monetary policy.[9]

Those opportunities dried up as inflation was brought under control in 1995. From late 1994 there was a sharp reduction in the use of direct central bank credits to finance the budget deficit and loans to commercial banks were provided only on market terms. This required new strategies from the banks. But, as Tompson puts it: 'Banks, too, felt the strain of stabilization, but, with a near monopoly on ruble liquidity in a liquidity-starved economy, they found it easy to exploit the situation.'[10]

One way that they made use of their liquidity was to become heavily involved in the government securities market. As part of the stabilization process much more reliance was placed on the sale of government securities, particularly short-term securities (GKOs) and bonds (OFZs). Russian commercial banks were heavy buyers of government debt. While interest rates and yields fluctuated considerably over the next couple of years, depending on the government's budgetary situation and the Central Bank's policy on market intervention, generally yields were very good and the banks did well. Indeed they borrowed heavily from foreign sources to fund their GKO purchases. Before the crash the financial oligarchs were among the few able to make money in these circumstances. While they made money out of inflation, other economic actors, industrial enterprises in particular, were impoverished by it. This left the financial institutions in a strong position when they developed an interest in buying industrial assets.[11]

While it was in the financial sector that the G7 oligarchs made their first major fortunes, in the public eye they were neither the main players nor the villains of the pre-1998 financial sector. That distinction belonged to the pyramid schemes such as MMM and Chara-bank. While the pyramid schemes were flourishing around 1993–4, the oligarch banks had relatively little direct contact with the public. It was only as relative stability came in 1994–5, and after the inevitable collapse of the pyramid schemes, that the oligarch banks paid much attention to retail banking. They then did so to a sufficient degree that many private citizens lost their savings in the August 1998 financial crisis, as banks collapsed and shifted what assets remained into new corporate structures and offshore. As Bunin suggests, it was this aspect of the 1998 financial crisis that did the oligarchs the most harm. Most survived commercially relatively unscathed, but their links with scandalously 'bankrupt' banks did serious damage to their image in the eyes of the general population.[12]

Privatization

Unsavoury as these activities and events might have been, it is not their years as bankers for which the oligarchs are now best known or most maligned. It is their ownership of resource assets and therefore their role in various forms of privatization that now attract the most attention. That applies as well to those oligarchs who never had major financial involvements, the bulk of the new oligarch sample.

Privatization is a complex and highly controversial story,[13] and the oligarchs' involvement in it is no less complex or controversial. Privatization took many forms, beginning with the 'spontaneous' privatizations of the late Gorbachev and early Yeltsin periods. Official 'mass privatization' took place from late 1992, with its peak in 1993. It went through a number of stages, from the initial allocation of shares to enterprise workforces, then voucher auctions and investment auctions and tenders. The shares-for-credit privatizations of 1995 were particularly controversial. Sales of residual state shareholdings in privatized enterprises have continued in a rather desultory fashion since then.

Spontaneous privatization. One of the most common justifications for the mass privatization of the early 1990s was the need to put a stop to the so-called 'spontaneous' privatizations that had been going on since the late Gorbachev period. In responding to a demand from Arkadii Volsky, at the time the spokesperson for the Red Directors, that privatization be slowed down, Egor Gaidar the acting prime minister and chief architect of shock therapy reform, claimed that 'calls to slow the pace of privatization are beneficial above all to those who are appropriating (*razbazarivaet*) state property'.[14] There were different ways of going about it. Sometimes special decrees from the state were obtained for the privatization of individual enterprises. Many of Russia's biggest enterprises, such as the automobile factories GAZ, AvtoVAZ and KamAZ, were privatized by special presidential decrees. On other occasions enterprises took advantage of the chaotic legal situation of the time simply to do it themselves. Gorbachev's legislation on cooperatives, small enterprises and leasing, all provided good opportunities.[15] In smaller enterprises management often set up under cooperative legislation private firms into which enterprise earnings were siphoned and then used to buy shares in the enterprise.[16] Another popular approach was for an enterprise to borrow money from a commercial bank with very close links to the enterprise's managers, using the enterprise's fixed assets as security. The loan was not repaid and the bank took over the assets.[17] As the methods suggest, it was the management of the enterprises which both organized and was the beneficiary of the privatization. Some shares were usually allocated to the workforce, but management had privileged access.[18] In many cases management was given shares in recognition of its 'intellectual contribution': that is, for nothing.[19]

No oligarchs were involved in spontaneous privatizations. Alekperov and Bogdanov were vigorously involved at the time in the preparation of oil industry structures, the privatization of which they would subsequently dominate. But none of our oligarchs, from either sample, were

in the sort of management positions required to take advantage of spontaneous privatization.

Mass privatization. Our oligarchs of the future, who had not been in a
position to take advantage of spontaneous privatization, were no better
placed at the initial stage of the mass privatization programme. There
was a fierce struggle between the ideologists of reform and those who
can be called generically the Red Directors, at a time when the oligarchs
were still in the formative years of building up their financial empires
in the case of the G7 and often still studying or just beginning entrepreneurial careers in the case of the 'new oligarchs'.

The reformers wanted a privatization scheme that would get state-
owned assets into private hands as quickly as possible. As long as there
was post-privatization negotiability of shares they were not particularly
worried about who obtained the assets at the initial stage of privatization. If they were good owners, they would keep and increase the value
of their assets; if they were bad owners, they would choose or be forced
to sell out to better owners. The realization of value by the state through
the disposal of its assets was also not a priority.

The reformers' opponents, once they accepted that mass privatization
could not be avoided, defended 'socialist equity', claiming that if enterprises were to be privatized those who worked in them deserved to
obtain ownership. The preferred approach was collective worker ownership, in which no one owned individual shares and ownership rights
were lost if one left the enterprise. 'Worker' was carefully defined to
include management. The intention was that management would dominate both the workforce and the shares that it owned.

The reformers eventually accepted that privatization should include
a 'workforce ownership' component, but extracted some very important concessions from the Red Director lobby. First was the addition of
a voucher component to privatization. Every citizen would receive a
voucher representing a unit of value that could be used to bid for
shares in enterprises being privatized. It is hard to know what exactly
the reformers expected of the voucher component of privatization.
It was not their preferred option. They would have preferred straightforward 'sell to the highest bidder' privatization. But there were
commentators claiming even before the event that the voucher scheme
was designed in such a way as to allow the government ultimately to
get its preferred 'entrepreneurial' privatization, since the vouchers
would end up cheaply in the hands of business people.[20] The scheme's
populist element – that it gave everyone access to the nation's assets,

not just those who worked in enterprises being privatized – made it difficult to resist politically.

Just as important as vouchers was the reformers' insistence that individuals have the right to own the shares obtained through privatization and that they be fully negotiable. That opened the door for the post-privatization transfers of ownership that they saw as central to their plans. Those intending to benefit from *nomenklatura* privatization went along with this, since they expected that it would give them an unchallenged opportunity to add to their own shareholdings.

The eventual programme included the allocation of shares to the enterprise workforce (which included by definition management), voucher auctions, and investment auctions and tenders, in which packets of shares were sold to investors offering the best package of cash and investment undertakings. Workforces had the choice to receive a free allocation of 25 per cent of shares with no voting rights or buy, at a discounted price, 51 per cent with voting rights.

At first glance the outcome was a predictable victory for the Red Directors. Something like 70 per cent of enterprises opted for the workforce allocation option that allowed them to purchase 51 per cent of voting shares. Very often voucher auctions were then used to increase workforce holdings, as management arranged for workers' vouchers to be pooled and bid for more shares in their own enterprise. Management then used a variety of forms of persuasion and coercion to ensure that the workers voted at shareholder meetings the way it wanted. Persuasion took the form of promises to maintain employment and wage levels, as well as social welfare facilities. The crudest form of coercion was the threat of dismissal against those who voted against management.[21] At the time the reformers' critics ridiculed them for a privatization programme that had delivered the Red Directors even tighter control of their enterprises than they had enjoyed in Soviet times.

But very quickly the weakness of the position of the Red Directors, particularly in the sorts of enterprises able to produce real value, became evident. They were unable to guarantee control of the behaviour of their workforces, including middle management, with deleterious effects on enterprise performance to be described in more detail later. That inability to control the workforce was also reflected in an inability to control their shareholdings. In those enterprises where management had relied on promises of the maintenance of wages and employment to get the workforce to vote their shares in their favour, management's inability to guarantee either of these saw the workers either voting them out at shareholder meetings or selling their shares to outside investors. A prime example of the former is the Vladimir Tractor Factory. At the first post-privatization shareholders' meeting the incumbent general director, Grishin, was opposed for re-election by Iosif Bakaleinik. Grishin was a classic Red Director, a graduate of the Vladimir Polytechnical Institute who had worked his way up to the top job from a shop-floor position over a 40-year career in the plant. Bakaleinik, a much younger man, was a graduate of the Economics Faculty of Moscow State University and had pursued a research career before being recruited to the factory by Grishin as deputy general director for economic matters. Bakaleinik had then left to study business at Harvard, and now returned to the plant as a representative of Renova, the Blavatnik-Vekselberg investment vehicle much better known in this book for its part ownership of the TNK oil company and its role in the SUAL aluminium producer. Renova owned 12 per cent of the shares in the tractor factory, and its partner Alfa Bank another 10 per cent.[22] The workforce owned 48 per cent. (The state retained 29 per cent, but as was usually the case these shares appear not to have been voted.)

Grishin won the election, with the support of the workers' votes, by promising to maintain employment and social infrastructure. (It probably helped that proxies were arranged by shop foremen.) Grishin also played up Bakaleinik's foreign links and, it is suggested, his Jewishness.[23] But it quickly became clear that Grishin would be unable to keep his promises. He tried to keep things going by maintaining output and deliveries even when customers were not paying for what they received. He had to borrow at punitive interest rates, and eventually had no choice but to close down production lines and pay off staff. In January 1994 he resigned and at a shareholders' meeting in March that year Bakaleinik won the general directorship with 98.6 per cent of the votes, even as he promised a programme of cuts in staff and social infrastructure.[24]

Another example of a Red Director getting more than he had bargained for involves one of our new oligarchs. The Cherepovetsk Metal Combine, soon to be known as Severstal, was privatized in 1993, with the workforce opting to buy 51 per cent of the shares. In March 1994, 34 per cent of shares were put up for voucher auction. Iurii Lipukhin, the Red Director head of the steel smelter, arranged for his trusted young protégé, Aleksei Mordashov, to bid for the shares through Severstal-Invest, an insider trading and management vehicle. For a while Mordashov sat quietly, but in May 1996 he had himself elected general director at a shareholder meeting. In the words of one source, 'Yury Lipukhin went to the meeting not suspecting his imminent dismissal, as he considered Mordashov his loyal colleague.'[25]

Mordashov's involvement in the privatization was as the protégé and ally of Lipukhin. The only other oligarchs to be involved in the primary workforce allocation stage of privatization were Alekperov and Bogdanov, and that is because they were the established managers of their enterprises at the time. In the final months of the existence of the Soviet Union Alekperov was first deputy minister of the Soviet Ministry of Oil and Gas Industry. It was from that position that he worked for the creation and then registration in November 1991 by the Russian Ministry of Fuel and Energy of the 'corporatized' but state-owned company Langepas-Urai-Kogalymneft. For some, such corporatized companies were a last-ditch effort by Red bureaucrats to save the old way of doing things, for others the earliest stage of the Red Directors' campaign to gain private ownership of the enterprises they ran. Alekperov definitely saw things the latter way.

Langepas-Urai-Kogalymneft was made up of a number of production units in the West Siberian oil fields where Alekperov had worked for many years. (He had been general director of Kogalymneftegaz from 1984 to 1990.) Alekperov became president of Langeras-Urai-Kogalymneft at the time of its registration. Thankfully it quickly became known as Lukoil. Alekperov, who was very much its driving force, remained president when in 1993 about 20 per cent of the company was sold in various ways to the workforce. A share issue in April 1995 made more shares available. In 1995–6 convertible bonds were sold to Atlantic Richfield and the Lukoil-controlled bank Imperial. In April 1996 the bonds were converted to shares. Lukoil bought 5 per cent of itself in a shares-for-credit deal in November 1995. Alekperov did not then or since have the dominant shareholding that other oligarchs had in their companies.[26] However by 1994 he had created for himself the position that the G7 oligarchs were only able to achieve a year or so later, firm control of a major oil producer.[27] According to Kryukov and Moe Alekperov had the management skills to dominate the holding company and its many subsidiaries:

> Alekperov was a key figure in attracting external investment and solving internal financial structural problems ahead of Lukoil's competitors. From the outset, the leadership took steps to establish a strong, separate holding company over and above the co-founders of the company, the oil producers, refineries and distributors that were to become its subsidiaries. The holding company was clearly superior to the subsidiaries in both personnel and competence.[28]

In 1993 another two corporatized but state-owned companies were created in the oil industry, Yukos and Surgutneftegaz. They were then privatized in the same way as Lukoil. The established oil industry figures who had presided over the central production units of the new companies,

Bogdanov at Surgutneftegaz and Muravlenko at Yukos, remained in control. Bogdanov proved sufficiently adept as a manager to, like Alekperov, maintain control and promote good performance with a relatively small personal shareholding. He was also able to resist possible incursions from oligarchs and other outsiders.[29]

Yukos under Muravlenko was not so fortunate. It was poorly managed, having major difficulties getting payment out of customers, particularly its extensive agricultural clientele. The holding company management also had trouble controlling its subsidiaries, particularly its major production unit, Yuganskneftegaz. At the time of its creation in 1993 it was the second most important oil company, but by 1995, to quote Lane and Seifulmulukov, it 'lagged far behind LUKoil and Surgutneftegaz in financial strength and corporate character'.[30]

Two other oil companies whose owners feature prominently in any chronicle of the oligarchs are Sibneft and TNK (the Tiumen Oil Company). They were both created in August 1995. It is claimed that Berezovsky was the chief lobbyist for the creation of Sibneft and indeed, through a shares-for-credit deal soon after, Berezovsky, his partner Roman Abramovich and existing Sibneft top managers concentrated 85 per cent of shares in their own hands.[31] It was only after he was forced into exile that Berezovsky sold his shares in Sibneft to Abramovich, in a deal which still rankles with him.[32] There were such legal and lobbying battles around the formation of TNK that it was not until 1997 that a substantial block of shares were sold, with an Alfa-Renova partnership buying 40 per cent. They paid $820 million, way above the minimum bid, in a sign that cheap assets were running out.[33]

Privatization in the oil industry was always unusual. To return to the more regular mass privatization to which the metals sector was subjected, with the partial exception of Mordashov no oligarchs were involved in the initial workforce allocation stage of privatization, since none were incumbent managers. But they, along with many other 'outsider' entrepreneurs, both foreign and domestic, were heavily involved in the subsequent voucher and investment auctions. We have already seen that incumbent Red Directors took the opportunity of voucher auctions to add to the shareholdings obtained in the initial workforce allocation. But outsiders were also active at voucher auctions. A very large secondary market had quickly developed, often made up of vouchers being sold by 'fly-by-night' voucher funds that had collected vouchers from citizens and then promptly disappeared. While Red Directors had the organizational capacity to build up useful numbers of vouchers to bid in voucher auctions, they could not control the entire market. Nor did they have the financial resources to bid at the more expensive investment auctions and tenders. These were far more likely to be dominated by outsiders. By summer 1994 Khodorkovsky's Menatep had spent $40 million on the purchase of vouchers and shares, and had another $35 million set aside.[34] The titanium producer AVISMA was just one of the many enterprises Menatep gained control of through voucher auctions.[35] One of the best-known investment tenders is that won by Menatep to gain a 20 per cent holding in the apatite producer Apatit. It is for failing to meet the conditions of that tender that Khodorkovsky and his associate Platon Lebedev were arrested in 2003. That is a matter that will receive considerably more attention in a later chapter. As another example, Renova purchased a 20 per cent stake in the Irkutsk aluminium smelter in an investment tender, with an offer of $37 million-worth of investment.[36]

Outsiders also bought up shares on the secondary market. This was far more likely to be an informal, at times literally street, market than the stock exchange. The immediate post-privatization period is full of stories of outside investors buying up workers' shares, often by setting up outside the factory gates and buying shares on the spot. It was not always a straightforward process, as can be seen from a 1995 newspaper article describing the adventures of Kakha Bendukidze who, if he had shown more long-term interest in the resource sector, could well have featured in our list of oligarchs. In their efforts to buy up the 7 per cent of shares needed to gain control of an oil exploration enterprise, his representatives had to travel beyond the Polar Circle. They were arrested by the local police, refused landing rights at the airport, refused accommodation and food, had their telephone cut off, and threatened with violence. They were able to get only a further 4 per cent of shares.[37]

Even in those enterprises where management had managed to win themselves a secure majority shareholding, they often did not have access to the capital needed to maintain operations, much less for investment. To maintain operations they found themselves having to invite into their enterprises as equity investors outsiders with greater access to capital. The Krasnoyarsk Aluminium Plant (KrAZ) serves as a good example. KrAZ was privatized in late 1992, with the workforce buying a 51 per cent holding. In May the following year another 27 per cent of shares were sold through voucher auction, with the management team of the incumbent general director Mikhail Turushchev buying the shares.[38] But Turushev did not have the operating capital to run the plant, and he quickly had to look to outsiders for assistance.

The metals industry was unusual at this stage of transition in that the most prominent of the early outside investors were trading companies.[39]

Some were foreign, some were Russian. They had the trading experience and access to trade credits that Soviet-era managers did not have. The best known – some would say most notorious – of the traders was TransWorld Group (TWG), the company to which Turushev turned. TWG was at the time of the collapse of the Soviet Union a British trader on the London Metals Exchange. With the breakdown of the Soviet system it found its trading relationships and generally the stability of the market disintegrating. The company came into contact with Lev Chernoi, an exceptionally controversial figure in Russian business, who proposed a tolling arrangement with KrAZ.[40] Tolling is a system whereby a smelter processes alumina for a fee, without owning and therefore having to pay for the input. It is a useful scheme for processors short of operating capital, as KrAZ and other aluminium producers at the time were. As part of the deal TWG took a strategic stake in the company. Indeed TWG quickly built up significant stakes in a whole range of Russian metal enterprises, including the Bratsk Aluminium Plant (BrAZ), the Novokuznetsk Aluminium Plant (NkAZ), the Sayanogorsk Aluminium Plant (SaAZ), and the Novosibirsk Electrode Factory, as well as the steel producer NLMK. It claimed at one stage to control 45 per cent of Russian aluminium exports.[41]

Although well-equipped to provide the required expertise to take the metals producers into world markets, trading companies were also well-placed to capture the cash flows as well, something that made them difficult partners for management and controversial politically. This applied particularly to TWG. In the mid-1990s a shift occurred in the metals sector, and traders began to be replaced by Russian commercial banks as the outside investors. They had a new interest in the real economy, and promised to be less stingy with investment finance than the traders. For example, Inkombank was brought into the Magnitogorsk Metal Combine, Russia's biggest ferrous metals plant, and also into Sameko, the former Kuibyshev and then Samara Metal Combine, a major aluminium producer coming out of the old Ministry of Aviation Industry. In both cases insiders desperate for investment funds invited the bank in. In the case of Magnitka, Inkombank's arrival required the removal in a boardroom coup of the general director, Anatolii Starikov, one of the 'new' directors of the Gorbachev era.[42] In the case of Sameko, the relationship began with a credit agreement under which the bank undertook to find foreign investment funds for the enterprise, but the bank over time built up a majority shareholding. The move was seen as the abandonment by the enterprise's management of the trader Euromin, which had previously been the enterprise's strategic investor.[43]

To summarize, outsiders built up positions in privatized enterprises through voucher and investment auctions, buying up workforce shares on the secondary market, and by being offered equity stakes by cash-strapped Red Directors. It was a gradual process, and one that was not always recognized by commentators. Black, Kraakman and Tarassova write that 'in a few cases' outsiders bought out existing managers post-privatization.[44] It was rather more than a few. As stated by Dolgopyatova, in describing ownership patterns in the period 1993–8:

> The most distinct trends were a reduction of the state share (on the federal, regional, and local levels) and a significantly reduced share of insiders relative to outsiders ... In particular, [growing outside owner-ship] resulted from an active establishment of holding structures, including those within the framework of formal and informal finan-cial and industrial groups (FIGs).

As recognized by Dolgopyatova, the extent of redistribution of owner-ship to new owners depended on the attractiveness of the enterprise or sector in which the enterprise was situated.[45]

Although a number of oligarchs were among the outsiders involved in privatization and the corporate governance adventures that followed, it was not in any concerted way and certainly not to a degree that set them apart from many other outside investors at the time. (Often outside investors were local entrepreneurs or related enterprises in the supply chain, the so-called *smezhniki*.) Indeed many oligarchs were not involved at all – Smolensky and Melnichenko kept to the financial sector while Gusinsky turned his attention to creating new media firms. Particularly as far as the G7 oligarchs were concerned, the involvement was extremely scattered, almost random. Freinkman has described the oligarchs' involve-ment in voucher privatization as being a case of 'buy now, think later'.[46] Kets de Vries's comment on Khodorkovsky's Menatep could be more widely applied: the strategy 'was crystal clear: acquire anything that could generate cash at the lowest possible price'.[47] In the metals sector the only commercial bank with something vaguely resembling a strategic approach to acquisitions was Rossiiskii Kredit.[48] It never quite made it to full oligarch status and was greatly weakened by the 1998 financial crisis.

Corporate governance

While there were various ways for outsiders, including oligarchs, to build up shareholdings in the real economy, it was not always easy for them, even those that had been invited into enterprises, to exercise their newly acquired ownership rights. For a start, in the early post-privatization period the manipulation of share registers was rife. Enterprise manager-owners held their own share registers, and were more than willing simply to remove the names of unwelcome shareholders or – slightly less extremely – fail to include them in the register in time for the new shareholders to vote at shareholder meetings. It was not rare for two registers to be maintained by competing groups of would-be owners. At KrAZ, TWG and Turushchev were driven out by the plant's commercial director, Iurii Kolpakov. Part of the process was the removal of TWG's name from the share register.[49]

Shareholder meetings were also the forum for corporate governance shenanigans. Examples include the failure to hold such meetings, the manipulation of their timing and location, the refusal to recognize the voting rights of inconvenient shareholders at meetings, manipulating agendas, and so on.[50]

The other classic technique of the time was the share issue designed purely to dilute a minority shareholding. Johnson records, quoting a *Moscow Times* article of April 1996, the difficulties that the bank Rossiiskii Kredit had in gaining control of the Lebedinsk Enrichment Combine:

> Company directors diluted the bank's stake from 23 per cent to less than 6 per cent, manipulated proceedings to deny the bank a seat on the board, and hustled one of the visitors off the stage when he tried to speak.[51]

Given that these were all techniques designed to keep outsider share-holders at bay, naturally they were pioneered by the Red Directors who had first gained ownership rights through privatization. But once the oligarchs got a foothold in the real economy they were quick to use the same methods themselves. Khodorkovsky's Menatep was considered to be highly adept at the manipulation of shareholder meetings. At the Sayanogorsk Aluminium Plant, TWG fell victim to the share dilution approach at the hands of Oleg Deripaska, the future oligarch who had been placed in the plant as its own representative. In 1998 he turned against his patrons, and through a classic 1990s share issue diluted TWG's share holding from 37 to 15 per cent. He then cancelled their trading contracts.[52] The critics of the oligarchs provide many more examples of such dilutions.

The involvement of the oligarchs in mass privatization can hardly be described as the systematic and calculated theft of state assets. While such terms as *prikhvatizatsiia* at the time of mass privatization seemed to be directed primarily against the Red Directors and *nomenklatura* privatization, with time the target of the accusations changed.[53] The impression one might get from some accounts, that the oligarchs were the intended and actual beneficiaries of mass privatization, is wide of the mark. In terms of corporate governance shortcomings, they were as much the victims as the perpetrators, and certainly in no way stood out from the crowd in such activities. As already suggested their involvement was haphazard and at the time did not stand out from the involvement of many other participants. While there is no denying their willingness to use dubious corporate governance methods, they were as often the victims as the perpetrators, and again in no way did they stand out from the crowd in using such methods. Their holdings were not sufficient to suggest that the foundations were being laid for oligarch capitalism. More extensive incursions and tighter control of the most important parts of the real economy were needed before that could become a reality. They came with two new developments in the reallocation of Russian economic assets, the so-called 'shares-for-credit' deals and the 'second *peredel*'.

Shares-for-credit[54]

Shares-for-credit involved the transfer of some of the most valuable Russian resource enterprises to a small number of financial oligarchs. We are well advised to pay heed to Anders Åslund's observation that in fact only a small number of enterprises were disposed of to a very small number of oligarchs through shares-for-credit. That is, shares-for-credit is by no means the whole story of oligarch power in Russia.[55] Nevertheless it did involve handing over a very substantial proportion of the Russian oil sector and some juicy pieces of the metals sector, and the very small number of people who were the beneficiaries are the most important players in our story. It is also undoubtedly the most controversial component of economic transition.[56] It therefore deserves the considerable amount of commentary that has been devoted to it.

At a cabinet meeting on 30 March 1995 Vladimir Potanin gave a presentation on behalf of a banking consortium, the Inter-Bank Credit Alliance, in which it was proposed that the consortium would provide substantial credits to the state, with the state's shares in a wide range of major industrial and resource assets being given to them to manage operationally as security on the loans. The banks involved were Menatep and ONEKSIMbank as the core participants, with Stolichnyi, Inkombank,

MFK and Imperial also members. Allan claims that Alfa-bank, Sberbank and Vneshtorgbank were also interested. Rossiiskii Kredit expressed support, but did not join.[57]

To some extent the proposal was a reaction to a different proposal from another bank consortium, known as Nadezhnost. Although there was some overlap in the membership of the two consortiums, Nadezhnost was dominated by banks that had been hived off from Soviet banks, rather than 'oligarch' commercial start-ups. Each consortium had quite a different approach to large-scale private investment in the Russian economy. While Potanin's group was oriented towards complete private control of the assets to be included in the scheme, Nadezhnost's proposal was based on banks participating as partners in state investment programmes.[58]

The government leaned towards the 'oligarch' approach and approved the proposal in principle, asking that a more detailed version be prepared. Negotiations continued, and towards the end of 1995 a final scheme was approved and implemented. It now involved a much smaller number of enterprises than first envisaged (managers of many originally on the list succeeding in having themselves removed), but it still involved some highly strategic assets in the resource sector. Now the scheme was open to all, meaning that the original consortium lost its reason for existence. The assets were to be put up for auction, the winner of each auction being the bidder who offered the highest amount of credit to the state. The winner, as already mentioned, would hold the state's shares as security on the loan and have the right of operational control. If the loans were not repaid, the creditor would have the right to sell the shares at another auction in order to recover the debt.

The original auctions proceeded in an atmosphere of confusion and scandal in late 1995. The main players, ONEKSIMbank and Menatep, had clearly divided up in advance the assets they were interested in, with the main losers being Inkombank, Rossiiskii Kredit and Alfa-bank. When they had tried to enter the fray, their bids were excluded on the flimsiest of grounds. One of the most notorious was the exclusion of Rossiiskii Kredit's bid of $355 million for Norilsk Nickel, leaving ONEKSIMbank as the winner with a bid of $170.1 million, $100,000 above the starting price. Table 3.1 summarises the results of the auctions. To no one's surprise, a year later the loans were not repaid, and the banks holding the shares duly arranged the second round of auctions in such a way that they won them.

There are three main explanations as to what shares-for-credit was all about. According to the first it was a short-term political deal cooked up

Table 3.1   Results of shares-for-credit auctions

Asset auctioned	Percentage of shares auctioned	Starting price, $m	Winning bid, $m	Winning institution
Surgutneftegaz	40.12	66.7	88.9	Surgutneftegaz Pension Fund
Norilsk Nickel	38	170	170.1	ONEKSIMbank/MFK
Mechel	15	5	13.3	Imperial
Northwest Shipping	25.5	6	6.05	MFK/ONEKSIMbank
Lukoil	5	35	35.01	Imperial/Lukoil
Sidanko	51	125	130	MFK/ONEKSIMbank
NLMK	14.84	30	31	MFK/ONEKSIMbank
Murmansk Shipping	23.5	4	4.125	Menatep
Yukos	45	150	159	Menatep, Stolichnyi, Tokobank
Novorossiisk Shipping	20	15	22.65	Novorossiisk Shipping Company
Nafta-Moscow	15	20	20.01	Nafta-fin/ ONEKSIMbank
Sibneft	51	100	100.3	Stolichnyi/Menatep

Source: 'Rezul'taty auktsionov', *Panorama privatizatsii*, no.3, February 1996, pp.52–4.

by Yeltsin and his political cronies, worried about losing an upcoming presidential election and so looking to buy the political support of the most powerful economic actors in the country. As Freeland puts it, 'the loans-for-shares deal was a crude trade of property for political support'.[59] The second explanation, argued forcefully by Allan, is that it was an opportunistic grab of assets off a government that faced a desperate budgetary situation.[60] The third is that it involved a strong element of long-term strategic thinking among a powerful group of reform-oriented policy makers.

Allan's dismissal of the first, 'political deal', explanation is convincing. The oligarchs' funding of Yeltsin's presidential campaign in the first half of 1996 seemed in its conception and implementation too hurried and even panic-stricken to have been planned at least a year in advance. He also provides appropriate evidence of the government's waxing and waning in attitude towards a scheme about which it had always had strong reservations, according to the ups and downs of its budgetary situation. This is not what one would have expected of a carefully planned political strategy.

The waxing and waning of the government's support over most of 1995, depending on its budgetary situation, is what drives Allan's explanation. Although he does not address his argument so exclusively to shares-for-credit, Neil Robinson's basic argument is similar to Allan's. He suggests that governments are driven in their policy-making above all by fiscal concerns. In the Russian case those fiscal concerns made it necessary to deal with the oligarchs.[61]

The third view is that shares-for-credit was designed to achieve a strategic goal, laying the foundation for a privately owned big business able to operate competitively in global markets. The original shares-for-credit proposal of March 1995 came at a time when there had been a vigorous discussion underway in Russia for some months on the benefits or otherwise of large, integrated corporate structures. It was a time of considerable emphasis on the so-called financial-industrial groups (FIGs), with regular and positive references to Korean *chaebols* and Japanese *keiretsu*, the huge, privately owned conglomerates that, working in close cooperation with the state, were seen as the 'locomotives' of Korean and Japanese economic growth. The main – or most public – champions of such an approach were those whom we could call the 'statists'. Sceptical of the market, they saw large industrial groupings as being more easily managed by the state, particularly if the scattered residual state shareholdings in individual enterprises were consolidated into large holding companies.[62] The most immediate outcome was a burst of legislative and organizational activity devoted to 'official' FIGs. They were to a considerable extent a last-gasp effort of Red Directors and sectoral officials, and enjoyed the fate that one would expect of such creations.[63]

If it had been only the statists interested in FIGs, it is unlikely that the matter would have gone further than the rather sad 'official' examples. The original reformers, beyond a classical fear of 'combination' in general, had regarded the burgeoning commercial banks with particular suspicion. Those who preferred an Anglo-US style of capitalism to a German bank-dominated style (to say nothing of Singaporean, Japanese or South Korean models) feared the excessive power of banks. As a consequence there was a history of limitations on bank involvement in industrial investments.[64]

However there was a group of reformers whose desire for strong competitive private companies was such that they were prepared to accept the risks of an over-concentration of economic power. As ever Chubais was to the fore – even if not in a loud, public way. He championed the concept of non-official, privately owned FIGs.[65] His resulting willingness to support shares-for-credit caused considerable disillusion-ment among his one-time supporters. *The Economist* commented some time later that '[Chubais] has become closely entwined with an oli-garchy of bankers and industrialists who want at best only a freeish mar-ket in Russia ... [R]eform has long since parted company with the theories that once inspired it'.[66] The official FIGs were still-born, to a considerable degree because Chubais's State Property Agency (GKI) refused to hand the state's shares over to them. The private, commercial-bank-led FIGs were treated with considerably more respect.

One aspect of the strategy requires particular and unfortunately inconclusive attention. It appears to have excluded the possibility of for-eign involvement. This was particularly so in the case of shares-for-credit. There is no strong evidence as to the views of a reformer such as Chubais towards large-scale foreign involvement in the economy. He had not excluded foreigners from mass privatization. There were few foreign takers on that occasion, and it is by no means certain that there would have been greater foreign interest even in the attractive assets put up for sale through shares-for-credit.[67] The financial wobble of Black Tuesday, in October 1994, and the brief reign of the conservative Vladimir Polevanov at GKI had shaken investor confidence. Indeed according to Allan's argument regarding shares-for-credit, it was the lack of foreign investment, plus extreme revenue pressures on a government deter-mined to keep inflation under control, that made shares-for-credit an irresistible proposition for a sceptical government.[68]

The oligarchs, however, had a history of lobbying for the exclusion of foreigners, and there are claims that they were active again in this regard at this stage.[69] Potanin is reported as claiming that he wanted the bid-ding to be open to foreigners,[70] but given the long history of lobbying by the 'seven bankers' for the exclusion of foreigners from their fields of activity, and the vast benefit that their absence from the bidding for Norilsk Nickel brought Potanin, this is hard to believe. Allan, indeed, claims that a major impetus behind the shares-for-credit proposal from Potanin and the other oligarch banks was to forestall a possible govern-ment sell-off of shares in Russia's biggest companies to foreign interests.[71] But equally, in the Russia of the time, it would not have been hard to make a case for the exclusion of foreigners – indeed the oligarchs proba-bly did not need to make it. Public opinion would hardly have been assuaged by a higher return in what would have been seen as a pauper's sell-off of assets to foreigners. Once it had been decided that foreigners would be excluded, there was never any doubt as to who would win the assets. The financial oligarchs were the only possible bidders.

For those promoting the 'strategic' explanation of shares-for-credit the waxing and waning in the government's attitude towards the proposal through 1995 is not explained by Allan's ups and downs in the government's fiscal situation, but by political manoeuvring within the government, between statists, Chubais's FIG-oriented reformers, and the more classically pure reformers. In 1992–3 Chubais had made a strategic alliance with the Red Directors over privatization, albeit one that the latter were probably not aware they had entered into. Again Chubais achieved policy success by taking advantage of the statists, who, wanting their official FIGs, probably realized too late the extent to which they were being used.

Just because shares-for-credit was part of a deliberate and long-term strategy by the government, rather than a short-term political deal or reaction to a fiscal crisis, does not mean that it was a good thing, either in conception or implementation. For those who were horrified by shares-for-credit the outcome was that so much economic power had been handed to the oligarchs that they could only be prevented from arrogating to themselves excessive political power through the use of authoritarian methods. And it had been done in such a brazen and corrupt way – and at such obscenely cheap prices – that it finally killed off any remaining legitimacy that political or economic reform might have had. This made it very much easier for a politician adopting the authoritarian methods needed to control the oligarchs to do so with popular support. That is an argument we will return to when we examine the relationship between Putin and the oligarchs.

There are few who speak in public with enthusiasm for shares-for-credit. Åslund is an exception. He claims:

> Most of the enterprises involved in loans-for-shares did extremely well, notably Yukos and Sibneft. They led the revival of the Russian oil industry, and soon they paid as much in taxes in one single year as anybody possibly could have tried to sell those enterprises for in 1995. Thus, economically, the Russian loans-for-shares privatizations were an unmitigated success.[72]

It will take an examination of the economic performance of the business structures that resulted from shares-for-credit and the political consequences of their dominance of the economy before we can decide who has the better of the argument, Åslund or the critics. We will therefore leave a final evaluation of shares-for-credit until after we have looked at what the oligarchs did with the assets they obtained through the scheme.

The second *peredel*

As shares-for-credit ended, Russian industry, including the resource sector, was in a far from stable state in terms of ownership, at a time of considerable economic difficulty. The allocation of assets to new owners through mass privatization had taken place at enterprise level and had therefore been haphazard in terms of the relationships between enterprises. In the oil sector, where considerable efforts at consolidation had been made before privatization, there were as a result serious difficulties in sorting out the relationships between holding companies and subsidiaries. As far as the economy at the time was concerned, although the banking oligarchs had found a new way of making money in the government bond market, the real economy was suffering from a severe cash squeeze that produced the barter economy and a strong ruble policy that reduced the returns of exporters and the competitiveness of those producing for the domestic market. Nevertheless, despite the uncertainty of returns in the resource sector, the assets were clearly considered worth fighting over, sometimes all too literally. The second half of the 1990s saw a vigorous and often brutal struggle for corporate ownership and control, known as the second *peredel* (*peredel* being the word originally used to describe the redistribution of land by collective peasant bodies under Tsarism and now applied to major events in post-Soviet property redistribution).

There were two aspects of the second *peredel*. The first was obtaining new assets to fill in gaps in corporate holdings. This indicated a new awareness of the desirability of properly structured holdings. The early impetus was in the direction of vertical integration, particularly to secure inputs. Horizontal integration then became of interest as well. Both forms of integration generally involved acquiring privatized assets from other private owners, whether they be Red Director beneficiaries of privatization or outside investors. This aspect of the second *peredel* was typical of the metals sector, which had been privatized through the regular mass privatization process, and so was characterized by individual production units existing as juridically independent companies.

The other form of the second *peredel*, more typical of the oil sector, was securing dominant majority shareholdings in companies in which the oligarchs already had equity holdings. This applied particularly to the subsidiaries that the oligarchs had obtained with their oil holding companies. There had been a considerable degree of integration, both vertical and horizontal, in the oil sector *before* privatization. That meant that those who had succeeded in gaining control of a holding company, whether it be Yukos, Sibneft or TNK, had a lot of subsidiaries and a lot of minority shareholders in those subsidiaries to deal with. It often involved the rough treatment of those minority shareholders. (In the metals sector the second *peredel* could quite possibly involve the rough treatment of majority shareholders!)

Minority shareholders were dealt with in time-honoured fashion, using the techniques pioneered by the Red Directors and described earlier in the chapter, above all manipulation of share registers, shareholder meetings and their agendas, as well as the dilution of share holdings. Attempts had been made to deal with these abuses in the mid-1990s by a series of presidential and governmental decrees and some of the provisions of the Civil Code. The basic principles of shareholder rights and corporate governance were then set out in a consolidated piece of legislation, the Law 'On Joint-Stock Companies' (*aktsionernye obshchestva*, AOs), which after a long passage through parliament was passed by the Duma (the lower house) on 24 November 1995 and signed by Yeltsin on 26 December 1995, to come into legal force as of 1 January 1996. The Law had some success in reducing the incidence of the early forms of corporate governance abuse, share register abuse in particular and to a lesser extent shareholder meeting abuse.[73] Despite the legislation making it the exclusive right of a shareholders' meeting to approve share issues, and requiring that new share issues be offered in proportion to shareholding, share dilution remained a major problem.

Share dilution. Share dilution episodes can be found in almost all oligarch-held companies of this time. For example, in 1998 Sibneft pushed through a shareholder meeting of its main production unit, Noyabrskneftegaz, a vast share dilution scheme, which was upheld by a local court.[74] Norilsk Nickel's restructurings have also involved very controversial dealings with minorities as Potanin worked to consolidate assets in a single corporate entity. Shareholders suffered a 50 per cent dilution in early 1998,[75] and another controversial restructuring was pushed through in late 2000. After much manoeuvring, that restructuring appeared to end in an 11.5 per cent dilution of minorities.[76]

Not surprisingly minority shareholders were often not happy about these dealings, and vigorous approaches to controlling the relevant shareholder meetings had sometimes to be adopted. During 1997–8 Khodorkovsky borrowed from Western banks, using Yukos shares and subsidiary guarantees as collateral. The August 1998 crisis left him unable, or perhaps unwilling, to repay the credits, meaning that 30 per cent of

Yukos shares were liable to be taken by Western banks. Khodorkovsky proposed a huge asset transfer and share dilution deal to shareholders. Khodorkovsky had 51 per cent of shares, but needed a 75 per cent vote to get the deal he wanted. On the day before the shareholders' meeting, he got a court decision that disqualified the votes of minority share-holders, on the grounds that they intended to act in concert, something forbidden under anti-trust legislation. After long and loud protests and threats of court action, eventually most minority shareholders gave up, and accepted the Khodorkovsky proposal.[77]

Value transfer. The transfer of value from one company to another within an oligarch-controlled group, almost always from a subsidiary with substantial minority holdings to a more fully owned holding com-pany, took two forms: the simple transfer of assets at less than fair value, and the shift of earnings through transfer pricing. One of the criminal cases involving Yukos executives related to the decision of a subsidiary to transfer its assets to Yukos. Svetlana Bakhmina, of Yukos's legal department, was charged with the theft of the assets of Tomskneft in the years 1998 and 1999. Tomskneft became a subsidiary of Yukos in 1998, when the latter obtained control of the Eastern Oil Company (VNK). Bakhmina was a member of the council of directors of Tomskneft and, it is claimed, used that position to arrange for Tomskneft assets worth more than R8 billion to be sold to various Yukos front firms for R3.38 billion.[78]

Yukos was also criticized from the time it was taken over by Khodorkovsky for the use of transfer pricing in the relationships between the head company and production subsidiaries. This was a major component of the tax evasion charges against Yukos, to which we will return later in this book. However the transfer pricing also had the effect of shifting value from the subsidiaries, who suddenly found them-selves selling oil to the head company at well below market value. As a consequence subsidiaries that had been making good profits were suddenly booking huge losses.[79] Similar stories can be found in the activities of Abramovich at Sibneft. Sibneft's main production unit was Noyarbrskneftegaz, of which it owned 61 per cent. In 1996, before Sibneft's involvement, Noyarbrsk earned $600 million; the next year its earnings were zero.[80]

There is little doubting the predatory nature of both share dilution and value transfer schemes. The value of the assets and the income streams of the minority shareholders were greatly weakened. However some further comments on these events are in order. When Menatep won the shares-for-credit auction for Yukos, it not only paid $150 million, but also took over debts of $3 billion.[81] Presumably before Khodorkovsky had become involved the losses within the operation, mostly unpaid-for deliveries, were being borne by the holding company, and what transfer pricing there was operated in favour of the subsidiaries. As we will see in the next chapter, this was typical of the management decentralization that ruled in late Soviet and early post-Soviet industry. Although to make the point is not to justify the transfer of the losses from the holding company to the subsidiaries, with their higher levels of minority shareholders, it does serve as a corrective to the view presented in some of the anti-oligarch literature that the Russian oil industry was thriving until Khodorkovsky and his ilk came along to destroy it, as evidenced by the sudden losses of subsidiaries.

As a further comment, although one has to be wary of the public relations wars that were just as vigorous at this time as the board and court room battles, there were doubts expressed at the time about the bona fide intentions of many of the minority shareholders. Kenneth Dart, Yukos's main protagonist, has been described as a 'greenmailer'.[82] Without suggesting that greenmailers should have no property rights, it is indeed hard to see Dart as a serious strategic investor, willing to match the investment intentions of the majority owners. In later years, when the investment plans of the oligarch companies became much more ambitious, there were clear cases of minority investors blocking those plans. When an oligarch owner wanted to put more equity into the company, hard-up or disinterested minorities did not contribute. When Norilsk Nickel's revenues improved post-1998 and the company announced ambitious investment plans, minority shareholders were unhappy at the effect on their immediate returns.[83]

Bankruptcy. In the metals sector the second *peredel* was more about new acquisitions than establishing control over subsidiaries. Here the favoured new technique was bankruptcy. The first post-Soviet bankruptcy code had been designed to make it easy for creditors to bankrupt debtor enterprises and then arrange to have existing management replaced. Creditors could go to court to have the debtor enterprise bankrupted and simultaneously recommend the appointment of an administrator to run the company. It seemed to suit the needs of a transition economy – to make it harder for corporate dinosaurs to survive but without requiring liquidation.[84]

In practice the process was used largely as a form of hostile takeover, and not usually of corporate dinosaurs. A would-be new owner would set out to gain control of the target enterprise's debts, at a time when most enterprises were heavily indebted. The secondary debt market could be used for this purpose, but if need be a cooperative state, whether at federal or regional level, would help 'create' some debts through the new and often retrospective interpretation of tax liabilities or essential service charges. Once in possession of the debtor's ledger, the raider would go to court to have the enterprise declared bankrupt and a bankruptcy administrator sympathetic to its interests put in place.[85] Steps would be taken, sometimes of a bizarre character, to ensure that debtors who were able and willing to pay off their debts were not given the opportunity to do so.

A classic example of the use of bankruptcy can be found in the aluminium industry. Remembering that Oleg Deripaska had used a share dilution to seize control of the Sayanogorsk Aluminium Plant from TWG, in doing so he took over the beginnings of a vertically integrated structure of Siberian enterprises that had been taking shape under TWG's control and which was known as Siberian Aluminium.[86] He wanted to add the Novokuznetsk Aluminium Plant (NkAZ) to his rapidly growing empire, and used the bankruptcy approach to do so. Aman Tuleev, the governor of Kemerovo region, had the local power company retrospectively raise power rates. In reports at the time this action was explained by the fact that the majority shareholder of NkAZ, Mikhail Zhivilo, had got sick of paying into the governor's slush fund. The benefit that came to Deripaska from subsequent events makes it hard to believe that he was not involved from an early stage.[87] When NkAZ was unable or unwilling to pay the new power bill, Tuleev had the local court bankrupt NkAZ and appoint a Deripaska representative as administrator. To ram the point home Zhivilo was forced to flee the country as charges were about to be brought against him for attempting to murder Tuleev. He eventually sold his NkAZ shares, which then quickly ended up in Deripaska's hands.[88] Zhivilo was by no means a Soviet-era dinosaur Red Director. Although presumably using the connections made possible by an uncle who was a long-standing senior official in the Soviet metals sector, he was a brash young trader, more in the mould of the oligarchs than the Red Directors.

Zhivilo was at the same time being subjected to similar treatment by Tuleev at his other investment in the Kemerovo region, the steel producer, the Kuznetsk Metal Combine. There was some rough justice here, since Zhivilo himself had used the bankruptcy method to get control of the Kuznetsk plant, although only after the previous owners had allegedly used an illegal dilution against him.[89] This time Abramov's Evrazkholding was the beneficiary when Tuleev arranged for the court to dismiss and arrest Zhivilo's administrator and appoint an Evrazkholding representative.[90] Tuleev then assisted Evrazkholding gain control of another local steel producer, the West Siberian Metal Combine (ZSMK), using similar methods, this time against Fridman's Alfa Group.[91]

Another major bankruptcy battle raged around the Achinsk Alumina Combine. The plant had been purpose-built to process local nephelite ore into alumina, to feed the nearby Krasnoyarsk Aluminium Plant. Control of Achinsk, and therefore control of the prices at which its alumina was sold to KrAZ, was vital to the financial health of the latter. By the violent standards of KrAZ it was a relatively peaceful, if bitter, struggle, with multiple changes of administrator and juggling of debts. At the centre of the struggle was Alfa Bank, which for a number of years controlled the debts and therefore the administrator of the enterprise, and various KrAZ owners with differing relationships with Alfa.[92]

A new bankruptcy law was brought to parliament in 2002, which significantly shifted the balance of power back towards the debtor.[93] There are those who would claim that it was no coincidence that the new law was introduced after the oligarchs had consolidated their control over the resource sector.

We have seen in the stories told in the last few pages not just accounts of the use of share dilutions, value transfers and bankruptcy to strengthen oligarch control of assets and cash flows. Those techniques could work only if the oligarchs also had privileged access to the instruments of enforcement. Those instruments could be either official or unofficial, that is, the courts, both civil and criminal, or organized crime. There are indeed those who accuse the oligarchs of being organized crime.

Use of the courts, civil and criminal

In the early stages of transition there was considerable optimism regarding the development of a civil justice system to be used for commercial purposes. Kathryn Hendley wrote in 1998:

> The fact that economic actors have indicated a willingness to submit these disputes to the *arbitrazh* courts and to make use of the appellate process, when appropriate, indicates a burgeoning trust and acceptance of the reconstituted institution.[94]

Still today one might be encouraged by the willingness of business people to use the civil courts, despite all the manifest shortcomings of the latter.[95] Nevertheless in practice, so far, they have shown themselves to be at best open to manipulation and at worst totally corrupt.

In the case of the bankruptcy of NkAZ described above, the person who controlled the court was the regional governor, a not atypical case. But once an oligarch came to dominate a region, he also was likely to gain control over the local courts. Another strong feature of the time was the shopping around for a friendly court anywhere in Russia. Many an ill-timed injunction in these years appeared from obscure local courts in the general civil justification situated thousands of kilometres from the site of the commercial activities under dispute. The result was not just commercial chaos, but also sometimes physical violence among those sent in to enforce the decisions of different courts. The misuse of the courts also produced a very low level of trust in the legal system, with the obvious consequences for the rule of law. Business has been campaigning to restrict commercial disputes to the commercial court of the place of registration of the defendant.[96]

Perhaps even more fraught with unpleasant consequences was the willingness to use the criminal justice system in commercial disputes. For a good example we return to the aluminium industry, specifically KrAZ. TWG had been driven out by an insider manager, Iurii Kolpakov, in 1995, using share deregistration and the 'authority' of Anatolii Bykov, a reputed local underworld figure.[97] Over the following years Bykov became something of a fixture at the plant through various ownership changes. Once Deripaska got an entrée to the plant in 2000, through an alliance with Roman Abramovich, who had recently bought out TWG, he decided to deal with Bykov, and did so in classic style. As well as having been the enforcer for a number of owners of KrAZ, Bykov also had a substantial shareholding in his own right, enough to represent a blocking minority at shareholder meetings and obtain troublesome board representation. As Deripaska moved in, Bykov suddenly found himself forced to flee the country to avoid prosecution on money laundering and conspiracy to murder charges. He was eventually extradited from Hungary.[98]

Although those charges were eventually dropped, Bykov was immediately rearrested on somewhat bizarre charges of attempting to murder a former business associate. The initial murder charge was reduced to attempted murder after it was discovered that the victim was still alive – in fact had been observed walking down the street by Bykov's lawyer. The prosecutors then claimed that the 'murder' had been part of a sting, to entrap Bykov when his hired killer reported his successful completion of the job. While in prison Bykov expressed willingness to sell his KrAZ shares 'in a civilized fashion – without threats and pressure', although he did add that 'until I sell my shares in KrAz, I will not be left in peace'.[99] While awaiting trial Bykov duly sold his KrAZ shares, and although he was found guilty was immediately released after receiving a suspended sentence.[100]

We have already seen a similar use of the criminal justice system against Mikhail Zhivilo, who also sold his shares in a disputed company after fleeing the country to escape charges of attempted murder. Deripaska was the beneficiary on that occasion as well.

The effect of all this on a 'law ruled' society is to be looked at again when we look at Putin's campaign against the oligarchs, Khodorkovsky in particular. It is worth mentioning at this point, though, that when the state moved against the oligarchs in the form of Khodorkovsky and his company Yukos, using the full force of both the civil and criminal jurisdictions, a strong theme in the oligarchs' self-defence strategy was regret for their past use of the justice system in their competitive struggles and a strong desire that such techniques no longer be used.[101]

The use of criminal 'authorities'

If the misuse of the criminal justice system is of greater cause for concern than misuse of the civil jurisdiction, then recourse to unofficial, extra-legal enforcement systems must be of even greater concern.

It is often claimed by their critics that the oligarchs themselves were criminals or were the partners of criminals. The title of Klebnikov's book about Berezovsky, 'Godfather of the Kremlin', presents the picture. Stiglitz refers, very circumspectly, to 'the small band of people (some of whom owed their origins, reportedly at least, partly to mafia-like connections)'.[102] A former Soviet military intelligence officer, Stanislav Lunev, speaks in the same breath of criminal involvement in privatization and drug and prostitution rackets. '[T]he battle at the privatization auctions was waged between representatives of former underground mafia structures, who by that time had become respectable financial-industrial groups, firms, companies, and banks.' He cites a Russian parliamentary report to the effect that privatization 'is the main cause of the criminalization of society and the progressive growth of crime in Russia'.[103]

The degree of criminalization of the oligarchy is an interesting but difficult theme. It is a matter of great definitional complexity and obvious evidentiary difficulty. In the claims of criminalization more is being spoken of than the possible criminality of the oligarchs' commercial activities – the stripping of assets, the minimization of tax and so on. The claims are that the oligarchs or their associates had their origins in the criminal, 'thieves' underworld; that like most mafia members they are engaged not only in the regular economy, but also in traditional criminal activity such as prostitution, drug running, protection rackets and so on; and that they use extreme forms of violence up to and including murder.

We have noted already, in our accounts of struggles for corporate control, the use of 'enforcers' and 'authorities', including the rise and fall of Anatolii Bykov at KrAZ. The aluminium industry has been a particularly violent one.[104] Despite that, there is in fact not much evidence of criminal backgrounds among the oligarchs, in the sense of having come from the Soviet or even post-Soviet mafia and bringing mafia money into the real economy. Some of the G7 had blackmarketeering backgrounds, including legal difficulties as a result; of the new oligarchs, Abramovich had early legal difficulties relating to his commercial activities. But there is nothing of the mafia about any of this. As already mentioned, regular claims have been made about the organised crime origins and connections of the Chernye brothers, who through TWG provided a start to Deripaska and Lisin.[105] Deripaska has no clear criminal background in the way that Bykov does. Nevertheless he was for many years denied a visa to enter the US on the grounds of his criminal connections. It is said that it took the personal intervention of President Putin with George Bush to have the ban lifted. The criminal connections in question were apparently the Chernye brothers.

The case against Bykov of a criminal background seems better based in evidence, at least evidence available in the public arena, than that against Deripaska. Similarly strong claims are made about another would-be metal magnate, Pavel Fedulev.[106] But in terms of the criminalization of the oligarchs, the fate of these two – and the Chernye brothers for that matter – is instructive. They were all driven out of the industry. It could be claimed that the oligarchs have proven tougher than the crooks.[107] One notes the 1998 comments of an unnamed leading banker regarding Smolensky, by no means the most important or toughest of the oligarchs. While he might once have had criminal connections, now 'I am sure no gangster can reach Smolensky, or even talk to him today.'[108]

There is no more evidence of involvement in such typical organized crime activities as prostitution and drug running than there is of criminal origins. There are the occasional little titbits, but they never go beyond that. One newspaper published what appeared to be a leaked dossier from the Prosecutor General's office about activities in the aluminium industry, claiming that TWG spirited money out of Russia, through an unnamed but shady scheme which is obviously tolling, and used the proceeds to fund drug and terrorist operations.[109] These are presumably part of the claims about the organized crime links of the Chernye brothers. Another version of what appears to be the same story is that the aluminium magnates of the 1990s used tolling schemes to launder and export criminal earnings within Russia, by artificially inflating the cost of tolled inputs. This is more than simple transfer pricing in order to reduce taxable earnings. Some of the inflated sums flowing offshore were in fact earned in criminal activities outside the aluminium industry.[110]

In September 2005 a US court finally dismissed a case that Mikhail Fridman and Petr Aven had been pursuing against an American NGO, the Center for Public Integrity, since 2000. In 1999 the Center had published on its website an article which claimed, more in an aside than as the main theme of an article which was in fact about the alleged influence-peddling of Halliburton, that Fridman and Aven's company Alfa 'was involved in the laundering of narcomoney of the Russian and Colombian mafias and in the transhipment of narcotics from the Far East to Europe in the early 1990s'. It should be noted that the judge made no judgement on the truth of the claims, but ruled on the basis that under the US First Amendment comment on 'public figures' could not be found to be libellous.[111]

In more recent times there have been reports of investigations in Europe and Israel of the money laundering activities of Gusinsky and Khodorkovsky's colleague Leonid Nevzlin (in Israel avoiding murder and tax evasion charges).[112] The reports of the investigation of Nevzlin's alleged activities came at a particularly embarrassing time for Khodorkovsky, as he was on trial in Moscow. Berezovsky is also occasionally subjected to searches of his houses in pursuit of evidence relating to similar vague charges.[113] None of the investigations appear to have come to much. Even if there is some basis in the claims of money laundering, it appears likely that what is involved is the processing of the proceeds of their commercial operations in Russia, that is, part of 'normal' capital flight from Russia. As Buiter puts it:

> Even when the funds channelled abroad were acquired in legitimate activities, the manner of their transfer abroad will often have criminalized them.[114]

Those on the receiving end of the accusations usually point to their coincidence with developments in the foreign relations between Russia and the states involved: an Israeli desire to have Putin on their side in the Middle East conflict, a recent visit of Chirac to Moscow and so on.[115]

The other component of the accusations of criminality against the oligarchs is that they have used the methods of organized crime in pursuing their commercial activities. We have already seen the role of Bykov as an 'enforcer' for various owners of KrAZ. The finger is also pointed at the private armies employed by the oligarchs. The public faces of the big corporate security forces are in fact usually former military or KGB types, not people from the criminal world, with former KGB deputy chair Fedor Bobkov at Gusinsky's MOST being the most commonly cited example. That of course does not mean that they are averse to using extreme methods. Aleksandr Pichugin, the Yukos security official found guilty of murder and attempted murder, has a background in the security services, not the mafia. (The charges against Pichugin will be described in more detail in a later chapter.) However usually the more concrete accusations that are made against corporate security forces are of industrial espionage and counterespionage and the gathering of *kompromat* (compromising materials) on business competitors and politicians and officials.[116] Oligarchs themselves see their security departments as being used to guarantee the probity of their companies' operations, not undermine it.[117]

We have already come across claims that the criminal activities of big Russian corporations went as far as murder. There were a number of murders in the aluminium industry in the mid-1990s, although it remains to this day obscure who was involved and why. More recently in December 2005 Aleksandr Shoror, the chairman of the board of directors and co-owner of the Stupino Metal Combine, was arrested on a charge of the 2002 murder of another businessman. His defence claims that the false accusation comes from Shoror's co-owners, with whom Shoror had argued and one of whom is himself the subject of a search warrant relating to charges of falsification of evidence and pressuring witnesses.[118] It should be pointed out that no oligarchs are involved in the Stupino Metal Combine. As already mentioned, part of the recent campaign against Yukos has been the arrest and sentencing of one of its security officials, Aleksandr Pichugin, for murders and attempted murders carried out on the orders of major Yukos shareholder Leonid Nevzlin. We will devote more attention to those cases in the later chapter which concentrates on the Yukos affair.

The picture drawn so far in this chapter is not a pretty one. Even allowing for the falsifications of the PR campaigns of competitors and the exaggerations of the ideological opponents of market reform and oligarch capitalism, the evidence is clear of – at best – serious corporate governance abuses by the oligarchs. They themselves admit as much, Khodorkovsky being particularly frank and penitent in recent times.[119]

One might argue that the predatory treatment of subsidiaries and minority shareholders was inevitable in the circumstances of the time and had a positive economic logic to it. The minority shareholders were usually no angels themselves, and had entered into their investments with their eyes open. Consideration will be given in the rest of this chapter to the suggestion that the consolidation of oligarch control of their assets might have had such positive benefits, for both corporate governance and commercial performance, that a conciliatory approach to judgement might be appropriate.

The misuse of the court system is a more serious matter, since the victims of such misuse end up being all of society rather than a limited number of minority shareholders. A corrupt and compromised legal system is not sustainably compatible with the sort of economic and political development that the reformers and their supporters among the population hoped for when they undertook the transition.

There can, of course, be no justification for the use of violence in business competition. The best that can be said about the oligarchs in this regard is that there are major problems of evidence with regard to most of the more lurid accusations, and that the more 'colourful' figures involved in Russian business have been driven out by the oligarchs.

Any defence of the oligarchs' violations of corporate governance and legal rules and procedures has to be based on two grounds: that they were temporary, 'a natural stage of development'; and that they brought about changes in corporate behaviour and performance that were in net terms beneficial to the Russian economy and society, changes that might not have happened otherwise.

Corporate governance 'enlightenment'

Whatever the methods used, by the end of the 1990s or the early 2000s the oil and metals sectors, non-ferrous in particular, were well consolidated, as is reflected in the presence of oil barons and metal magnates in both our oligarch samples. Not only was there a considerable degree of consolidation of the sectors into a relatively small number of large corporations, but those corporations were held quite tightly by their oligarch owners. Minority shareholders in both the holding companies and their subsidiaries had been reduced to virtual insignificance, with indeed the basis being laid for the consolidation of oligarch holdings into single balance sheets and share registers often as a prelude to the public sale of shares.[120]

The consolidation of oligarch control brought a significant shift in the style of corporate governance and behaviour of the oligarchs. Kets de Vries quotes Khodorkovsky, generally credited with being the pioneer of the shift towards improved corporate governance and transparency:

> Previously we were all focused on the cash revenues of our business, since no one believed that the situation would last. Now that things are stabilizing, people are more interested in increasing the value of their property.[121]

Guriev and Rachinsky note the importance of the oligarchs now having secure controlling shareholdings for producing a strong incentive to restructure and increase value, 'rather than for diverting cash flows and stripping the assets'.[122] Roland Nash puts a lot of emphasis on gaining a 75 per cent + 1 shareholding, at which level minorities are unable to block the policy preferences of the controlling shareholder. The change in the economic environment – the strengthening of ownership control – allows asset value to become more important than mere revenue streams. The secure ownership 'provides both the security and the incentive to manage those assets more sensibly and therefore profitably. Most important from a shareholder perspective, it also provides the incentive to encourage the share price upwards.'[123] According to this view, there was now a new stress on increasing the value of the asset in order to ensure a long-term flow of returns from it. A number, at least, of oligarchs saw the expression of the increase in terms of market capitalization. Often this was further expressed in terms of wanting to prepare the company for a future stockmarket flotation. We will deal with the problems of using share price and market capitalization as a measure of the performance of Russian firms in the next chapter.

Even for those oligarchs concerned to keep tight control over their share registers and so less concerned with share values, there is a new desire to have the value of their companies publicly measured and acknowledged. As their empires grew and required long-term capital for their future development, the oligarchs found it increasingly necessary to attract external funding. For some this was through partnership with a strategic investor, not someone who would be interested in the day-to-day movements of the share price and market capitalization, but nevertheless who would need a good understanding of the core value and prospects of the asset. But even more important, given the continuing reluctance of most oligarchs to give away too much equity, is access to debt financing. A good public reputation is important for reducing the cost of debt, and oligarch firms have shown a new interest in international auditing and credit ratings.

How did this new approach express itself? Khodorkovsky created a sensation when in early 2002 he declared publicly the ownership structure of his company and his own income. He began to publish the accounts of his companies, and brought a large number of independent directors, many of them foreigners, on to his board of directors.[124] By doing so he put pressure on other oligarchs to do the same.

Once the oligarchs were willing to produce such believable accounts, and given that they were in most cases now dominant shareholders, they had no reason not to put more emphasis on dividends as the preferred way of distributing returns. Previously, when a substantial proportion of dividends would have gone to minority shareholders and when there were good reasons not to produce realistic accounts on which dividends could be based, dividend payments were a rarity. In recent years they have become very common. We will examine dividend policies in more detail in the next chapter.

Khodorkovsky also claimed that the new approach required greater respect for the law. Taking the West as a model, he said in an early 2002 interview (published for the first time in 2005):

> There they have various rules, including in business, which serve to make life normal. And since pickling money in jars is not a goal in itself and one wants to live a normal life, then those rules are not completely superfluous. Even if tactically they might sometimes get in the way, in the medium term they help you live.[125]

The implication is that in earlier times Khodorkovsky might have allowed the tactical considerations to hold sway. But now a longer-term view, based on what he believed to be secure tenure of his assets, had brought home to him the benefits of rules.

Socially responsible business

A contentious aspect of the oligarchs' 'enlightenment' was a very public concern for the social responsibility of business. The oligarchs, like other big businesses, had never been able to avoid entirely their social responsibilities. They usually controlled a very significant proportion of the economic activities in the localities and regions in which they operated, and were under irresistible pressure to maintain employment and social facilities. This is not to say that there were no redundancies and no transfer of kindergartens, rest homes and all the other paraphernalia of the Soviet 'corporate welfare state' to local governments. Nevertheless the entire burden could not be denied, and business owners who wanted to maintain good relations with local politicians in particular had to be restrained in their cutting of social expenditures.[126]

In the early years of the new millennium social responsibility became a declared policy of big business, particularly through the business association into which the oligarchs had just moved, the Russian Union of Industrialists and Entrepreneurs (RSPP). Social responsibility generally took the form of providing funding for local projects, whether it be sponsoring sporting events or facilities, cultural events and so on. The RSPP estimated in 2003 that Russian business had been spending in recent times about $500 million a year on philanthropy and social programmes. In 2002 Severstal had spent $30 million on philanthropy. Between 1997 and 2003 Norilsk Nickel had spent $100 million resettling 23,500 retired workers from its far northern settlements.[127]

Occasionally social responsibility was seen in broader terms. Three large charity funds had been created, the Potanin Fund, Khodorkovsky's 'Open Russia', and Berezovsky's Fund for Civil Freedom. The names of the latter two suggest that in the eyes of Khodorkovsky and Berezovsky social responsibility included a major civic component. Khodorkovsky's fund became well-known in misfortune, as it became a pawn in the state's attacks on its patron. Khodorkovsky put great emphasis in his statements on his philanthropy on the civic education of young people, and he sponsored schools, youth camps and youth forums. He famously described himself as combining three generations of Rockefeller in one, from Robber Baron to philanthropist.[128]

As we will see in the chapter devoted specifically to the Yukos affair, Khodorkovsky's charitable work became controversial not just because of its political sensitivity, but also because of the state's claims that most of his charities were in fact nothing more than tax evasion schemes. The social responsibility of business in general became a major theme of business-government relations as the Yukos affair dragged on. As big business, mainly through RSPP, tried busily to attract public support by speaking ever more loudly of its commitment to social responsibility,[129] the government made it very clear that social responsibility included paying taxes in full and that its philanthropic component would be recognized by the state as a contribution to society only if it were in areas identified by the state as being worthy of such attention.[130] 'Social responsibility' as a civil society concept was further damaged in 2005 and 2006 by the debate over the registration of NGOs and their foreign funding.[131] The effect can be seen in the public's attitudes towards charity and philanthropy. A March 2005 poll of Muscovites found that 24 per cent believed that philanthropy was just a cover for spying, and 55 per cent for money laundering. Only 51 per cent considered charity to be more beneficial than harmful, and 59 per cent believed that charity was a matter for the state, not private bodies.[132]

The sceptics would claim that the oligarchs' commitment to social responsibility was never more than rather thin window dressing, and that it became an increasingly pathetic response to the government's attacks on Yukos. Those who regard the oligarchs more positively would like to think that here was a genuine commitment, as one would expect of business people who feel more secure in their place in the economy and society, and therefore feel the need to make a broader contribution to social development than purely commercial activity. While some further discussion of the government's tax accusations against Khodorkovsky's charities will be relevant, the author's view is that generally one should not look a gift horse in the mouth.

Conclusions

After a decade of privatization and *peredel* the 'Chubais reformers' had what they wanted – big, powerful private companies, with a considerable degree of vertical and horizontal integration. There were a small number of oil majors, covering everything from exploration to retail. The aluminium industry was divided between Deripaska's Rusal and Vekselberg's SUAL,[133] while nickel and copper were covered by Norilsk Nickel and Makhmudov's UGMK. While there were still perhaps more steel groups than the industry could bear, those groups that did exist were looking increasingly coherent in terms of input security, technological regimes and market strategies.

While one is suitably aware that there might have been some gap between oligarch propaganda and reality,[134] the author is prepared to accept that there was a change in the oligarchs' attitudes towards their own assets, admittedly after they had worked with a degree of brutality to put themselves in a position where they could assure themselves that they did own the assets. It is undoubtedly easier to treat minority shareholders well when there are none of them left. However to the extent that the change took the form of the adoption of a longer-term approach to managing their assets and the wealth flows from them, not only was the result an improvement in corporate governance behaviour, but also a willingness to recognize that continued growth of the business would require the attraction of outside investment. The major reliance was on debt finance, with its reduced implications for ownership control. But inevitably and evidently consideration had to be given to the readmission of outsiders to the share register, as the search for strategic investors and preparations for IPOs became increasingly serious.

In the end, though, all of this, even if it happened, is relevant only if it were accompanied by improvements in business performance and in the mechanisms for allocating a share of the benefits to society. In the next chapter we look at performance, and then in subsequent ones at the political arrangements and – that most controversial of mechanisms for the reallocation of the benefits of economic activity to society – the tax system.

4
The Economic Performance of the Barons and Magnates

How the oligarchs obtained their assets is hardly irrelevant: perceptions of morality, equity and social justice are too important to the legitimacy of any politico-economic system, much less one in as difficult and delicate a transition process as Russia. Indeed, for some, whether or not our oil barons and metal magnates make good use of the assets they obtained is irrelevant. A thief cannot justify theft by claiming to have looked after the stolen property well.

But to most of their critics it is clear that the oligarchs can lay no claim to such a justification anyway. They are guilty not just of having obtained their assets in inappropriate ways, but of not having looked after the stolen property as well. This is important not just for economic but also political reasons. The economic consequences of rapacious and incompetent business leaders are clear enough. The political consequences are also clear. An economy that is being driven into the ground by those who dominate ownership of assets cannot provide the material welfare needed for the bulk of the nation's citizens in order to provide the foundations for stable, democratic development. The lack of legitimacy of big business, derived not just from how it obtained assets but also the poor use made of them, leaves room for populist, anti-market politics. The inability or unwillingness of the oligarchs to contribute to the material prosperity of society makes it difficult for them to resist attacks from the state. As Rajan and Zingales put it:

> Not only do these oligarchs oppose the development of free markets and free access to finance, but they also offer little countervailing force to a powerful state. Since their empires are not built on competence, they can be taken away as easily as they were acquired.[1]

The accusations of incompetence came particularly as the financial oligarchs moved into the real economy. The mildest of critics simply declared them to have been poor managers, without strategic grasp or workplace managerial skills. Referring to the early stages of their real economy empires, Paolo Borzatta, head of the TACIS project on financial-industrial groups in the 1990s, said in an interview:

> To be honest, I believe that corporate planning, which is an instrument of corporate strategy and one of the most important management instruments, to all intents and purposes does not exist in Russia. I have formed the impression that people here have no idea what it means, to develop a corporate strategy.[2]

The apparent lack of strategy of the oligarchs as they moved into the real economy was commented on in the previous chapter. They seemed uncertain, even, whether their purchases were long-term or short-term, investments for growth and dividends or quick restructurings to increase value for rapid resale. A former Menatep executive writing in 2005 about Khodorkovsky's early days at the company says:

> Young energetic entrepreneurs with self-made banking experience, taking over the highest management posts in gigantic industrial companies with post-Soviet management cultures, could not possibly have the time to develop a long-term management strategy for their new business, nor the experience to choose a management model.[3]

He did go on to note that the new owners learned quickly. In 1998 Vladimir Lisin of NLMK, presumably speaking as a professional manager rather than budding oligarch, stated that the oligarchs bought up industrial companies, 'but did this insufficiently systematically. The oligarchs have not learned how to manage their empires. All that they have succeeded in doing is get Western credits on the security of their assets.'[4]

These are gentle views. Most critics sum up the oligarchs' approach to their assets simply as looting and asset stripping. These are words that have a relentlessly negative tone, but which are not usually defined with great precision. Sometimes, indeed, they seem to mean no more than taking an excessive personal return out of the business, at the expense of taxation, but with no explicit suggestion that the assets are badly managed and reduced in value. That is an accusation which is worth taking seriously and one to which we will return later.

Usually, though, the suggestion is that the oligarchs take out more value than is created under their ownership, meaning that the business is worth less and less as time goes on. The most extreme version of asset stripping sees the owner literally selling off all the business's assets until there is nothing left. Klebnikov, the subtitle of whose book is 'Boris Berezovsky and the looting of Russia', describes Berezovsky's business activities in such terms:

> As I looked into Berezovsky's meteoric career, I discovered a history replete with bankrupt companies and violent deaths. The scale of the destruction was extraordinary, even by contemporary Russian standards. He had soaked the cash out of the big companies he had dealt with, leaving them effectively bankrupt, kept afloat only by lavish government subsidies.[5]

Of those who benefited more generally from shares-for-credit Klebnikov says:

> Having squeezed the cash out of Russia's prime industrial companies, the financial companies who won the first round of the loans-for-shares auctions ensured that none of Russia's best industrial companies were financially viable on their own.[6]

Stiglitz claims that 'privatization, accompanied by the opening of the capital markets, led not to wealth creation but to asset stripping'. The evidence that this is so is the level of capital flight.[7]

A less harsh accusation is that the oligarchs try to run their assets as businesses, but that they persist in extracting excessive returns. It is not just a matter of returns being appropriated at such a rate that the state and people do not get their fair share through taxation, but also that there is inadequate investment. Black, Kraakman and Tarassova, for example, recognise the difference between asset-stripping and what they call self-dealing, that is, the appropriation of returns that belong to others, those others being minority shareholders, suppliers, the workforce and the state. They would expect true asset-stripping only when a firm has no prospects of being profitable. Indeed, as other commentators suggest, asset-stripping in these circumstances might even be desirable.[8] Self-dealing is more likely to happen in profitable firms. Indeed, as Black, Kraakman and Tarassova suggest, it should be possible theoretically to self-deal and create value at the same time. But, they claim, in practice it does not work. Those claimants on value who are not receiving their due return eventually will refuse to deal with the self-dealer. Minority shareholders will not provide finance, suppliers and labour will not provide their goods and services, and the state will take coercive action. 'For all these reasons, self-dealing will decrease a profitable firm's value.'[9] The end result is the same as that of the more rapacious form of asset stripping – the business loses value until there is nothing left. It might just take a little longer.

What causes behaviour which ultimately destroys the assets one possesses? Two broad explanations can be identified. One is simply greed, or what Dzarasov and Novozhenov call an adventurist personality.[10] Those putting forward this point of view are likely to look at the black-market or criminal backgrounds of at least some of the oligarchs (and often imply that they all have such backgrounds). Some see high levels of cynicism as typical of the late-Soviet generation to which the oligarchs belonged. As Andrei Yakovlev, of the Higher Economic School in Moscow, put it:

> The younger generation of the Soviet elite and intelligentsia, which was pushed forward during perestroika, was characterized by a high degree of cynicism and pragmatism, hidden by declarations on democratic and market reforms.

Yakolev goes on to claim that in the 1990s this produced a devaluation of the values of democracy and competition, and very short-term views of the world.[11] One would not expect those with such personalities to change as circumstances change. They will strip the assets of everything they can get their hands on no matter what the circumstances. These are roving bandits who will never become sedentary, Robber Barons who will never become philanthropists.

The other, more benign, explanation is that their behaviour is what one would expect of owners with the short-term time horizons that come from lack of confidence in the future, most specifically in the future security of property rights. Presumably there is some hope if this is the sort of behaviour we are dealing with. We can expect quite different behaviour if time horizons can be changed. Before returning to look at that possibility in more detail, let us review the evidence regarding performance.

The accusations against the oligarchs are essentially three-fold:

- that the businesses they took over performed worse in their hands than they had previously;

- that the returns that they extracted from their assets were excessive and indeed rapacious;
- and that as a consequence of that they neglected investment and the long-term development and reproduction of their assets.

In this chapter we will examine each of these accusations in turn.

Are oligarch companies worse off than they were before?

If companies are under the control of asset strippers, one would expect to see them performing worse and worse over time until, presumably in reasonably short order, they collapse altogether. Experience of the African mining industry suggests that asset-stripping can lead to the closure of the operations at even the richest deposits in a few years.[12] On what basis do the oligarchs' critics find that they run their companies badly, in a way and for whatever reason, that leaves them worth progressively less? A lot of critical attention is devoted to the market capitalization of oligarch-owned companies. Rajan and Zingales, in noting that Russian oil companies trade at values one hundred times less than they would trade at in the United States, claim:

> Such an enormous difference cannot be explained simply by differences in market liquidity or risk preferences of participants in the two markets. The only plausible explanation is that the market expects that Russian oil companies will be systematically looted by insiders.[13]

Black, Kraakman and Tarassova take the same approach. They estimate the 'true' values of oligarch-based companies based on developed country multiples, and rhetorically ask why their market capitalizations are so much below the results of their calculations. They then state, presumably in response to their own question:

> Russian share prices can be understood as out-of-the-money options: Investors expect that the firm's entire value will likely go to the government or the firm's controllers.[14]

The government possibility is one we return to later. But the general tone of Black and his colleagues' article is relentlessly that the firms' owners represented a far greater threat than the government.

Fox and Heller also claim that one can see the effect of corporate governance problems in the low share prices of oil stocks. For them good corporate governance entails two things: the maximization of residuals (residuals defined as 'the difference between what a firm pays at con-tractually pre-determined prices for its inputs and what it receives for its outputs') and the distribution of wealth in a pro rata fashion. They use the maximization of residuals rather than the maximization of share values, because they recognise that share ownership is not the only or necessarily best form of ownership. But they then state, in a way that seems to make the residuals/share values distinction quite redundant, that for firms with shareholders, since residuals should go to them, 'maximizing share values is equivalent to maximizing residuals'. That is then the measure they use in the Russian case. They claim that 'Russian firms are falling far short of maximizing their residuals', presumably on the basis of the fact that their share prices are lower than one would expect given their assets. They are of the opinion that the pro rata dis-tribution requirement is important only over the long term, since it is on that basis that firms are able to raise capital. But, they note, quoting a *Moscow Times* reporter, owners, in this case specifically those in the aluminium industry, were not looking to raise money through equity issues.[15] As we have already seen, in the 1990s share issues were designed to dispossess shareholders, not raise money from them.

None of the approaches outlined here for measuring the value of oligarch-owned firms are satisfactory. As Fox and Heller hint, what does low market capitalization tell us about the performance of a firm if its controlling owners do not care about its market value, and indeed have no desire to encourage outside equity holders at all? To put it bluntly, not very much. This is particularly so when one cannot help feeling that those arguing the market capitalization approach rather too easily dis-miss other factors that could well have contributed to low share values, above all political risk and barriers to foreign investment.

Market capitalization is not in fact the only measure that the oligarchs' critics use. One statistic that they like to cite as direct evidence of cata-strophic declines in performance once oligarchs arrive is the worsening of the balance sheets of the subsidiaries of such oil holding companies as Yukos and Sibneft. It is true that these subsidiaries suddenly went from making substantial profits to large losses. But at the same time the holding companies went from large losses to very large profits (both declared and undeclared). Before the oligarchs arrived it was the owner-managers of the subsidiaries that dominated the companies, and so they made sure the profits were concentrated where they were. Once stronger owners arrived in the holding companies, they quickly reversed the arrangement. It was hard on the minority shareholders of the subsidiaries, but says nothing about their performance or the performance of the holding company as a whole. As we will see in a moment, overall performance was indeed lacklustre in very difficult circumstances in the second half of the 1990s. As conditions improved performance improved, and any losses that remained on the balance sheets of the subsidiaries were there overwhelmingly for tax purposes and had little relationship to performance.

It should be no surprise that in the Russian conditions of the 1990s balance sheets and market values were poor measures of enterprise performance. Guriev and Rachinsky, who are not on balance critics of the oligarchs, take a different approach, and look at productivity. They note that up to 2002 oligarch firms had lower total factor productivity levels than privately owned domestic non-oligarch firms (foreign-owned firms were even more productive; state-owned firms less), and there were insignificant differences in productivity growth. In 2002, however, oligarch firms were 8 per cent above non-oligarch private domestic firms in terms of total factor productivity growth. It appeared that they had achieved this result by increasing output while retaining inputs at the same level (including holding employment at levels higher than they needed to, for politico-social reasons). They note that it is unclear whether the improvement is in firms they took over around 2002 or the result of lagged improvements in firms they had taken over earlier. While also urging caution on the grounds that the superior performance of oligarch firms might be explained by political connections, rather than superior management skills, they nevertheless conclude that 'the evidence is consistent with the view that oligarchs do manage their firms better than other Russian domestic owners and better than regionally owned firms, and almost as well as foreign owners'.[16]

If it is true that the oligarchs managed their firms better than their previous owners, a conclusion which will be supported in a moment in brief descriptions of what happened in individual firms, what did they bring to the enterprises?

Despite the claims of some that oil production units were thriving before the arrival of the oligarchs, most of the businesses they took over were in a parlous state as they did so. Most Russian businesses were, of course, in a parlous state at the time. Nevertheless the businesses that were targeted by the oligarchs were different from the rest of Russian business. They were already resource exporters. In the case of the oil industry they had been so to a considerable degree since Soviet times; in the metals industry the Red Directors had already shifted their sales strategies towards exports early in transition. Access to export markets did not seem to help. Their condition was indeed so parlous that commentators at the time were predicting that those commercial banks, such as Menatep, that became too committed to long-term investment in them in order to create an industrial empire were running an unacceptable risk of being dragged into bankruptcy and collapse by the voracious financial demands of their newly acquired assets.[17] Why were even these companies, with good foreign markets, in such difficulties?

One reason, identified by Jerry Hough, is that the Red Directors who had gained ownership control of enterprises at the time of privatization had themselves particularly strong incentives to strip. Because of a total lack of investment funding and so capacity to increase value, and with good reason to believe they would be dispossessed, they were in the classic situation of roving bandits – take as much as you can and get out while the going is good.[18] Bim describes the 'destructive' strategy of owners, particularly in vulnerable sectors such as light industry and food processing, who realize that 'their core businesses cannot be reliable sources of prosperity for a considerable period of time':

> So managers make immediate efforts not to adapt enterprises but first of all to extract income and capital for their personal benefit. These efforts sometimes may be easily defined in terms of barbarism or robbery.[19]

Hoffman, in explaining Chubais's actions in bringing outsiders into enterprises, states that the latter 'knew that the factory directors, siphoning off the profits into their own pockets, were poison for the market'.[20]

But the problem was not just asset-stripping Red Directors. The late Gorbachev period produced considerable management chaos within enterprises. Although his experiments with work-place democracy, in the form of elected general directors and work-place councils, were short-lived, they were enough to leave a legacy for some time of senior managers having to bargain with and pay off middle managers and the work units gathered around those middle managers. The situation was made worse by the cooperative movement of the same time. Middle managers were able to set up cooperatives linked to and feeding off the work units over which they had management control. Burawoy and Hendley set the scene for the process of managerial disintegration in the late Soviet period in their eyewitness account of a Moscow factory, as the differences in the interests of middle managers with top management and between themselves became ever starker.[21] Most commentators focus on the advantage taken by top managers of the cooperative movement to privatize cash flows. Middle managers were able to do the same. Mass privatization did nothing to improve matters. Top managers again had to bargain with middle managers and staff as shares were allocated and voted at shareholder meetings.[22]

The outcome was the looting of companies by everyone, from top management down. It was not just the oligarchs who built up start-up capital in the late Soviet period. A huge range of middle-level managers took their share in the late Soviet and early transition periods. Sometimes it was to seize just enough in hard times to live on. But the author has met those who built up their start-up capital in this way in order to leave the enterprise and set up private entrepreneurial endeavours of their own, as well as embittered communist managers who took enough to build themselves a good house. Added to the problems at middle management level were the relatively undeveloped skills of top managers of all levels in commodity export, and therefore their need to make use of expensive and not always honest middlemen. In the circumstances it is not surprising that the leakage of cash flow was enormous.

Even energetic and apparently honest Red Directors managed to drive their enterprises into the ground. Anatolii Pukhov at Tulachermet, the pig iron producer, was sufficiently infected by the decentralization ideology of the late Soviet period that as a matter of policy and apparently voluntarily he created multiple profit centres within the enterprise. He brought new entrepreneurial energy to the Soviet practice of self-sufficiency and diversification, opening new enterprises for a range of non-core activities, including the production of consumer goods. It was all too much for a company whose core area of activity was facing serious market problems, and in the end the edifice collapsed in a sea of debts and barter. Pukhov was replaced by the representative of outside interests.[23]

At the Nizhnii Tagil Metal Combine the Soviet-era general director, Iurii Komratov, with great enthusiasm took advantage of new opportunities to invest and develop the plant in ways that had been planned for years. He borrowed large sums of money to do so, but had neither the cost controls nor marketing skills to keep the business afloat. He continued with his investment programme even while he was having to engage in the most elaborate barter arrangements to get anything in return for domestic deliveries and to continue exports even though they were loss-making in order to bring in some cash. Even so he was unable to cover operating costs. Eventually Eurasian Metals, the Abramov-owned trading company and precursor of Evrazkholding, that had bought into the plant at Komratov's invitation, lost patience. With promises to pay off R100 million of wage arrears Eurasian Metals persuaded the workforce to vote against Komratov and he was dismissed.[24]

In these circumstances it is not surprising that the main priorities of the new owners were to enforce strict financial controls and highly centralized trading arrangements. Although hardly born-and-bred financial and trading specialists, they did have recently acquired skills in those areas. Their first actions were to take control of all the financial accounts and trading contracts within the enterprise.[25] It would be easy to say that they did so only in order to ensure that they could keep everything for themselves. That may well be the case, and is something we will look at in the next sections. But the evidence suggests quite rapid turn-arounds in performance once oligarchs arrived in real economy enterprises. Dzarasov and Novozhenov devote considerable attention to the opportunistic behaviour of middle managers, and grudgingly accept that the management discipline introduced by the oligarchs was an improvement.[26] We will now provide more detail of their efforts in specific enterprises.

Norilsk Nickel

Norilsk Nickel was privatized in 1994, although the state retained a 51 per cent shareholding. Shares were very widely held, and operational control was retained by Anatolii Filatov, in what could be described as a typical case of 'worker/management privatization'. Filatov had worked at the Norilsk plant all his life, and had been elected general director by the workforce during Gorbachev's short-lived experiment in workplace democracy.[27]

The company was in a mess, seemingly suffering badly from the breakdown of central management control described above. Norilsk Nickel was particularly susceptible to this, since many of its units had been brought together, very controversially, only in 1989. The effect was management and, in particular, financial chaos. With large numbers of independent trading and financial units within the firm, operating capital disappeared, resulting in high wage and tax arrears, declines in output, lack of investment, and high levels of labour discontent.[28] Johnson describes it as having been 'a badly run, top-heavy company with indebtedness of over $1.2 billion to federal and local governments'.[29]

It appears probable that Vladimir Potanin's ONEKSIMbank bought into the company at the initial privatization (since Norilsk Nickel was a founding shareholder of the bank). In 1995 the bank began providing credits to the company,[30] and in the same year took control of a state-owned 38 per cent stake through one of the notorious shares-for-credit deals (the stake cost $US170.1 million). The bank struggled to remove Filatov in 1996, and in 1997 gained ownership of the 38 per cent stake in the second stage of the shares-for-credit deal.

Once they gained control in 1997 Potanin and his team concentrated on centralizing trading arrangements, paying off debts and increasing output. The company claimed that the centralized trading arrangements replaced the dozens of agents for individual enterprises within the group, many of whom competed with each other. The new arrangements led to a better capacity to negotiate freight deals and shorter payment periods. The need for trade credit was virtually eliminated.[31] K.P. Zlotnikov, the head of the company's planning department, said in 2000:

> Opportunities to economize on all forms of resources were found through the introduction of elementary order, [including] strict centralization of all financial flows, contractual arrangements and hiring of staff.[32]

Zlotnikov claimed that by 2000, through a combination of firm management control and an improvement in market conditions, it was possible to shift from survival mode to a development strategy, including increased investments.

While not free of the ups-and-downs of the market, nor enjoying ideal labour relations, and while by global standards still suffering from staggeringly inefficient labour productivity, the company is a sturdy and profitable global operator. It is certainly very different from the company of the first half of the 1990s. It does not sound like a story of asset stripping, although one should note that some commentators claim that ONEKSIMbank financed its regeneration of Norilsk Nickel by taking money out of Sidanko, the oil company that the bank had gained control of through shares-for-credit.[33]

Apatit

Like Norilsk Nickel the apatite producer Apatit, situated in the north west of Russia, was privatized in 1994. Mikhail Khodorkovsky's bank Menatep bought up shares, including a 20 per cent stake obtained through an investment tender. (It is that tender, and the $US280 million of investment it called for, that has caused Khodorkovsky and his associate Platon Lebedev so much grief in recent years. We will return

to the details of the tender in a later chapter.) The company had suffered the usual collapse in output in the early 1990s. There was some
pick up in output and sales from 1994, but the company's general
director from 1997, Sergei Fedorov,[34] later described the situation up
to 1996 as critical, and then the period 1997–9 as one of stabilization.[35]
Capital investment greatly increased from 1998, and by 2002 the
company had a turnover of R15.9 billion and net profit of R900 million.[36] The company's new owners might well have been guilty of not
meeting the terms of the investment tender. But certainly when Platon
Lebedev entered prison in mid-2003 the company was in better shape
than when he signed the ill-fated tender document nine years previously.[37] In November 2004 Menatep sold Apatit in a management
buyout, and for the first three quarters of 2005 the company reported
a loss of R2.7 billion on revenues of R15.3 billion.[38] The sudden losses
probably reflected difficulties the new owners were having renewing
the contract for the sale of its nepheline ore to its sole alumina-
producing customer, the Pikalevo Alumina Plant, owned by Vekselberg's
SUAL.[39]

North Urals Bauxite Mine (SUBR)

SUBR is one of the few commercial bauxite deposits in Russia. It has
been the main source of bauxite for the Urals alumina producers at
Bogoslovo and the Urals Aluminium Plant since they were built. The
mine has always faced major mineralogical and geological difficulties.
The mineralogical problems mean that it takes seven tonnes of North
Urals ore to produce a tonne of aluminium, rather than the typical figure of five.[40] Geological conditions are also difficult and particularly
since going underground the mine has suffered serious flooding problems. In 1979 its biggest shaft was so badly flooded that it was closed for
two years. In 1995 it was said that half the power used by the mine
was devoted to pumping 16 million cubic metres of water per year.[41] It
suffered declines in output through the 1990s, and in the mid-1990s its
financial situation was so critical that it was having to pay wages in
kind.[42]

When SUAL moved into the mine, it was forced to recognise that
serious investments were needed to maintain and expand capacity. In
1998 it was said that $24 million a year would be required to keep out-
put at 3–3.2 million tonnes per annum over 10 years, including opening
a new shaft at Novo-Kalya. The decision was taken to make the required
investment. The Novo-Kalya mine was opened in August 2005, and the
subequent talk has been of the need to reopen the closed Cheremukhovo

mine at a deeper level.[43] In 2000 Vasilii Anisimov, the then partner of SUAL, said of their efforts:

> Over a short period, sorting out the financial bottlenecks and normalising financial flows, we were able to cut the costs of producing alumina from bauxite in half and get SUBR's balance sheet back into the black.

While the costs of production of Australian bauxite producers were still half SUBR's, the Russian mine's locational advantage allowed it to operate profitably.[44]

Yukos

Before dealing with Yukos specifically, a brief outline of the background debate over the contribution of the oil barons as a whole to either the collapse or resurrection of oil output is useful. Russian oil output peaked in 1988. There was then continuous decline until 2000, when increasing output again became the pattern. There were particularly marked declines in the mid-1990s.

It is the decline in the mid-1990s which has led to claims that the oligarchs, who moved into the industry at that time, were responsible through incompetence and a failure to invest. The figures do not support the argument. While there are complicated issues of investment involved, especially in exploration, the declines from 1988 on can be put down to the maturing of the major West Siberian fields and big declines in demand, particularly exports to CIS countries.[45] The fact that, as can be seen from Table 4.1, oil exports held up quite well throughout the period, while CIS purchases in particular declined dramatically, suggests that demand was the issue, not supply. There are

Table 4.1   Russian oil production and exports, 1988–98, million tonnes

	1988	1990	1992	1994	1996	1997	1998
Oil production	568.8	516.2	399.3	317.8	301.3	305.6	303.4
Oil exports	—	220.3	137.7	129.8	126.0	126.9	137.1
non-CIS	—	99.7	66.2	91.7	105.4	109.8	117.9
CIS	—	120.6	71.5	38.1	20.6	17.1	19.2

Source: Yegor Gaidar (ed.), *The Economics of Transition*, MIT Press, Cambridge MA and London, 2003, pp.667–9.

indeed commentators who speak of a new 'West Siberian miracle', the expansion of output from these mature fields, brought about by the investments and technological rationalizations of the oligarch-owned oil companies.[46]

To look more specifically at Yukos, according to Kets de Vries (clearly a fan of Khodorkovsky), when Khodorkovsky first became involved in Yukos in 1995, the company had 11 000 wells badly in need of repair, 90 000 unpaid workers, non-transparent accounts and $3 billion debts. To quote Kryukov and Moe:

> The leadership of the holding company could not prevent resistance from Yuganskneftegaz [the company's main production unit] to its policies; nor was the holding company able to control the main material and financial flows within the larger integrated organization.[47]

This is the familiar administrative decentralization problem. To further quote Kryukov and Moe, 'it took a new owner to remedy the situation', that owner, of course, being Khodorkovsky's Menatep.

Menatep adopted the standard strategy of strictly centralizing administration. And what for some was skimming its subsidiaries was for others 'to rationalize their operations and money flows'.[48] Khodorkovsky quickly laid off 11 000 workers and divested the company of its non-core businesses. In September 1996 the proceeds of a share issue, $80 million, were used to pay off wage arrears.[49] He developed a very centralized administrative structure as part of his struggle with managers who wanted to continue to drill new wells rather than increase output from existing ones, and who were also unwilling to give up their own regional support services and infrastructures. He brought in advanced new technology through a tie-up with Schlumberger, but also relied on old, depreciated equipment to keep investment costs down.[50] The focus was on cost cutting until 1998, after which a more strategic approach was adopted.[51]

Aleksei Golubovich, a former Menatep executive, provides a detailed, if not always friendly, account of Yukos's strategic and managerial approach. He is more positive in his opinion of the pre-Yukos management than this author has been, and so is more critical of Khodorkovsky's centralizing approach. Nevertheless the management style he identifies is very similar to that seen in the other brief case studies presented here, both the crisis management up to 1999, and then the turn to a more growth-oriented approach.[52]

A topic of debate with regard to oil sector corporate governance is the relative performance of different companies and the relationship between performance and ownership. The supporters of the most 'entrepreneurial' of the oil companies, Yukos in particular, claim that its performance under Khodorkovsky and his team outstripped that of more 'Red Director' companies such as Lukoil and Surgutneftegaz.[53] For Nash this occurred most noticeably after Khodorkovsky's team gained a dominant shareholding.[54] Alekperov reacts icily to such comparisons by pointing out that it is easy to perform well when one does not pay taxes (not of course that Lukoil has not had its moments with the tax man).[55] He has support from Black and his colleagues, who describe Lukoil and Surgutneftegaz as being the better-respected companies, with shares which have traded at higher prices per barrel of reserves.[56] Those claims aside, the comparison to a state-owned company such as Rosneft is even more flattering to the oligarch.[57] Given the purchase of Yukos's main production unit, Yuganskneftegaz, as a result of the Yukos affair, that comparison becomes a particularly important one.

While perhaps too panegyrical for some, the words of Vladimir Milov, the president of the Institute of Energy Policy, regarding Khodorkovsky are worth attention:

> In 1995 oil experts sadly sighed: well, they 'gave' Yukos to Khodorkovsky – now he will loot it and run. But he didn't loot it or run. Khodorkovsky invested intellect, effort and money in growth. He turned a dying asset, looted by its Red Directors, into a brilliant company of global significance. He became the leader of the phenomenal growth in oil output in Russia – a minor economic miracle.[58]

To return from the brief case studies to the broader picture, the oligarchs took over companies in management and financial crisis. Through some basic centralization of financial and managerial functions, rapid improvements were achieved. But market conditions in the resource sector from roughly 1995 to the financial crisis of 1998 were not conducive to high profitability – domestic demand was weak and the ruble corridor badly hit profits on exports.[59] But the devaluation of 1998 and the improvement in both domestic and export demand that became evident around the beginning of the new decade allowed the shift from survival mode to development mode. It is very hard to see in this evidence of either managerial incompetence or asset stripping. Golubovich and Dzarasov and Novozhenov, while acknowledging the positive aspects of the centralized management style of companies such as Yukos, do worry that it might have gone too far, producing ultimately a stultifying corporate culture. But these are concerns that are familiar to any reader of the Western management literature, and are a very long way from accusations of asset stripping and self-dealing. It is hard to find in the evidence presented here support for the view that the oligarchs, including the most entrepreneurial of them, have performed worse than the previous owners, much less run their assets into the ground.

Even if we find in favour of the oligarchs in terms of competence and the ability to keep enterprises going in difficult conditions and then develop them when circumstances improve, can we nevertheless accuse them of the self-dealing types of activities described by Black, Kraakman and Tarassova that will eventually, even if not by design, lead to the running down of the enterprise? In other words, do they extract excessive returns from their enterprises, even if they might be adding value to them? We will now examine the levels of extraction of returns, and then look at the possible consequences in terms of levels of investment.

Extraction of excessive returns

The oligarchs have been accused of the relentless extraction of value from their assets, mainly through transfer pricing, and then the transfer of that value abroad as reflected in capital flight data. We have already seen the use of transfer pricing to transfer value from subsidiaries to the holding company in the oil industry. The next stage was to get the value out of the country. In the metals industry and to a considerable extent the oil industry as well, this was done through the use of transfer pricing between the production unit and an offshore-registered but principal-owned trading company. That is why control of trading companies was always such an important part of an outsider moving into a company. In some of the current cases against Yukos officials, the alleged scheme for transferring money abroad was based on the profits of domestically registered trading companies that bought oil from the production subsidiaries at well below market prices, being transferred abroad as dividends to the owners of the trading companies, who were again Yukos principals. Those cases will be examined in more detail in the later chapter devoted to the Yukos affair.

It would be a rash person who claimed that none of this happened. But it is difficult to know to what extent, and whether that extent was 'excessive'. The indirect evidence is capital flight data. But this in itself is very problematic, particularly to separate out that part of it which is oligarch corporate flight, and even then what part of that represents reasonable returns, what part reasonable investment abroad, and what part unreasonable extraction of value.[60]

The first few years of oligarch presence in the real economy were claimed as years of limited profitability. While there are those who would claim that there were particular tax-related reasons for reported low profits, it certainly was a time, from around 1995, of difficult market conditions (particularly after the Asian crisis of 1997) and of the negative effects on profitability of a strengthening real value of the ruble. Remembering the claims made at the time that the banks were taking an enormous risk moving into the real economy, to have kept enterprises already in bad shape going at all in difficult circumstances suggests that the returns that were extracted were not 'excessive' in the asset-stripping sense. Indeed at a time when the oligarchs were still enjoying good returns in the financial sector, some subsidization of their resource assets seems entirely possible.

As described in the previous chapter, it was only when their control was total, and so they were able to extract returns legally in a more transparent way and in a way that they did not have to share them with other shareholders, that they turned to dividends as the favoured form of value extraction. Although the data are thin, consolidated companies appear to pay about 15 to 25 per cent of net profits in dividends. But when there is a strategic foreign investor there is pressure to pay more. TNK-BP pays 40 per cent or more, while Lukoil is under pressure to increase its dividend to that sort of level.[61]

There is a difference between foreign and Russian rates of return and the levels of tax actually paid. It is said that in 2002 Sibneft made more after-tax profit from revenues of $4.8 billion than Chevron did from revenues of $99.1 billion. That is not surprising when we consider that Chevron paid 72.8 per cent of its profit in profits tax, compared to Sibneft's 12.3 per cent.[62] It appears that it is in the level of tax that we are most likely to find evidence of excessive, at least by international standards, extraction of value. Tax is such a special case that the next chapter is devoted to it entirely. It will also feature prominently in the chapter on the Yukos affair.

Investment

While tax is probably the key issue in the debate about the reasonableness of the oligarchs' value extraction policies, it could be argued that the most fundamental indicator of economic performance is investment. In terms of the long-term efficient running and development of the business, investment is the key input. Whether or not the oligarchs pay tax is very relevant to the future of the state and society but for the future of the company it is investment which is more important.

Asset strippers in the strict sense of the phrase and by definition do not invest in their assets. The oligarchs are regularly accused of precisely that. Most such accusations are crude, blunt and without supporting evidence. Klebnikov claims that their being looted starved the best companies of investment which led to their ruin.[63] Black, Kraakman and Tarassova state:

> The new investment that the privatizers hoped for rarely occurred. The kleptocrats often reneged on investment promises that they made when acquiring shares, or that their companies had made before the kleptocrats acquired them.[64]

Their first claim refers to the failure of the oligarchs (and many others) to fulfil the conditions set out in investment tenders. The most notorious of these was Menatep's winning bid for 20 per cent of Apatit, the details of which will be examined in a later chapter. The claims made in defence of Khodorkovsky and Lebedev were that the specific details of the investment conditions set out in the tender were inappropriate, if not actually foolish, and that the more sensible investments that actually ensued were greater than those required by the tender conditions. Our brief account of the performance of Apatit under Menatep's ownership offers prima facie support for the defence. Black, Kraakman and Tarassova's second claim, that the kleptocrats reneged on investment programmes agreed by previous owners, seems to be based principally on Menatep's treatment of Amoco when Khodorkovsky's bank took over Yukos. On gaining control Khodorkovsky cancelled a contract to develop jointly the Priobskoe field in Western Siberia.[65]

Their point does prompt some speculative reflection on the oligarchs' investment policies. Earlier in this chapter evidence was provided that the oligarchs brought to health enterprises that had been seriously struggling in the conditions, both within and outside the firms, of the early transition years. The emphasis in these earlier accounts was on straightforward strengthening of management and financial discipline. Some mention was made then of investment, but let us now pay more attention to that issue. In what follows particular attention will be devoted to investment in the metals sector.

As already described the oligarchs moved into the commodity sectors of the economy at a time of poor profitability, as a consequence of difficult market conditions and an appreciating ruble, and took over firms facing serious debt and operating capital problems. At the beginning of 1997 40 per cent of ferrous metal enterprises were loss-making, as were 60 per cent of those in non-ferrous metals. For the metals sector as a whole the debit side of the balance sheet outweighed the assets side by 1.6 times. In these circumstances, the oligarchs claim, when they moved into the real economy they had no choice but to focus for a period on pure survival. The money they put into their new assets, whether it be their own or borrowed money, went into operating accounts, to pay wages, including arrears, and trade credits. As late as 2000 six out of ten Sberbank credits to the metals industry recorded in press advertisements were for operating funds.[66]

This meant that there was not a lot of money available for investment. When the official government programme for investment in the metals sector (1997–2005) called for annual investments of $3 billion, the net profit of the whole sector was estimated at $500 million.[67] While those data almost certainly overstate the problems of the biggest exporters, it is not hard to believe that investment needs were greater than the internal resources available to meet them. Nor should we exaggerate the amount of cash that the oligarchs had available to bring across from the financial side of their businesses, even if they were inclined to do so. Johnson, in stating that the total assets of the commercial banking sector in January 1997 were $62.5 billion, was clearly sceptical that that included enough to meet the investment needs of their real economy assets.[68]

Unsurprisingly, therefore, capital investment declined, in ferrous metals in particular. Government figures show that capital investment per tonne of steel between 1992 and 1995 was $20–25. In 1996 it was 12 and in 1997, $8.[69] For the metals sector as a whole capital investment in 1993-95 was $2.7 billion per annum, and in 1996 $1.8 billion.[70]

It is in the context of the shortage of investment funds that claims were made that reduced levels of investment were both possible and desirable. Soviet enterprises had been notoriously overcapitalized, and Red Directors had got even more carried away with investment plans when they were given more control over such things. We have already described the fate of Iurii Komratov at the Nizhnii Tagil Metal Combine. He was removed from his position by Aleksandr Abramov's Evrazkholding after running up enormous debts to undertake a beloved modernization programme. Only with the most careful husbanding of resources, and coal investments that gave them some control over input prices, were the new 'oligarch' owners able to fight off bankruptcy claims, get the enterprise back on its feet and continue the investment programme.[71] Another Urals steel producer, the North Siberian Metal Combine (ZSMK), ended up in bankruptcy because of what was described as an 'insufficiently balanced policy in use of credit'. It was in that context that an article on the technical re-equipment of the plant could be called 'Modernization without investment'.[72]

When Mordashov took over Severstal he severely cut the investment programme. He stated very openly his belief that the Russian steel industry could get by with relatively modest investments in new technology. His views were set out in most detail in an *Ekspert* interview in September 1999.[73] In what was for the time a not-unusual but nevertheless eerie mixture of management new speak and Soviet-style agitation, he spoke of the need to get the cooperation of the workers in the search for ways to cut costs rather than relying on huge investment projects. One such workers' suggestion was to extend periods between maintenance work. That might indeed be a sensible approach to reducing the Soviet legacy of extremely high maintenance expenditure, but it could also be grist to the mill of those who believe that Mordashov and their ilk are deliberately running their assets into the ground for short-term personal gain, as would be his decision to reduce Severstal's investment programme from $1.1 billion to $130–50 million. However, Severstal's performance since 1999 is not that of a company that is being run into the ground.[74] Two Western commentators, admittedly not in the anti-oligarch camp, agree with Mordashov that a reduced level of investment could have been an appropriate response to the circumstances of the time. Åslund, in summing up the oligarchs' performance, says:

> They eliminated the most criminalized parts of an enterprise, reduced the work force, expanded production and improved its quality by astute small investment in bottlenecks, drawing on old equipment and engineering skills.[75]

Kets de Vries suggests also that it was a judicious mixture of modern Western technology and fully depreciated old equipment that allowed Khodorkovsky to increase output while keeping costs under control at Yukos.[76]

Some clear and conscious decisions were made to adopt 'half-way house' technological strategies, most particularly in the approach to anode technology in the aluminium industry. The big Siberian smelters were built in the 1960s and early 1970s, and so missed out on the now-standard pre-bake technology. They were built with vertical-stud Soderberg technology. Only the later Tadzhik (1975) and Sayanogorsk (1985) smelters used pre-bake technology. Considerable amounts of money are being spent on refitting Russian smelters – Rusal has allocated $270 million to KrAZ (which had already gone through a modernization programme in the mid-1990s) and $250 million to the Bratsk smelter. While new capacity is built to pre-bake specifications, the decision has been consistently made that the replacement of existing Soderberg technology with pre-bake is financially unsustainable. At the end of the 1990s still only 20 per cent of Russian aluminium was produced using pre-bake technology, whereas the Western figure was 80 per cent (85 per cent in the US and 100 per cent in Australia).[77] The Russian producers, however, claim to be leading the world in getting the best out of Soderberg technology.[78]

While some might consider these accounts of investment cutbacks and technological compromises to be window dressing for oligarchs who have been extracting value to their personal benefit at such a rate that there is nothing left for investment, there were notable shifts in the second half of the 1990s in the technological structure of the metal industry. This is most noticeable in the ferrous sector. The percentage of Russian steel output coming from open-hearth furnaces declined from 50.6 in 1991, to 39.3 in 1995 and 27.8 in 1998. Continuous casting capacity increased from 17.9 per cent in 1991 to 37.1 in 1995 and 46.5 in 1997.[79]

After 1998, with an improvement in world prices and a devalued ruble increasing returns, and therefore greater internal cashflows and greater creditworthiness, the metal companies undertook some serious capital projects. In 2000 NLMK undertook a five-year investment programme worth $1.1 billion, in what was not an unusual commitment in the sector.[80] In 2001 the Magnitogorsk Metal Combine, having raised its profitability to over 40 per cent from 6.49 per cent in 1996, claimed to have spent about 90 per cent of its undistributed profit of R7.79 billion on capital investment (11.3 per cent went on dividends and 10.4 per cent on 'social expenditure' and philanthropy).[81] In the aluminium industry, in 2004 Rusal invested $534 million, including $278 million on plant modernization. These figures were up from $284 million and $180 million respectively in 2003. The intention was to spend $1.5 billion in 2005 on an extensive list of projects. Up to half that sum was to come from the company's own revenues; the rest from credit. Recently Rusal joined its much smaller competitor, SUAL, in the latter's development of the Timan bauxite deposit in the Komi Republic, with its associated alumina plant in nearby Ukhta. This is one of the few greenfield projects in the post-Soviet mining sector. The start up costs for the mine itself were said to be $77.4 million; the alumina plant, on which construction started in 2004, is estimated to cost $1 billion. The difficulties SUAL was having in financing the project led it to bring Rusal in, for $100 million and a 50:50 split of future costs and output.[82] These are not the activities either of asset strippers or of managerial incompetents.

Conclusions

There is some contradiction in the arguments of the critics of the oligarchs. On the one hand the oligarchs are accused of having stolen enterprises for a song that are now worth a fortune. On the other hand they are accused of running their assets into the ground through asset stripping. It is certainly the first accusation that demands the more attention. There is undeniably a huge gap between what they paid for their enterprises and what they are worth now. Clearly the oligarchs cannot claim all the credit for the gap. But the gap is far too big to be compatible with claims of incompetence and asset stripping.

It is the gap which produces the biggest problem for the oligarchs today. Indeed in a sense they are the victims of their own success. It is the enormously increased value of their assets that subjects them to insistent demands from other stakeholders in society to 'pay up' (*delit'sia*). This creates a political problem for them, and it is to the political aspects of their position in Russia's transitional society that we now turn our attention.

5
Oligarchy and Political Power

Although it was deliberately avoided in the title, the word 'oligarchy' has appeared very often in the book itself. It is a word almost as controversial as the group of individuals to whom it is applied. The reason is that it is a word which is inherently, in its etymology and its use over the millennia since Plato and Aristotle first coined it, about political power and indeed ruling power.

It is not the primary purpose of this book to determine whether the oligarchs have had enough political power to justify the use of the word oligarchy. Nevertheless, in anything less than that specifically definitional sense, the political aspect of their place in the Russian political system is clearly of fundamental importance. How much power did they have, how did they obtain it and then use it, and to what ends did they use it? What were the implications for Russian political culture and democracy of the oligarchs' political activities? An inevitable part of answering those questions is a detailed examination of the Yukos affair, which will appear in a later chapter. The issue of whether the oligarchs could or did work collectively in the political arena will be part of the analysis, not so much as part of an attempt to decide whether they really deserve to have the collective noun 'oligarchy' applied to them, but as part of the empirical consideration of the extent and nature of their political involvement. An important part of the story, the place of regional government, will receive only fleeting mention, far less than it deserves if the story were to be complete.[1] The story will be told by breaking the transition years up into a number of periods over which oligarch political power waxed and waned.[2]

1991–5

In the early stages of transition the oligarchs of the future were barely politically active, much less influential. No one in our samples was involved in the politics of the collapse of communism or the early steps in the creation of a new post-Soviet politico-economic system, either as activists or as leaders. We have already described how many of them depended on the support of state institutions, or of individuals working within institutions, to get their businesses beyond the stage of glorified street trading. But these were individual arrangements, with no direct political content and certainly no collective 'oligarchical' implications.

The first political involvement of anyone later identified as an oligarch came at the time of gathering tensions between the Supreme Soviet and Yeltsin over the replacement of Yegor Gaidar as head of the first post-Soviet government. A group called Entrepreneurs' Political Initiative-92 emerged, with Bendukidze, Vinogradov, Gusinsky and Khodorkovsky among those involved. In the words of Hans-Henning Schröder, 'the initiative called for a compromise between President and Supreme Soviet, but it had no significant influence on the course of events . . . At that time . . . [the so-called oligarchs] hardly had enough money and power at their disposal to actually influence politics.'[3] This was the time of Red Director power, and it was they who won on this occasion.

The first half of the 1990s did see increasingly assertive lobbying for something that could be called a collective interest. The most important was the lobbying effort to keep foreigners out of the banking sector.[4] This was the first of what commentators would see as many examples of the oligarchs lobbying to pursue a narrow 'oligarchical' interest rather than the interests of business as a whole. As Guriev and Rachinsky put it: 'Oligarchs work hard to reduce their own cost of doing business in Russia, but do not lobby for other entrepreneurs to have access to an improved business environment.' Indeed on many occasions they tried to ensure that their benefits were not shared with others, especially new entrants.[5] Anyone with any knowledge of business lobbying anywhere in the world will of course be aware that there is nothing unusual about such an approach.

For Bunin it was the choice made by the government on the issue of foreign ownership that laid the basis for oligarchic power, first economic and then political:

> The Russian political authorities were faced with a choice in the first half of the 1990s – to put their money on either 'their' business or on

foreign investors. The active lobbying of big capital (what we now call 'oligarchical') led to the adoption of the first scenario, and not only in the fuel sector, but also in other areas ... Such a situation created the ideal circumstances for the growth not only of the economic, but also the political influence of big capital.[6]

It was the fact that it was the state, not business, that made this strategic choice that, for Bunin, makes this early period one in which the state dominated. He starts his next period – the one during which in his view the oligarchs were stronger than state institutions – from 1996. This implies that he sees shares-for-credit as within the first period and therefore as one of the choices made by the government.

That is essentially the position put by this author following the detailed examination of shares-for-credit in Chapter 3. Shares-for-credit was not so much a case of powerful economic actors using their political clout to seize new assets. Rather it was a case of the government, as a strategic economic choice, giving them new assets. While it might have been pushed into something it was less than happy about, the government did not do so because it was under the control of the businessmen who profited.

1996–8

For Bunin, and many other commentators, shares-for-credit gave the oligarchs the economic and financial clout that led directly to the political clout they bought by financing Yeltsin's election campaign and victory in 1996.[7] It is the next couple of years, to August 1998, that are the most contested in terms of the debate over the political power of the oligarchs. For example, for Bunin they had the power to see off the opposition of prime minister Kirienko and his ministers Nemtsov and Fedorov. For others it was their inability to persuade the Kirienko government not to proceed with the default and devaluation which brought them such enormous losses in August 1998 that demonstrated their lack of power. Analysts such as Aleksei Zudin and Yakov Pappe have argued against the picture presented in the press at the time that the oligarchs were running the country.[8]

There is also a mixed record when we look at other economic policy outcomes over this period. It could be argued that in terms of policy up until 1998 they got good outcomes in the financial sector, but not so good in the real economy. When financial stabilization from 1994 onwards reduced the profit opportunities in their traditional areas of agency banking and foreign currency speculation, the government gave the oligarchs new opportunities on the GKO market. But in the real economy the basic policy settings worked against their interests. We will see in the next chapter the debate over whether tax regimes worked in their favour or not. The oligarchs certainly did not believe they did. The ruble corridor was also particularly damaging to their resource export businesses, although one might conclude that since most of the lobbying on the ruble corridor came from the formal lobbying structures of the metals sector, rather than the oil barons, then it was not yet for the latter a key issue. Their commitment to the real economy was not yet so great that that was where their policy priorities lay.

Stronger forces than the oligarchs were determining policy in that area, specifically the Chubais reformist block, supported by international institutions. Their main priority was the control of inflation. Chubais was happy to give the oil barons and metal magnates their empires and to intervene on their behalf with Yeltsin on a number of crucial occasions.[9] But he was not going to give them everything they wanted, especially an inflationary devaluation of the ruble.

To sum up the power of the oligarchs at this stage: while there was no doubting their entrepreneurial energies and skills, their policy role in the broad, system-creating sense, even in the economic sphere, was minor. They reacted to opportunities created by politicians and the politicians' ideologists, dating as far back as Gorbachev's cooperative legislation. They took advantage of, rather than created, the major economic transformation policies that were to follow: the opening of the economy, privatization, and perhaps most importantly the pursuit of a 'big business' strategy, including through shares-for-credit. These were major policies devised by a policy-making cabal of academics, many of whom transformed themselves into politicians and policy-making bureaucrats. The oligarchs were not of their number. One of the chief ideologists of all this was Anatolii Chubais, who could hardly be described as the tool of the oligarchs. The reverse, indeed, sounds more plausible.

The collective action problem. One of the most common arguments against the existence of an oligarchy in the true sense of the word were the overwhelming collective action problems they faced. In discussing it we will go beyond the 1996–8 period. Both in terms of their personalities and their rationally determined interests, these were not people likely to cooperate together for substantial periods of time. Their origins as entrepreneurs – a rather individualistic vocation – suggested people not inclined to cooperate with others. In 2003 Oleg Deripaska caused a scandal by representing a tax cut proposal as coming from RSPP, when it was in fact his own work. In speculating how Deripaska had got himself into such a mess, a journalist said that

> It was his temperament that undid Deripaska. The staff of Rusal and Bazel say that their boss rarely accepts opposition. It's clear that Deripaska is uncomfortable in RSPP, where every word has to be agreed with 27 members of the bureau.[10]

The unkind might suggest that as well as being intolerant of others they were extremely greedy people. Bunin is not alone in characterizing the period as one revealing the oligarchs' complete lack of collective spirit. He wrote of the politically connected entrepreneurs 'not having succeeded in working out precise rules of the game among themselves . . . Each player thought only about his own interests.'[11] Schröder writes:

> The 'oligarchs' do not represent organized interests of a social group at all, but are acting egoistically for gains in power and profit alone – often by avoiding or ignoring existing formal and informal rules.[12]

For Zudin it was the individualistic pursuit of personal interest by each oligarch, and the fact that when they did act collectively it was a sign of weakness not strength, that made oligarchy an inappropriate description of their place in Russian politics.[13] Pappe adopts Zudin's approach, citing Zudin's phrase, 'oligarchs without oligarchy'. For Pappe the oligarchs acted collectively rarely and only for localized and short-term purposes. Because of that, in his view, they could not and would not stand up to a united state, despite their many victories over individual state agencies.[14]

The argument is made that the collective action problems increased over time, particularly as there was less and less of the pie left for the oligarchs to divide among themselves. Initially the pie had been big enough that there was little need to compete, in the early 1990s financial sector and in mass privatization. But shares-for-credit and Svyazinvest revealed greed-based tensions. The ill-tempered battle over the sale in 1997 of the state's share in the telecommunications company, Svyazinvest, is particularly heavily cited as evidence of the oligarchs' serious collective action problems. Johnson writes of the period:

> With money tight, the government no longer pandering to their every wish, and no threatening presidential election to unite them in common cause, the leaders of the bank-led FIGs turned on each other.[15]

To take the argument beyond the 1996–8 time-frame, there have been ongoing claims that the oligarchs have throughout transition used the state and its coercive agencies in pursuit of their individual interests in commercial competition with each other. One of the earliest examples was the extraordinary 'faces in the snow' episode in late 1994, in which a dispute between Berezovsky and Gusinsky over Aeroflot culminated in an armed standoff outside Gusinsky's office building between the security forces of the presidential bodyguard, representing Berezovsky, and of Moscow mayor Luzhkov, representing Gusinsky.[16] In more recent times there has been continuing speculation, fuelled by insiders who should know, that there was an oligarch competitor involved in the igniting of the state's actions against Khodorkovsky and Yukos. Certainly in its response to Khodorkovsky's arrest the business community made much of its contrition over past use of such methods and promises not to do so in the future.[17] Nevertheless, ever since then there have been claims of the involvement of business competitors in the state's harassment of businesses in which Mikhail Fridman has an involvement and the recent arrest warrant for former Fridman partner Oleg Kiselev.[18]

Because of their inability to cooperate and indeed their propensity to use underhand methods to compete with each other, it has been claimed that the oligarchs have been unable and unwilling to defend each other when a dangerous common enemy appears. When a new president became a truly serious threat, much was made of their failure to defend their own when they were in difficulty. No serious measures were taken to defend Gusinsky, Berezovsky and above all Khodorkovsky.

The extent of the collective action problem is clear. Nevertheless a case can be made that it has not been as severe as often suggested. Shares-for-credit and Svyazinvest were 'normal' business and in the end accepted as such. When the oligarchs really needed to cooperate they did so. The 1996 presidential elections, the joint reaction to the 1998 financial crisis and the Kirienko government, and perhaps even the rise to power of Putin and the removal of Berezovsky could be suggested as examples. The response to the victimization of Gusinsky and

Khodorkovsky was not as conspicuous by its absence as often made out. Public and private protests over the arrest of the former were made. In the case of Khodorkovsky the originally strong collective reaction disappeared quickly as Putin gave stern warnings against which, it was recognized, no resistance was possible. But individual oligarchs have continued to speak in critical terms of what happened. Mordashov of Severstal has called for the end of 'Basmannyi justice'.[19] In reaction to the guilty verdicts against Lebedev and Khodorkovsky, Arkadii Volsky spoke of 'there having been born, in a society which gains nothing from the verdict against Khodorkovsky, a "beat the rich" mood, from the capital to the smallest villages'. He spoke in one breath of the negative effect on Russia's image abroad of events in the Caucasus and the Moscow courts.[20] We will see elsewhere the complaints of Deripaska and Potanin about the apparent expectation arising from the Yukos affair that business be socially responsible.

The oligarchs were always aware of their collective action problem, and took measures to combat it. At times they worked at their own internal conflict resolution mechanisms, from the Sparrow Hills meetings of the 1990s to the 'ethical behaviour' committees and arbitration court of RSPP.[21] But generally they relied on the use of political authority, specifically the president, as a referee.[22] A good example of their using Yeltsin in this way was the September 1997 meeting called by the president to resolve the 'bank war' over the Svyazinvest sale. For Zudin, with his requirement that an oligarchy work together cohesively, any possibility that the oligarchs made up a true oligarchy after the 1996 presidential election was ended by the 'bank war'.[23] It could alternatively be claimed that the actions of Yeltsin, calling six top bankers to a meeting and arranging some sort of truce, allowed the oligarchy to survive.[24]

The same role could be ascribed to Putin at his round-table meeting with the oligarchs in July 2000, following the issuing of an arrest warrant against Gusinsky. While undoubtedly seen by the oligarchs as an opportunity to express to Putin their collective dismay at the measures being taken by the state against one of their number, it was also an occasion at which Putin declared that the nature of the individual relations of the oligarchs with political power had to be re-assessed. In using what was to become a much-quoted word, he spoke of the need for *ravnoudalennost'* (equidistance) in the relationship between the state and the oligarchs, making it clear that the state would no longer play favourites and demanding that the oligarchs' individual opportunism be toned down.[25] Chubais had noted before the meeting that the apparent conflict between the oligarchs and the political authorities was in fact a case of the former carrying out their 'competitive struggle via the authorities' – in other words, the oligarchs, or some of them, were cheating. He found the situation highly alarming and requiring the rigorous intervention of Putin.[26] Commentators often interpret Putin's use of the word *ravnoudalennost'* as referring to the state refusing to do any favours for any oligarchs, that is, what he had in mind was equidistance between the oligarchs and other sectors of society. But it is possible to suggest that he rather had in mind that he would not play favourites in the way that Berezovsky had become a Yeltsin Family[27] favourite. The principle is cited as the grounds on which Putin was reluctant to get involved in a conflict between Potanin and Deripaska in the Krasnoyarsk region.[28] One unnamed oligarch, in referring to a round-table meeting that Putin had held with RSPP in February 2003, stated that 'each of us is entirely capable of resolving our problems alone, but that is precisely why we want to meet together – so that it is clear that we are not pursuing personal (*shkurnye*) interests'.[29]

Putin was being asked to address a standard difficulty of any small internally competitive oligarchy, the temptation to cheat, in particular cheating by trying to strike up a special relationship with the referee.[30] The most blatant and persistent cheater was Berezovsky, who tried to establish direct personal links with the president through the Family. Berezovsky's cheating was seen by the other oligarchs as excessive and dangerous to the oligarchy's continued existence.[31] In these terms Berezovsky's fall from grace under Putin was not an attack by Putin on the oligarchy, but rather a move to restore and strengthen it. Berezovsky's cheating looked so likely to succeed that first the referee was removed, for failing in his duties as a referee. The new referee then removed the cheater.[32] After Berezovsky's departure from Russia, RSPP issued a statement disowning him and rejecting the view that business could monopolize control of the country and use the media to impose its will on government.[33]

The problem with this approach to dealing with cheating is that if some players are trying to undermine the referee, others have to react by giving more power to the referee, including the right to hand out red cards. But such referees end up with genuine power in their own right, particularly if they have their own constituencies, and particularly if those constituencies include those excluded from the game who want to join in. This is the situation the oligarchs found themselves in under Putin. We will return to that period and Putin's performance as referee soon.

In discussing the oligarch's collective action problem we have leapt forward in our chronology. We will now go back in time. The collective action tensions that were evident in the lead up to the financial crisis of August 1998 became a little less sharp following the crisis as each oligarch struggled for survival.

1998–2000

The 1998 crisis was of major importance for the oligarchs. It destroyed only a couple financially, but it finished the process of pushing virtually all into the real economy as their priority area of operation. That became a very lucrative move for them, in conditions of crisis-induced devaluation and then major shifts in favour of resource commodities in global markets. That meant that the crisis was not in fact as great a financial blow for most oligarchs as at first expected.

It did, however, have some political negatives that would not have been immediately obvious. First, there was the major moral damage done to them by being connected to defaulting banks, in which private citizens lost their savings but the oligarchs demonstrably did not.[34] No less important was the effect of the Primakov government. Although ultimately unsuccessful and brought to a premature conclusion not without oligarch influence, the Primakov government showed that it was possible to oppose the oligarchs and to be popular at the same time, with there probably being some connection between the two.[35] That was a lesson probably not lost on the then-head of the FSB, the successor body to the KGB, Vladimir Putin.

This was also the period of the rise to dominance in internal Kremlin politics of the Family. This was disruptive for the oligarchy because, although the Family was generally pro-big business, it clearly had some favourites, not least Berezovsky. This did not help the collective action problem – a weak referee being manipulated by a small number of players. In terms of our referee analogy, it could well have been this fact that encouraged the oligarchs to push for, or at least welcome, the replacement of the weak referee with a tougher one. At the end of 1999 they got their new referee, and they would have had high hopes for the future. Their economic situation was much better than was expected a year earlier and commodity prices were about to turn in their favour. They would have been confident of their capacity to control the policy-making process to the extent needed to ensure they reaped the benefits.

2000–03

Bunin calls this period the 'period of compromise'. It could perhaps also be known as the period of Putin biding his time. The first attribution would suggest that the two sides, Putin and the oligarchs, were genuinely trying to reach an arrangement that they could both live with. The second suggests that Putin meant what he said in the quotations at the beginning of this book, and that when the time came – probably after he had finished dealing with the regions – he would deal with the oligarchs. If one paid attention to Putin's words, it would have been hard to believe that he was interested in compromise. But there was compromise in his actions. The essence of the negotiated compromise was the famous *shashlychnoe soglashenie* (shashlik agreement), so known because in at least some accounts it was reached at a barbecue,[36] although more conventionally it is attributed to a formal meeting Putin held with 21 top business people on 28 July 2000. Tompson notes the great uncertainty as to what if anything was agreed, and indeed describes the agreement as 'something akin to a foundational political myth.'[37] However to the extent that there is consensus on what the agreement involved, it is as follows: the oligarchs would stay out of politics, Putin would leave them to get on with their businesses; they would pay their taxes, he would provide them with services in return.

While Bunin talks of the period of compromise, the oligarchs themselves, including most particularly the Family, could well have thought they were at the height of their political power. Their businesses were settled and increasingly profitable, unlike the crisis-prone years after 1996 which are usually seen as their peak years. They no longer had to cope with the troublemaker Berezovsky and prickly Gusinsky. They were increasing their influence in the regions, and they had powerful allies in the central government, including prime minister Kasyanov and head of the presidential administration Voloshin. They had demonstrated the capacity to defeat the *siloviki* in struggles for economic assets, specifically in the battle for the oil company Slavneft when it was privatized in December 2002. That was a battle between Abramovich's Sibneft and Rosneft, state-owned and controlled by the *silovik*, Sergei Bogdanchikov, operating in alliance with Sergei Pugachev's *silovik* bank Mezhprombank.[38] They had a president who was unable to resist them, but who was playing a useful role as referee. They were building an institution, the RSPP, through which they hoped to sort out their internal problems and present a common interest to the outside world. RSPP was also working on presenting an image of a socially responsible big business to the outside world. They were building up a powerful presence in the Duma, which as we will see later was proving its worth as a means to maintain favourable tax and other arrangements. Generally they were making a lot of money, spending it on business and pleasure, and appeared to have enough control of the policy-making process to ensure they continued to do so.

But if the oligarchs thought that they were at the peak of their powers, there were serious indicators of trouble brewing. Their businesses were increasingly subjected to searches, summonses and charges from various government agencies, usually related to tax and privatization issues.[39] At the same time an ever-increasing number of *siloviki* were being brought into positions of power. The pressure on the oligarchs from the *siloviki* was enough for them to complain with increasing bitterness that the terms of the *shashlychnoe soglashenie* were not being observed. As usual Putin gave the appearance of listening with sympathy, but the harassment continued.[40] They faced a general population who refused to like them despite their pretensions to social responsibility, and a president who put great store on his public opinion ratings. One suspects that it was not purely for show when Putin could not hide his true feelings towards them in occasional outbursts. His feelings took on dramatic form in his famous exchange with Khodorkovsky over corruption in February 2003. Kirill Rogov interpreted the meeting and the corruption exchange in the following terms:

> A week ago Putin made it clear that he remains president in the well-known sense of an anti-oligarch mandate. He rejected the oligarchs' suggestion to 'freeze the situation' and give up former (corrupt) methods of the distribution of resources with a firm 'no'. If the oligarchs had earlier divided up the resources in their favour, then there is nothing shocking if now state companies use similar methods to correct the situation a little in their favour.[41]

To remind us, however, of the very mixed messages that Putin is capable of sending: literally a few days before the arrest of Yukos shareholder Platon Lebedev and the beginning of the so-called Yukos affair, in a speech at a ceremony marking a major share swap between the Western oil company BP and the Russian company TNK, he had spoken positively of big business, noting that its lobbying activities were now within acceptable limits, that it was not the job of business to be 'patriotic' but to make profits wherever they could best be made, and that it was the task of the government to provide the best conditions for them to do so.[42]

Along with an unpredictable referee, the business elite faced one of the biggest threats to an oligarchy, one of its members getting ahead of the pack. Khodorkovsky was not, like Berezovsky, currying favour with the referee. Far from it. Indeed, his crime was not treating the referee with respect. As we will see in a later chapter, after his arrest a number of oligarchs claimed to have been worried by Khodorkovsky's behaviour and the threat it represented to them.

Other than the public dispute between Khodorkovsky and Putin over corruption, there were other specific events in the first half of 2003 that indicated trouble not far over the horizon. There was the publication of the infamous report prepared by Stanislav Belkovsky's private but *silovik*-linked think-tank, the National Strategy Council, warning of preparations for an oligarchic coup. In the report it was claimed that the oligarchy had decided that the president, in person and as a post, was no longer the 'guarantor of the stability of the ruling elite, but a potential source of a dark threat to them'. They had therefore decided to weaken the presidency by moving towards a more parliamentary form of government, as agitated for in particular by Khodorkovsky, and by achieving the 'personal unification of political power and super big business', that is, placing business people in positions of state power.[43] The report created a sensation at the time, and led to a response from the Family's 'ideologist' within the Kremlin, Gleb Pavlovsky, that the coup that was being prepared was being organised not by the oligarchs, but by the *siloviki*. He referred specifically to the troika of Sergei Pugachev, the *silovik* banker at Mezhprombank, Igor Sechin, an old St Petersburg colleague of Putin now working as the 'grey cardinal' in the Kremlin, and Viktor Ivanov, another St Petersburg *silovik* in the Kremlin.[44]

Another sign of potential problems was an enquiry in mid-July 2003 to the prosecutor's office from Sergei Bogdanchikov, the *silovik* head of the state-owned oil company Rosneft (and the ultimate beneficiary of the Yukos affair), regarding Yukos's acquisition of a 19 per cent shareholding in Eniseineftegaz (a transaction over which the Russian authorities have since been seeking the extradition from Britain of the Yukos executive Aleksandr Temerko).[45] On 21 June 2003 a senior member of Yukos's security service, Aleksandr Pichugin, was arrested for murders and attempted murders carried out a number of years previously. The immediate and formal triggers for what was to come were official queries from two members of the Duma regarding the 1994 investment tender that was part of the privatization of the fertiliser producer Apatit and the tax affairs of Yukos.[46]

If the oligarchs thought that their positions were powerful, then they were about to be disabused of that impression. Before we analyse in detail what happened next, the place of tax in the oligarch-state relationship needs to be described. Tax was always going to be an important and sensitive part of the relationship between the state and business people whose businesses were providing a significant proportion of the state's tax revenues. Tax was also arguably the main component of the Yukos affair, and some reasonably detailed background is required for its proper understanding.

6
Taxation in the Resource Sector

The resource sector's dominance of the cash-generating part of the Russian economy is too great for its taxation not to be a matter of major contention between the state and the sector's oligarch owners. The state at times feels a desperate need to extract extra tax revenue from the resource sector as all other potential tax payers struggle financially. The oil barons and metal magnates, on the other hand, claim that they are operating in industries that are particularly likely to be disadvantaged by tax regimes.

Tax in the mid-1990s

As the oligarchs moved into both the oil and metals sectors in the mid-1990s the two sides of the argument quickly became evident. In the oil sector the pressure was already coming from the government to pay more tax – in the form of higher rates and paying off arrears – in very difficult fiscal circumstances. (Everything said here about the oil industry could be said with even greater force about the state-owned gas industry.) In 1995 the industry lost most of its export concessions, while excise taxes were repeatedly raised.[1] As the government's new willingness to enforce a hard budget constraint in the fuel-consuming sectors of the economy started to take effect, oil producers had increasing difficulty collecting payment from domestic buyers. The government then put pressure on them to continue to supply even when payments were not being made.

In conditions of low profitability – producers were beginning to feel the effect of the ruble corridor on their export earnings – their only possible response was increasing levels of tax arrears and payment in kind. In 1995 the fuel sector (including gas) was responsible for 73 per cent of debt to the federal budget.[2] In 1997 eight of the top ten tax debtors in

Russia were from the fuel sector.[3] It was strongly implied that the government was prepared to tolerate the arrears and payments in kind as part of a deal, the producers' side of which was to maintain supplies. Certainly in 1994 and 1995 prime minister Chernomyrdin persuaded the fuel industry to continue to supply without payment.[4] This is the deal, improvised rather than conscious though it might have been,[5] that is at the heart of Gaddy and Ickes' 'virtual economy' thesis: that the entire cashless economy edifice served to maintain the resource sector's subsidization of the value-subtracting rest of the economy. Vlad Ivanenko finds that the fuel sector at this time faced unsustainable statutory tax rates, but that effective rates, because of arrears, were sustainable. He presumes that this arrangement was negotiated in a 'non-cooperative strategic game of dividing the sector's value added'.[6]

The subsidization took not just the obvious form of supplying fuel to customers who had no capacity to pay for it, but also resulted from the inherently greater tax-bearing nature of the fuel industry compared to other sectors of the economy. Its product was produced under strict licensing conditions that gave the state access to reliable output data. Further, a large part of its product was sold for export, with delivery being made through state-owned transport and pipeline networks. Again the state was in a good position to collect reliable data. This meant that the state was in a far better position to calculate accurate tax liabilities in the fuel sector than in most other sectors, where the origins and destinations of products were far less transparent to the tax office.[7]

The opponents of the fuel industry found these arguments laughable. They retorted that the sector was notoriously non-transparent in its production and particularly trading operations, and the state agencies involved in collecting data notoriously incompetent and corrupt, a situation which was not going to change as the oligarchs consolidated their positions. In fact the sector was peculiarly well-suited to tax evasion, since it was so open to transfer pricing between production units and offshore trading companies. This reduced the tax liability of the producer and placed the great bulk of revenues offshore and entirely out of the grasp of the tax authorities. For these critics of the oligarchs, not only were the sector's export operations one big tax evasion scheme, but the cashless economy, far from being an arrangement for the subsidization of the rest of the economy by the fuel sector, was in fact another scheme designed to allow the fuel sector to evade tax on its domestic sales.

The situation in the metals sector was similar, although not so stark. The metals industry did not have the same degree of pressure on it to supply the domestic market at special prices and payment regimes. The sector did face some political pressure over the effects of high export volumes on domestic availability and prices,[8] and like the fuel sector metals producers found themselves subject to export duties designed at least partly to shift some output from export to the domestic market.[9] They also accepted very high levels of non-cash payments on their domestic sales, and passed the cash deficits on to the state in the form of their own tax arrears and payments in kind.[10] The sector also faced the same profitability problems as the fuel sector, something that was reflected in a steep decline in tax payments in the mid-1990s (see Table 6.1). However presumably social pressure to maintain metal deliveries to industrial enterprises could be more easily resisted than pressure to maintain fuel deliveries to cities, towns and farms. So the pressures on the metals sector were not as severe, and its tax arrears did not reach the levels of those in the fuel sector. In 1997 the metal sector held 5.79 per cent of tax indebtedness, the fuel sector 21.71 per cent.[11] A list of 46 major tax defaulters identified by the Federal Administration of Insolvency Matters in 1995 included three from the mining and metals sector.[12] In 1998, as there was talk of increasing export duties for metal producers, it was commented that while they could more or less cope with taxes, higher duties would be beyond them.[13]

While the tax issue might not have been so sharp for the metals sector, the same debate over its 'unfair' tax burden versus its tax evasion proclivities that was raging in the fuel sector was also evident in the metals sector. The industry claimed that it was susceptible to higher levels of tax, although on somewhat different grounds to those argued by the fuel sector. The metals sector complained about the way that certain taxes had a particularly negative effect on its enterprises, above all mining enterprises. It was said that the metals sector as a whole, including mining, bore a tax burden double that of the economy as a whole, with the mining burden being double that of the metal producers.[14]

Table 6.1   Profits and profits tax paid by the metals sector, billion rubles

	1995	1996	1997
Profitability, per cent	18.4	5.8	4.0
Gross profits	19.1	7.4	5.7
Taxable profits	17.6	4.6	2.9
Profits tax	6.2	1.6	1.0
of which to federal budget	2.3	0.6	0.4

Source: S.V. Kolpakov, 'Ekonomicheskie usloviia vozrozhdeniia metallurgicheskogo proizvodstva v Rossii', *Chernaia metallurgiia*, nos 7–8, 1998, p.6.

Further, it was claimed, an enterprise in the Russian metals sector bore a tax burden double that of the typical Western metals firm.[15] Table 6.2 shows average tax rates within the sector as a percentage of its contribution to GDP compared to the economy as a whole.[16] The table shows the sector as being more lightly taxed than the economy as a whole as transition got underway, but with a steadily and massively widening gap operating against the metals sector as the decade continued. Data for 1999 indicate that taxes represented 60 per cent of the contribution to GDP in the mining sector, 50 per cent among metal producers, and 35–40 per cent in industry (not the economy) as a whole.[17]

Table 6.2 Whole economy and metals sector as a percentage of gross domestic product

Year	Whole economy	Metals sector
1990	34.4	38.2
1991	33.2	27.8
1992	41.4	29.7
1993	48.2	30.6
1994	29.0	55.9
1995	26.1	62.9

Source: 'O polozhenii v metallurgicheskoi promyshlennosti i putiakh preodeleniia krizisa', *Chernaia metallurgiia*, nos 5–6, 1997, p.8.

Table 6.3 shows tax takes as a percentage of sales for metals producers and for mining. Again the mining sector is worse off. In 1997 the figure for the economy as a whole was 10–15.[18]

Table 6.3 Tax takes as a percentage of sales

	Mining	Metals
1990	12	
1994	25.4	12.7
1995	34.0	19.0
1997		22.0

Sources: *Metally Evrazii*, no.3, 1996, p.5; no.4, 1996, p.5; Anatolii Sysoev, 'Rossiiskaia metallurgiia: ot "monetarizma" k protektsionizmu', *Metally Evrazii*, no.5, 1998, p.9.

Table 6.4   Tax payments by the metals sector into the federal budget, billion new rubles*

Type of tax	1995	1996	1997
Assets tax	1.5	2.8	2.8
Profits tax	6.2	1.6	1.0
VAT	1.5	1.3	1.4
Resource taxes	0.3	0.3	0.3

* The table in the original source uses trillions of rubles as the unit of measurement. This was before the currency reform which removed three zeros from the Russian monetary unit.

Source: S.V. Kolpakov, 'Ekonomicheskie usloviia vozrozhdeniia metallurgicheskogo proizvodstva v Rossii', *Chernaia metallurgiia*, nos 7–8, 1998, p.6.

There were particular complaints about the reliance on non-performance-based taxes. Certainly the sector appeared to be paying relatively high levels of assets tax (see Table 6.4). In 1997 the tax paid on assets was only slightly lower than the total taxable profits of the whole sector.[19]

The data in the tables appear broadly to confirm industry claims of a significant tax bias against the metals sector, in particular mining, although one should note that the big decline in profits tax is not made up fully by increases in other taxes, as indicated in Table 6.4.

Those who were sceptical of the fuel industry's claims of an unfair tax burden were no more impressed by the arguments of the metals sector. As a sector even more dominated by exports than the oil industry, it was particularly suited to tax evasion schemes based on transfer pricing to offshore traders. The Audit Chamber made public accusations against the Novosibirsk Electrode Company and its owner, Vekselberg's SUAL, and then Minister for Taxation Pochinok made threatening noises about the tax-evading trading operations of Severstal in particular.[20]

There has always been tremendous excitement over one particular trading regime in the aluminium industry, the use of tolling, a system already described whereby a smelter processes alumina for a fee, without owning and therefore having to pay for the input. We have seen in a previous chapter that tolling was brought to Russia by TWG, but it quickly spread throughout the industry. Ever since it has been one of the perennials of Russian political and policy debate, primarily because of the particular tax arrangements it attracts, processing under tolling arrangements not being liable to VAT. Despite constant efforts to remove them, tolling still enjoys its tax advantages and something like 80 per cent of aluminium is still produced under tolling arrangements.[21]

Tax in the late 1990s and beyond

In the later 1990s, as the oligarchs moved ever more aggressively into the resource sector, tax payments if anything seemed to increase. While profits tax paid into the federal budget in the metals sector in 1997 was only R1 billion, by 1999 it had rebounded to R9.76 billion.[22] The sector also experienced a very big increase in resource taxes. In the mid-1990s the sector's resource tax payments were steady at around R300 million per annum. However later in the 1990s the level of payments increased sharply, reaching R1.6 billion in 1999.[23] Those payments by the metals sector can be compared to the R4.12 billion paid by the oil extraction sector, R1.48 billion by the gas sector, and R385 million by the forestry sector.[24] One source suggests that from 1998 to 1999 the metal sector's share of total tax revenues increased from 3.22 per cent to 4.35 per cent. Although the fuel industry's share declined from 11.55 per cent to 11.03 per cent over the same year,[25] its contribution to government revenues had increased from 6 per cent in 1994 to 22 per cent in 1998.[26]

The result of this was a big upsurge in lobbying activity.[27] The lobbying seemed to bear fruit with Putin's tax reforms early in the new decade. The changes were presented as highly beneficial to business, by reducing profits tax from 35 to 24 per cent and allowing a much wider range of business costs as tax deductions.[28] A little later changes were made specifically to the resource extraction tax regime that were seen as particularly beneficial to the oligarch oil producers and miners. Specifically a flat rate 'resource extraction tax' (NDPI, *nalog na dobychu poleznykh ispokaemykh*) replaced a whole range of differentiated resource taxes from the beginning of 2002. As a flat-rate tax it was seen as favouring low-cost producers: that is, the oligarchs with the biggest and most productive assets.[29]

But the oligarchs were not satisfied. Even a flat-rate NDPI, when combined with ever-higher export duties, represented what was seen as an excessive burden. There was particular disenchantment with the main tax reform package, it being claimed that the changes entailed the loss of investment offsets that left those businesses which were actually investing in themselves worse off.[30] Business representatives complained that this element of the reforms had been sprung on them in an underhand way.[31]

At roughly the same time the oligarchs had consolidated ownership of their holdings. They were interested in extracting returns more directly, giving a new emphasis on dividends. They also wanted to expand their businesses and had a new interest in raising outside capital. Both new interests required operating more transparently and leaving value in their corporate flagship, rather than shipping it offshore. The transparency left them much more vulnerable to tax demands from a state that was gaining in confidence under Putin.

The oligarchs responded with increased vigour in the use of tax minimization schemes. The focus shifted from the classic use of transfer pricing on the transaction between producer and offshore trading company. Because the oligarchs now wanted the financial statements of their flagship companies to look good, they wanted revenues clearly booked to them. However they did not want to pay any more tax, and so wanted after-tax profits to be as high a proportion of revenues as possible. The transfer pricing was therefore applied to the transaction between the producer, a subsidiary of the oligarch's holding company, and a domestically registered trader, whose revenues would show up on the holding company's results.

The traders were registered in so-called 'domestic offshore zones', in order to take advantage of special investment credits. The best-known of these zones were Mordovia, Kalmykia, Chukotka (an oil-bearing province where Sibneft head, Roman Abramovich, was governor), the Baikonur space base, situated in Kazakhstan but leased to the Russian government, and the village of Lesnoe in the Urals. They offered companies major profits tax discounts for registering their companies with them and making vague offers of investments. (It should be noted that the discounts applied only to the regional and local components of the profits tax. This made up 24 per cent of profits, as against 11 per cent that went to the federal tax authorities.)[32] Other schemes were based on tax credits granted to organizations employing invalids, a specialty of Sibneft,[33] and to charities. A number of Yukos officials have received very severe sentences for running the latter schemes, as will be described in the chapter on the Yukos affair.

Various calculations of the losses in government revenue are offered. The Ministry of Finance claims that in the first half of 2003 three regions – Mordovia, Kalmykia and Chukotka – provided the great bulk of tax breaks, totalling R29 billion, or roughly $1 billion.[34] For the whole of 2003 the loss of government revenue was put at $1.5 billion, in which year Sibneft, a major user of the schemes, paid an effective rate of 7 per cent tax on profits, against the set rate of 24 per cent.[35] At the end of 2002 Lukoil decided to pay the tax office $103 million to forestall claims based on its operations at Baikonur.[36] Yukos was an enthusiastic, although hardly solitary user of tax schemes, and we will see in more detail in the next chapter the enormous losses the government has claimed. The 'offshore' schemes were closed down by the Duma in November 2003, soon after the arrest of Khodorkovsky.[37]

Up until late 2003 the Duma had been a very useful ally of the oligarchs in maintaining the legislative ground for tax minimization. The oligarchs, Khodorkovsky most aggressively, activated powerful lobbying forces in the Duma, it being said that the resource sector came to 'own' hundreds of deputies from across the full range of parties, with their most loyal people in key parliamentary posts. Vladimir Dubov, a major shareholder in Yukos, was chair of the Duma's taxation subcommittee. He was instrumental in two particular victories. One was successful resistance to government proposals to increase radically the tax on dividends. The proposals were a response to a sudden increase in dividend payments by resource companies. The companies presented it as part of their move towards more 'civilized' corporate governance, by rewarding all shareholders through dividends. The Ministry of Finance saw it as a form of tax evasion, as shareholder-managers took lower-taxed dividends (6 per cent) rather than salary (13 per cent).[38]

Dubov's other achievement was the so-called 'Yukos amendment'.[39] This was an amendment to the Russian Customs Code which stated that the export levy on refined oil products could be no more than 90 per cent of the levy on crude exports. The amendment was a major source of irritation to the government, because it reduced its capacity to discourage exports of refined oil products, particularly at times of peak domestic demand, above all at harvest time. Such exports drive up the domestic price of refined products, creating great political and social difficulties for the government. Given that the domestic/export price differential represents one of the greatest wealth transfers away from the resource sector, the amendment was particularly important to it. It was reversed by the Duma, on the direct instructions of Putin, within a month of the arrest of Khodorkovsky.[40]

Conclusions

Tax is a key component of any business-government relationship. Transition Russia has been no exception and indeed, as is usually the case, when Russia is involved the tax issue has had a particularly sharp edge to it. If we accept that big exporters had severe profitability problems in the mid-1990s, then we can accept their complaints of an excessive tax burden with some sympathy. If we do not – if we find the declines in profits and profits tax suspicious in sectors highly open to profit minimization – then we would have no sympathy. As profits clearly rose, and resource sector owners had reasons not to hide their revenues, that debate became redundant. They then pursued tax mini-mization schemes with a degree of aggression that any objective observer would find disconcerting. It would appear that President Putin in particular did so. There are good reasons to believe that the Yukos affair was above all about tax, including the Duma's protection of the oligarchs' tax privileges. On that basis, we will now return to the narra-tive broken off at the end of the last chapter, with the storm clouds gathering over the heads of Yukos' senior shareholders in mid-2003.

7
The Yukos Affair

The arrest of Lebedev

On 2 July 2003 Platon Lebedev, considered to be Mikhail Khodorkovsky's second-in-command, left hospital to respond to a summons for questioning at the prosecutor's office regarding the 1994 investment tender through which a company called 'Volna', fronting for Menatep, had obtained a 20 per cent shareholding in the mineral fertilizer company Apatit. At the end of the interrogation he was charged with large-scale theft, the case being that he, and others, had fraudulently obtained the Apatit shares by winning an investment tender, the conditions of which were not fulfilled. Lebedev was held overnight and the following day an arrest warrant was obtained from a judge, allowing him to be held without bail.

Despite the warnings and omens described in Chapter 5, including the enquiry from Duma deputy Yudin to the prosecutor's office regarding the Apatit investment tender, Lebedev's arrest was a shock, particularly as the Apatit case had been settled out of court only a few months before. The business community reacted quickly, with the RSPP immediately preparing a letter for Putin on 11 July. Although cautiously not referring specifically to any particular event, the letter asked that the 'shortsighted campaign' against big business be halted.[1] RSPP head, Arkadii Volsky, handed the letter to Putin during a session of the State Council on 13 July. It is reported that Putin reacted by suggesting that the prosecutor's office should act with restraint.[2] At another meeting between the two on 16 July, Putin apparently stated that he did not believe that people should be held without bail while economic crimes were being investigated, but noted that he was not and should not be involved, since it was a judicial matter.[3] It was clear to all that Lebedev, as senior a figure as he was in the Yukos hierarchy, was not the true target of Putin's displeasure. Concern over the position of Khodorkovsky was evident in Volsky's address to journalists after the meeting. He noted that Khodorkovsky must use patience in resolving his problems with the authorities, and that his fate depended on 'whether he has learned the rules of the game and whether he will comply with them'.[4]

Another letter from the business community, this time a joint effort of RSPP and the medium and small business associations, Delovaia Rossiia and OPORa, was sent to Putin soon after. It referred vaguely to 'events of recent weeks', and called for a new 'social contract' between business and the state. The contract would protect privatization, including through a three-year statute of limitations on privatization deals, and the prosecutor's office would be made more accountable. In return business would take on greater ethical and social responsibilities, including the rejection of corrupt business schemes, the strict payment of taxes, and contributions to the solving of social problems.[5]

Various members of the government and presidential administration were cautiously critical of the arrest, including prime minister Kasyanov, Minister for Economic Development and Trade Gref, and two of his deputies Sharonov and Dvorkovich, and Minister for Industry Khristenko.[6] At the end of July Voloshin, the powerful member of Yeltsin's Family who was still hanging on as the head of the presidential administration, held an off-the-record briefing for foreign journalists, at which he suggested that he was working to resolve the matter, including the release on bail of Lebedev. He stressed that Putin had had nothing to do with the matter. Putin was indeed trying to find a way out of the situation, but was having difficulties dealing with the prosecutor's office.[7]

None of this helped Lebedev. Neither did the interventions of Khodorkovsky, who conspicuously failed to heed Volsky's advice to be patient. He demanded that the RSPP not legitimate the prosecutor's actions by adopting anything that could be seen as a beseeching (*prositel'nyi*) tone in its representations to Putin, and referred to the activities of 'bandits in epaulettes'.[8] He had a particularly vigorous exchange with deputy Prosecutor General Yurii Biryukov, referring to the latter and his colleagues as 'disgracing their uniform'. Biryukov responded that 'a transparent company doesn't hide documents in children's refuges and in suddenly constructed (*naspekh sdelannykh*) deputies' offices. In those circumstances, the question arises: is the money stolen.'[9] The reference was to searches at the time of a children's refuge sponsored by Yukos and the office in Yukos premises of Dubov, the former Yukos executive who was now a Duma deputy. Khodorkovsky was careful not to include Putin in his accusations, presenting events as part of a power struggle within Putin's entourage.[10] In the exchange just cited, he suggested that the prosecutor's office had spread around stories of multiple murders being part of Yukos's business model so that society would be so outraged that Putin would be powerless to intervene. Khodorkovsky travelled to, and then demonstratively returned from, the United States, and declared boldly that he would stay and fight, and go to gaol if need be.[11]

It was already clear in most of these statements that, despite all the stress on the arrest of Lebedev and whether he should be freed on bail, there was much more involved than one business executive and the Apatit investment tender. At the time it was made, soon after the arrest of Lebedev, an announcement that the prosector's office was responding to a query from Duma deputy Mikhail Bugera regarding Yukos's tax affairs received relatively little attention. But tax issues were quickly to take centre stage. The following week another query from a Duma deputy, this time Nikolai Daikhes, led to a prosecutor's investigation of Yukos's use of the Lesnoe domestic offshore zone.[12] Personal and corporate tax avoidance was added to the charges against Lebedev. In early October searches were carried out in the dwellings and offices of Lebedev and other Yukos shareholders and executives, including Dubov. It was noted that these were the people most involved in Yukos's financial flows.[13] Soon after there were further searches of schools funded by Khodorkovsky charities and of the office of his lawyer Anton Drel. The prosecutor's office claimed to have found evidence of flows of money overseas to avoid tax.[14]

The arrest of Khodorkovsky

On 23 October prosecutors attended Yukos headquarters to summon Khodorkovsky for questioning on 24 October. Khodorkovsky was on a very well-publicised tour around regional Russia, as was officially noted by Yukos staff on the summons. Nevertheless Khodorkovsky's failure to attend the prosecutor's office was the pretext for the storming of his plane on the tarmac at Novosibirsk airport the following day and his transfer to Moscow, where he was, like Lebedev, held without bail. He faced the same charges as Lebedev, and eventually the two cases were combined and heard as one.[15]

Although Khodorkovsky's arrest was not as great a surprise as Lebedev's – indeed there was an element of inevitability about it – the reaction was similar. An emergency meeting of the bureau of RSPP was convened, attended by Volsky, Chubais, Potanin, Bendukidze, Abramov, Yakobashvili of the Vimm-Bill-Dann dairy products company, and representatives of Delovaia Rossiia and OPORa, at which a corrective response from Putin was demanded. Acknowledging, as in previous statements, that it was those who had first and voluntarily adopted a transparent approach to business who were being persecuted, the businessmen noted:

> The crude errors of state power have thrown the country back several years and destroyed faith in its declarations as to the impermissibility of reviewing the results of privatization. The situation can be reversed only by the clear and unambiguous position of the president of the RF, V.V. Putin. The lack of such a position will make irreversible the worsening of the economic climate and the transformation of Russia into a country that is not conducive to the development of business.[16]

They were strong words, and suggested a degree of culpability that Putin did not like. He refused to discuss the matter, appealing to all to cease 'speculation and hysterics'.[17] However he did reiterate that any actions against Yukos had nothing to do with privatization and did not represent a precedent for action against others.

Soon after Putin attended congresses of both RSPP and the Chamber of Trade and Industry (TPP). It was made clear before the RSPP meeting that Yukos was not to be a topic for discussion. The oligarchs appeared to have already given up the struggle, and concurred with Putin in his refusal to discuss the matter. They promised to keep out of politics, and expressed relief that Putin was prepared to speak to them at all. Volsky said in closing the congress:

> Many wanted to use us as a political force, but we will not participate in politics. We have excluded ourselves from all political debates ... You have been reading in the newspapers in recent days the discussion along the lines: the president will come to the congress, the president will not come to the congress ... Thank god that that discussion is over. And to those who wrote in the press, we say: You were wrong! Vladimir Vladimirovich, thank you very much.[18]

Aleksei Mordashov summed up the mood of the oligarchs in responding to journalists afterwards:

> We assembled to work. The calling of the congress and the arrest of Khodorkovsky were a coincidence. We avoided questions about

Yukos because the congress assembled not for that purpose, but for the consideration of more important questions, for example, entry into the WTO. I am satisfied with Putin's speech. There was nothing didactic (*nazidatel'nyi*) in it.[19]

Others spoke of the oligarchs' participation in more demeaning terms. Mikhail Delyagin described the meeting as the 'congress of the defeated' (a reference to Stalin's notorious 'congress of the victors' in 1934).[20] Dmitrii Zimin, the now-retired founder of the telecommunications company Vympelkom, said it reminded him of the set-piece congresses of the Brezhnev period. Boris Fedorov, the long-time reformist foe of the oligarchs, put it thus:

> They didn't solve problems at the congress because they are frightened even to discuss them. After all if you start to discuss something, then you might be held to your opinion ... Now at the congress everyone is trying to display maximum loyalty. The president came, and they are already happy, even if their knees are still knocking.[21]

There was indeed no further collective intervention by big Russian business on behalf of Khodorkovsky or Yukos. Indeed some oligarchs proceeded to make it clear in various ways that they had always disapproved of Khodorkovsky's ways of doing things.[22] However there were the occasional comments made by individual oligarchs critical of the state's actions, sometimes in surprisingly strong terms from those considered the most loyal and cautious. They will be described in the next chapter.

The Yukos affair was addressed more directly at the TPP congress, the TPP presumably being seen by Putin as a less dangerous forum. The TPP, with its origins going back to Soviet times, had always been a more cautious body than RSPP,[23] and was now headed by that most cautious of political operators, Evgenyi Primakov. Putin reiterated yet again that there would be no revision of privatization, but was more threatening than he had been after the arrest of Lebedev, noting that his statements regarding privatization

> don't apply to people who didn't observe the law. We often hear that the laws were complicated and it was impossible to observe them. So say those who didn't observe them. This is nonsense. Those who wanted to did observe the law ... If five or seven people did not observe the law, it does not mean that everybody else did the same.

The reference to five or seven who had broken the law led to frenzied speculation as to who he might have had in mind. It is no clearer now than it was then. 'Five to seven' could be seen as pretty close to the number of oligarchs of whom he would have had a dim view. But he might have been referring more narrowly to the top executives of Yukos. Perhaps he had no one in particular in mind.[24]

There was also criticism, albeit heavily muted, of Khodorkovsky's arrest among 'liberal' members of the government, immediately after the event and in the following months. Although Gref was silent, two of his deputies, Dvorkovich again and this time Mikhail Dmitriev, were reasonably outspoken, the former saying that the dialogue between business and the state should be carried out around a table, not through prison bars; the latter that it was the government which was the real threat to economic growth.[25] In summing up the year, Ilya Yuzhanov, the head of the Ministry of Anti-Monopoly Policy, said that the biggest negative had been the pursuit of the owners of Yukos. 'I haven't seen the case materials, but the way it is being done is like an elephant in a china shop.' He also said it was a blow to Russia's image.[26]

The most immediate victims, beyond the man himself, of Khodorkovsky's arrest were the mooted strategic investments of either Chevron or ExxonMobil in Yukos, and the political career of Aleksandr Voloshin. Although both US companies claimed a continuing interest in investment in the Russian energy sector, negotiations over an investment in Yukos were frozen by both companies immediately after Khodorkovsky's arrest.[27] Voloshin resigned very soon after the arrest.

Strangely, while Khodorkovsky's arrest was enough to end Exxon and Chevron's desire to invest in Yukos, it was at this very time that a merger between Yukos and Sibneft was brought to a formal completion. It was not until the end of 2003 that Abramovich moved to extricate himself from that ill-starred deal. We will return to it later.

The threat to Yukos

With audits of Yukos's accounts proceeding quietly in the background, the first open threat to the company itself, as distinct from its senior shareholders, came from the Ministry of Natural Resources just before Khodorkovsky's arrest, with the ministry announcing a full review of the company's licences. This apparently was in response to a request from the prosecutor's office, which was in turn responding to a query from Duma deputy and chairman of the joint venture Rosneft-Dagneft, Gadzhi Makhachev.[28] The significance of the Rosneft connection would become evident later in the year. In early November the Minister of Natural Resources, Vitalii Artiukhov, threatened to withdraw all licences, regardless of the results of the review, on the grounds that a 'company whose controlling shareholder is under arrest is hardly an appropriate partner for cooperation with a licensing federal agency'.[29] As was to happen again in the future, the ministry's offer to help in Yukos's persecution was not accepted, with Putin expressing doubt that withdrawing licences would bring positive results. 'I am counting on the government to abstain from such measures.' Kasyanov wasted no time in issuing the necessary orders.[30]

The real blow to Yukos the company came in January 2004, when the tax office presented a claim for tax arrears, including penalties (*peni*) and fines (*shtrafy*), of $3.4 billion, flowing from the audit of the company's 2000 accounts.

In the same month, as they left the country, Yukos executive Leonid Nevzlin and Dubov were placed on the wanted list. (Nevzlin subsequently obtained Israeli citizenship.) Another Yukos executive, Vasilii Shakhnovsky, was put on trial after his aborted effort to gain immunity by getting himself a seat on the Federation Council as a representative of the Yamal-Nenets Autonomous Region. All the charges against these Yukos shareholders were related to tax minimization schemes. In the same month Rafael Zainullin, chairman of the board of the Yukos subsidiary, the Kuibyshev Oil Refinery, was charged with tax evasion.[31] Although the next few months saw the occasional search and blocking of accounts, there were no new charges, with the exception of Vladimir Malin, who had been head of the Russian Property Fund at the time that Yukos had resolved its dispute with the state over the Apatit investment tender. In March he was charged with 'exceeding his powers' in arriving at that deal.[32] There were also no new tax claims in the following six months, which were a period of considerable debate within Yukos as to what should be done and by whom, and of apparent negotiations with the government.

As Khodorkovsky and Lebedev, perforce, removed themselves from the affairs of the company, a new chief executive was appointed. Semyon Kukes was a US citizen of Soviet origins. The shareholders did not like his style of negotiating with the government, and he in turn was replaced by what became a double team of Steven Theede, a US citizen, as CEO and the veteran banker Viktor Gerashchenko as chairman of the board. The desperation of the company to find someone who could negotiate 'Soviet-style' is demonstrated in the surprising choice of Gerashchenko: he was notorious for being described as the 'world's worst central banker' by Jeffrey Sachs when Gerashchenkor ran Russia's loose money policy as chairman of the Central Bank in the early 1990s. Although Khodorkovsky was quickly dissatisfied with Gerashchenko,[33] he has shown typical staying power and is still in his post.[34] Despite the arguments within the company, between shareholders and management and perhaps between groups of shareholders, and a multitude of plans, a general line was arrived at. It was that, somewhat inevitably, management would be entrusted with both the running of the company and negotiations with government. Although refusing to recognize any guilt in the charges against it and its shareholders, the company would make every effort to meet any claims made on it. Although there were occasional tactical threats of seeking bankruptcy, the company's approach in practice was consistently to seek to 'trade its way out of difficulties'. This entailed the willingness of shareholders to put up their shares for sale or to transfer them to the government or government-approved entities, as well as the willingness of the company to sell off assets.[35]

While Yukos managers claimed to be negotiating with the government along the lines just outlined, the government itself was never forthcoming about the existence, much less substance, of these negotiations. An outsider could easily gain the impression that if such negotiations were taking place, the government was not a serious participant and that it was simply biding its time while the prosecutors and tax authorities prepared future cases. The government, with some small success, presented Yukos as too untrustworthy to be negotiated with, with its spokespeople noting that the company was still paying dividends, paying off commercial loans, running up debts to its subsidiaries, and running 'domestic offshore' tax minimization schemes, at the same time as it was claiming to be focused on meeting its tax obligations.[36] By early July 2004 Yukos was claiming that the negotiations had been broken off. Minister of Finance Kudrin stated bluntly that the government was not interested in a schedule for paying off tax arrears.[37] Prosecutor General Ustinov made the situation very clear when, following a vague hint from a deputy Minister of Finance that a deal might be possible, he pointed out that there were still a few years of tax audits to come, and that 'this is a snowball. This matter has had a beginning, but it is very hard to see an end . . . Where are the dividends that the company's shareholders have received? They're huge, many billions.'[38]

It was indeed at precisely this time that new tax demands appeared. A demand for $3.3 billion came out of the tax audit for 2001 in early July 2004. In November the 2002 audit yielded a demand of $6.4 billion, and it was in that month that tax bills began to be presented for Yukos's subsidiaries: $3.2 billion for Yuganskneftegaz for 2001–02 and then $1.2 billion for 2003; $0.5 billion for Samaraneftegaz; $40 million for Tomskneft for 2001; and so on. A large proportion of the amounts charged were penalties and fines. As was pointed out at the end of December 2004, the total tax arrears charged to Yukos and its subsidiaries were now about the same as the Russian defence budget.[39] By November 2004 Steven Theede was saying in public what many had long believed to be the case:

> In my view it is entirely clear that this is not a matter of Yukos not paying enough tax. I see here an effort to arrive at the level of tax claims needed to justify what is in fact the theft of the assets or a change in the ownership of the company.[40]

It was not just that new claims for arrears were constantly presented, but attempts to sell assets in order to pay off the arrears were frustrated by court arrests on the sale of the shareholders' and company's shares and fixed assets. It was increasingly clear that Yukos was the mouse being baited by the cat. Part of the game, as ordered by Putin in June, was not to drive Yukos into, or allow it to voluntarily, declare bankruptcy. The government presumably did not want the free-for-all grab for assets by creditors that would ensue. Nevertheless, by the end of 2004 the company was unable to meet the demands on it.

The second half of 2004 also saw a new wave of charges brought against Yukos shareholders, senior and middle managers, executives of subsidiaries, lawyers and consultants. A good proportion of them were able to get abroad in time. Some of the charges were related to what Black, Kraakman and Tarassova refer to as the 'skimming' of subsidiaries, specifically the sale of their assets to the holding company for clearly understated values. The main cases of this type were those against Aleksandr Temerko relating to Eniseineftegaz, and Svetlana Bakhmina relating to Tomskneft.[41] Another was related to the use of charities for tax avoidance purposes – the case of Kurtsin. But most were related to the use of domestic offshore zones for the avoidance of tax and, increasingly in the second half of 2004, for money laundering. Accusations of money laundering seemed to be the prosecutor's approach to dealing with the transfer of revenues to foreign offshore companies. There were also of course the cases brought against Lebedev, Khodorkovsky and others for personal income tax crimes. There were also conspiracy to murder charges against Nevzlin, now formally identified as the Yukos executive controlling Pichugin's contract murder operation. We will look at some of these cases in more detail later.

The sale of Yuganskneftegaz

With Yukos unable to make any progress in meeting its obligations, in late 2004 the process got underway that many believe was what the affair was all about from the beginning – the government sale of the company's assets. The bailiffs had first announced their intention of selling Yuganskneftegaz (Yugansk), Yukos's main production unit, in July 2004.[42] Yugansk contributed 62 per cent of Yukos's output (54 million tonnes of crude a year) and 70 per cent of its reserves, and provided the Yu in the company's name. At that stage both the main players to appear later on the stage, Gazprom and Rosneft, denied any interest in purchasing Yugansk (although there were rumours Rosneft did approach the Federal Anti-Monopoly Service for a preliminary opinion on approval from that agency for a bid in August).[43] However it took until November for the arrangements to be put seriously into place, with the auction eventually taking place in December. The sale was conducted with what can only be called typical Russian chaos and murkiness.

The first issue was what price would the government try to get. Everyone's assumption was that the government wanted to sell Yugansk to one of its own companies or one very closely linked to the Kremlin. If that were the case it was desirable and indeed essential that the price be low, since no Kremlin-friendly company had the money to pay a fair price for Yugansk. And to set a very high price would not be a friendly gesture to one's friends anyway. On top of that the government did not want Yukos to get so much for Yugansk that it would be able to pay off its tax arrears. Early in proceedings Yukos's outstanding tax debt had been in the $3 billion range only, and there were rumours that the government was planning to fix Yugansk's price at that level, so as not to give Yukos any spare cash. But handily, in November, a new tax bill for 2002 was presented to Yukos, for another $6.4 billion.[44]

The government realised early on that the valuation of Yugansk was going to be a controversial matter, and in mid-August hired the international investment bank, DKW, to do the job for it. DKW's involvement did not prevent scandal. DKW was wary enough to provide considerable room for manoeuvre in its range of valuations, but nevertheless made it clear that it believed that the fairest value was in the range $18.6 to $21.1 billion. If one deducted from these values Yukos debts for which Yugansk was a security and tax claims on the subsidiary, a value in the range \$14.7 to \$17.3 billion was arrived at. Most analysts were prepared to accept those figures as reasonable. However they were too high for the government. DKW had diplomatically left the government with some leeway, by mentioning a valuation of \$14.4 billion based on the most pessimistic rating of Yugansk's reserves, which with debt and tax deductions would leave a figure of \$10.4 billion. Unsurprisingly the government, despite DKW's protests, latched on to this figure. It then apparently applied a discount in recognition of the fact that not all shares were being sold,[45] and a final figure of about \$8.8 billion was arrived at or, more precisely 246,753,447,303 rubles and 18 kopecks.[46]

The next issue was who could and would bid. There were stories of interest from a great range of overseas companies, most strongly the Chinese.[47] Gazprom had denied any interest when the intention to sell Yugansk was first announced, and in September Gazprom head, Artur Miller, was still denying interest, on the straightforward grounds that the company did not have enough spare cash, but also on the more surprising grounds that Gazprom did not want to destabilize either Yukos or the markets. That comment was in the context of Putin's statement that he had no objection to state-owned companies being involved in the purchase of Yugansk.[48] Despite Miller's disavowals, most people's bets were on either Gazprom, because of its declared interest in entering the oil industry, or Surgutneftegaz, because it had considerable cash reserves.

In October Gazprom and Rosneft announced merger plans. This was a complicated and always somewhat fraught deal designed to get Gazprom into the oil industry, and in such a way that the state would get a majority shareholding large enough to keep control while having some shares left over for sale. This required the swap of Gazprom shares for a packet of Rosneft shares at a sufficiently high value. All this was enough to convince most commentators that Gazprom's specially created oil entity, Neftegazprom, to be run by the *silovik* head of Rosneft, Sergei Bogdanchikov, would be the victor in any auction of Yugansk. Bogdanchikov duly announced that Neftegazprom would be bidding, and registered its intentions with, and received the approval of, the Federal Anti-Monopoly Service. Gazprom also lined up a 10 billion Euro line of credit from a consortium of Western banks headed by Deutsche Bank to pay for its purchase.[49]

The day before the auction a major spanner was thrown in the works. Yukos succeeded in getting a Houston judge to order a stay on the sale of Yugansk while its application for bankruptcy under US law was considered. That left any Russian company with assets in the US – as

Gazprom certainly did – liable to the arrest of those assets if it partici-pated in an auction that proceeded despite the injunction. That was enough to frighten off the Western consortium.[50]

Perhaps it was this that contributed to the even-more-than-usual con-fusion in the conduct and outcome of the auction. Representatives of two participants attended, Neftegazprom and the entirely unknown Baikal Financial Group. According to *Kommersant's* account,[51] the auc-tioneer began by calling for an opening bid. The Baikal Financial Group representative mumbled something. The auctioneer seemed to take it as being the official opening bid – the ruble price mentioned above – and asked the Neftegazprom representative if he wished to go higher. He in turn looked confused and asked if he could make a phone call. When he returned, the auctioneer reminded the participants that Baikal Financial Group had opened the bidding at the official starting price. The Baikal representative protested that he had in fact made a higher bid – 260,753,447,303 rubles and 18 kopecks (no wonder the auctioneer was confused). In dollar terms this was about $9.7 billion, more than $500 million higher than the starting price, and at least five steps up in the set scale of bidding. The auctioneer accepted the Baikal claim, and asked Neftegazprom if it would go higher. Its representative declined and Baikal Financial Group was declared the winner. We must assume that, unlike the auctioneer, the Neftegazprom representative had known that Baikal had opened the bidding higher than the starting price. Otherwise he would have been ringing to get permission to raise the bidding above the starting price. It would seem, if that was indeed the case, that he had not expected the opening bid to be so high. We will speculate more on what was going on at the auction in a later section.

The biggest mystery of the moment was what was and who was behind Baikal Financial Group. The Russian Federal Property Fund, the agency that ran the auction, claimed to know nothing of the company, although it confirmed that the company had provided the $1.7 billion deposit required for participation in the auction from a State Savings Bank (Sberbank) account. The author has seen no reports that its partici-pation in the auction had been cleared with the Federal Anti-Monopoly Agency, or on what basis it would have made a determination if it had been approached. It was quickly revealed that Baikal Financial Group had been registered a few days before at a nameplate address in the provincial city of Tver, which ironically had in recent times housed the Tver branch of Menatep Bank.[52]

Some commentators believed that it was Gazprom behind Baikal Financial Group, the strange approach being not just because it was traditional in Russian auctions to have more than one front company bidding on one's behalf, but in order to present itself eventually as a bona fide buyer of Yugansk and avoid the wrath of the Houston court. Most commentators, though, were putting their money on Surgutneftegaz, with one newspaper claiming that the Baikal representatives at the auction had been identified as Surgutneftegaz employees.[53]

The mystery lasted several days, with Putin doing little to clarify the situation by declaring that 'as far as I know, the shareholders of Baikal Financial Group are exclusively individuals (*fizicheskie litsa*). These are people with many years experience of the energy industry.'[54] Increasing suspicion was directed towards Igor Sechin, Putin's close *silovik* ally within the presidential administration, even though he had very limited experience of the energy industry, having become chairman of the board of directors of Rosneft only in August 2004. Unlike his CEO at Rosneft, Bogdanchikov, Sechin did have a *silovik* background, having served as a 'technical' interpreter and then in the army in Angola. He also had close links with Putin in St Petersburg in the first half of the 1990s. The suspicion proved well-founded: soon after it was announced that Rosneft had bought Baikal Financial Group, and with it Yuganskneftegaz.[55]

The next big scandalous mystery was how Rosneft would pay the $9.7 billion. No official statements have ever been made, but analysts have pieced together what they believe to be the story by tracing unusual payments in the published accounts of various banks and Rosneft itself.[56] The $1.7 billion deposit to participate in the auction was provided as a long-term credit, at 8 per cent per annum, by Sberbank. The great bulk of the rest of the payment, $6 billion, was eventually provided as credits by Chinese banks. These credits represented advance payment on the delivery of 48.4 million tonnes of oil up to 2010. In the period between final payment for Yugansk at the end of December 2004 and the Chinese credits becoming available in February 2005, Rosneft subsidiaries provided the money by selling short-term bonds. Those bonds, it seems, were bought by Vneshekonombank, the state bank for foreign operations, using money transferred to it from the Federal Treasury, ostensibly to pay off foreign debt. The bonds were bought back when the Chinese credit came through. It would appear, therefore, that the purchase was financed by the Chinese, with payment to be in oil, but with Russian state banks and treasury providing both long-term and bridging finance.

While Rosneft was sorting out paying for Yugansk, the other major problem it had on its hands was its merger with Gazprom. As soon as it was revealed that Rosneft had bought Yugansk, Gazprom put the merger on hold.[57] Bogdanchikov, with presumably Sechin behind him, was now even less happy about being absorbed into Gazprom than he had been before. There was talk of the merger going ahead, but with Yugansk being spun off as a separate company for Bogdanchikov.[58] That would not have satisfied either Gazprom or Bogdanchikov. In the end the whole merger was abandoned,[59] with a little while later Gazprom getting its entrée into the oil industry by buying Abramovich's Sibneft for $13 billion.[60] The government would achieve the goals of the aborted merger by buying enough Gazprom shares for cash, and then selling off shares in both Gazprom and Rosneft. We will examine the Kremlinological aspects of Rosneft's purchase of Yugansk, including its apparent outmanoeuvring of Gazprom in the process, later in this chapter.

The purchase of Yugansk left Rosneft with greatly increased crude oil production capacity and reserves, and a correspondingly improved market value. However it had also purchased some major problems. There were particular operational and structural problems. Rosneft does not have the refinery capacity to handle the amount of crude that Yugansk provides, and the Yukos refineries that had processed Yugansk's oil promised to be difficult partners.[61] Other problems included a big increase in an already high level of debt; among the assets on its books an unpaid loan by Yugansk to Yukos, that would be recovered only with great difficulty; Yugansk debts to the tax office and Yukos debts to a Western consortium that were secured on Yugansk; and Yukos threatening to sue anyone and everyone involved in the Yugansk deal.[62]

We should remember that the starting price for Yugansk was calculated taking these debts, and the tax arrears to be discussed in the next paragraph, into consideration. Nevertheless Rosneft, using Yugansk as the plaintiff, has been pursuing Yukos in Russian courts for massive compensation for the damage done to Yugansk while it was owned by Yukos. By July 2005 claims of over $15 billion had been recognized by the courts, with promises of more to come. (A Yugansk spokesperson claimed that between 1999 and 2003 Yugansk's losses had totalled R226.1 billion as a result of Yukos's use of transfer pricing.)[63] It is not entirely clear why Rosneft should be entitled to recovery of the losses made in the past by its new possession, but the claims have allowed Rosneft to have arrests placed on Yukos's other subsidiaries with not very subtle hints that it might have an interest in receiving them in compensation. As Bogdanchikov put it, 'In Russian terms, they are ours (*Oni u nas, po-russki govoria*).'[64]

Another headache that Rosneft purchased with Yugansk was the latter's tax arrears. These were arrears that were considered at the time they were imposed to be a government tactic to reduce the price for which Yugansk would be sold. (We will not ask how Yugansk could have such huge arrears on profits tax given the losses it had incurred.) As already mentioned they were included in the calculation of Yugansk's worth before its sale. The authorities have presumably felt sufficiently embarrassed about the debts not to simply write them off at the stroke of a pen. Indeed for a while the tax office was demanding full and immediate payment.[65] However some relief was not long in coming. In February 2005 a Moscow court agreed that there had been numerous errors in the calculation of Yugansk's tax liabilities for 1999, reducing the bill by $30 million, and a further reduction of $20 million was allowed in October.[66] In November, in reporting on its first half accounts for 2005, the company expressed the expectation that $3 billion of the $4.7 billion tax claims on Yugansk would be reversed.[67] There are no signs of such 'errors' being recognised in the calculation of the arrears charged to Yukos and its remaining subsidiaries.

The feeling that there is a double dose of 'selective justice' here is reinforced by evidence that Rosneft has been using transfer pricing in its relationship with Yugansk. In early 2005 Yugansk agreed to sell Rosneft its crude output at $13.60 per barrel, three times below the world price. In Yugansk's accounts for the first three quarters of 2005, it showed an increase in revenues of only 26.8 per cent on unchanged output, when the increase in world prices was at least double that. There was an even smaller increase in after-tax profits, although that seems to be explained by greatly increased tax payments.[68]

Yukos responded to all this by suing everyone involved in the sale of Yugansk, including Rosneft, in the Russian courts,[69] while holders of Yukos shares listed abroad pursued the Russian government in US courts.[70] One doubts that Yukos will get what it wants in either jurisdiction. Its shareholders will probably have to be satisfied with relieving their feelings of an injustice having been done by using the approach taken by Khodorkovsky. He claims to feel sorry for those 'who have so crudely and senselessly behaved with regard to the tens of thousands of Yukos shareholders . . . They face many years of fear, of new generations of those who want to "take and divide", and of genuine, not *Basmannyi* justice.'[71]

One problem acquired by Rosneft with it purchase of Yugansk ultimately worked in Rosneft's favour. That was a Yukos debt to a Western consortium of banks led by Société Generale secured on Yugansk. The loan, of $1.6 billion, had been taken out in September 2003, with responsibility for repayment being transferred to Yugansk in May 2004. Initially

Rosneft had trouble avoiding responsibility, through its ownership of Yugansk, for the debt. It agreed in late 2005 to pay some of it off, although it still disputed its responsibility for a considerable portion.[72]

In March 2006 a Moscow court dismissed a Yukos claim on Yugansk for the outstanding amount, on the grounds that Yukos's transfer of the debt to Yugansk had been a deliberate effort to pervert the course of justice.[73] At that point the Western banks, who had already received a judgement from the High Court in London that Yukos was liable for the debt, began bankruptcy proceedings in Moscow. If at the time it might have seemed that the Western banks were providing cover for Putin, who had in mid-2004 declared that the Russian state had no interest in bankrupting Yukos, even that tiny fig leaf was removed a few days later when it was announced that Rosneft had bought the debt off the banks and would now pursue the bankruptcy itself. The court, presided over by a judge with a background in the military procuracy, duly appointed an administrator with claimed close links to the *siloviki*, after a rushed, three-hour hearing. The court is to reconvene in early August 2006 to decide whether Yukos is to be allowed to continue operations or to be broken up.[74]

How that decision goes might be determined by the willingness to cooperate of Yukos management. While the bankruptcy proceedings were getting underway a struggle between the Yukos 'management-in-exile' in London and the management team in Moscow came to a head. The former, seeing the latter as too willing to cooperate with the authorities, granted the power to run Yukos on-the-spot to a long-time executive Vasilii Aleksanyan. He was promptly called to the prosecutor's office to be informed that a criminal investigation against him had been opened and to be warned, in his words, 'to keep away from Yukos'.[75] He responded with a vigorous statement of his intentions to run Yukos, and was arrested the next day.[76] While this might be enough to ensure a compliant Yukos management, the betting is nevertheless that the bankruptcy court will determine that the company should be broken up, with Rosneft being the main beneficiary of the process.

While that might be the end of Yukos's agony, what of its founder? There is no evidence that the state is intending to exercise mercy, and one can predict that as long as he shows any willingness and mental and physical capacity to play a prominent role in Russian society once a free man, he will remain where he is.

What was it all about?

The first question to be answered in trying to understand what the Yukos affair was about is whether Putin was in charge or not. If Putin was not in charge, and that was an image that he tried assiduously to promote, then who was? One popular explanation is that the *siloviki* were in charge, primarily in order to obtain for themselves a major economic resource.[77] Of course, the fact that the transfer of Yugansk to Rosneft was all about giving a major resource asset to the *siloviki* does not necessarily mean that Putin was not in charge – he might have been doing it, fully in control, for his clan colleagues. But if he was not in control, the *siloviki* are strong candidates for those who were.

Another possibility is that bureaucratic agencies initiated and made the running in the affair. The agency most involved was the prosecutor's office,[78] but the tax office, going through wrenching re-organizational change at the time, and the Ministry of Natural Resources might have seen organizational benefits to themselves. It seems unlikely that such relatively junior government agencies could have initiated and run such a controversial process but it is possible that at times they pursued it more aggressively than their masters intended.

The final contender for responsibility, if it was not Putin himself or the *siloviki*, is one or more of Khodorkovsky's business rivals, presumably from within the oligarch group. We have already seen their penchant for using political and coercive weapons in their competitive struggles, and this might have been another example on a spectacular scale. We will speculate later on who might have been involved.

Clearly very serious consideration has to be given to the view that Putin was in fact in charge, that he knew what was going on from the very beginning and all that happened happened with his approval, if not on his initiative. If he was in charge, what was it that was driving him? One possibility is that he was simply doing the only thing that he knew: to fight for power and to strike at anyone who looked in any way at all a threat to that power, even if only in the 'protocol' sense of not showing due respect. That attitude might have been directed against Khodorkovsky personally or against the oligarchs as a group. Either or both had clearly got too big for their boots. Part of his resentment of their behaviour might have been a feeling that they had reneged on an agreement that he had negotiated in good faith.

If there was more to it than cutting down tall poppies, three possibilities present themselves. Firstly, there is the possibility already mentioned, that the Yukos affair was carried out to provide the *siloviki* with some serious economic resources, although in this version because Putin wanted to, not because they were in a position simply to take it. Secondly, he might have wanted above all to extract more revenue from the resource sector, presumably in order to spend it on other things that would in his view contribute to the growth and strength of Russia and to the maintenance of his popularity. The final possibility is that, for presumably the same reasons, he wanted to do more than extract more revenue from the resource sector – he wanted actually to nationalize it.

These are the possibilities. Almost certainly they were all involved one way or another, but is it possible to identify one that might carry more weight than the rest?

We will begin by considering whether Putin was in charge. He constantly claimed not to be, stating that the whole process was a matter for the courts.[79] A more serious argument would be that he was unable or unwilling to control events, since they were initiated and pursued to benefit the *siloviki* on whom he depended for his position. As evidence, on those occasions when Putin expressed a public opinion on what should happen, in particular when it came to Rosneft's role, the reverse in fact occurred. In June 2004 he said at a press conference that the state was not interested in bankrupting Yukos[80] and in September the same year he assured a group of Western investors that 'no Rosnefts or anyone of that ilk (*nikakia Rosneft'*) would ever buy Yukos'.[81] He might choose to argue that Rosneft bought Yugansk, not Yukos, but such pedantics aside the state-owned, *silovik*-controlled Rosneft has brought about both outcomes.[82]

These cases can of course be interpreted in two ways. They might be an indication of Putin not being able to control the *siloviki*. But they might show the extent to which he is prepared to lie and be hypocritical to get what he – and his *silovik* cronies – want. On the very big issue of whether the Yukos affair represented the beginnings of the wholesale reversal of privatization, so far events have not contradicted his repeated statements that it did not.

Clearly we are not in a position to know conclusively whether Putin was in charge. For what it is worth, in the author's view it is extremely unlikely that he was not. How much control he had over day-to-day events would have depended entirely on how much he trusted subordinates to do things the way he wanted, not whether or not he had enough power to keep things under control. If at any stage he was tricked or ignored by subordinates who took matters into their own hands – we have already reported Khodorkovsky as suggesting that the prosecutor's office came up with murder charges to make it impossible for Putin to end the matter – he had many opportunities to bring it to an end. His own public pronouncements were sufficiently sphinx-like to leave him room to blame subordinates for things getting out of control. The affair escalated so steadily that there were many points at which it could have been stopped. And there were a number of occasions when there were wide expectations that things would be called off: Lebedev and Khodorkovsky would be released or given symbolic sentences; judges would find errors in the substance or calculations of tax liabilities; these things would happen after the parliamentary elections, after the presidential elections, under various amnesties, when the oligarchs had shown suitable humility, and so on. None of these opportunities were ever taken advantage of. The relationship between Putin and the *siloviki* is undoubtedly a subtle one, but it is unlikely that they – or anyone else in Russia today – act in ways that Putin does not want them to act.

If Putin was in charge, what was he trying to do? We will begin with what was probably the most popular explanation in the early stages, that Putin decided that he had to put a halt to Khodorkovsky's political ambitions.

Politics and personality

Khodorkovsky's political ambitions consisted of vague statements that he did not intend remaining at Yukos beyond 2007 (taken to mean presidential ambitions at the elections in 2008); the funding of a number of political parties, primarily Yabloko (although Yukos executives also funded the Communist Party and indeed stood as candidates for that party);[83] the funding of organizations designed to promote civil society, particularly among young people; and general talk of the need for a parliamentary republic in Russia.

None of these seem threatening to Putin's personal political ambitions, although there were suggestions that a good showing by Yabloko might threaten the chances of Putin's preferred party, United Russia, getting a constitutional majority.[84] Those pushing the electoral political explanation were disappointed when the parliamentary elections passed, with the results entirely satisfactory to Putin, with no sign of leniency towards Khodorkovsky. Regarding Khodokovsky's presidential ambitions, given the public opinion survey results regarding him and his oligarch colleagues cited in other places in this book, it is hard to imagine Khodorkovsky representing an electoral threat to Putin or even a Putin-backed candiate in 2008.

If the concern was with public politics, it must have been a broad general concern rather than with specific electoral results. Perhaps it is required of a Russian political leader that he not allow talk, no matter how vague, of constitutional changes, in this case talk of a parliamentary republic, that would diminish his position. It seems more probable that what played a role here is the inability of a Russian leader – particularly one of Putin's background – to allow insubordination in any form, for reasons of political prestige and standing, to go unpunished.

Khodorkovsky had long been outspoken. His famous challenge to Putin regarding the corruption within the state was seen as particularly provocative.[85] He was warned, by the arrest of Lebedev, and was given the opportunity to leave the country. Although he was careful to exclude Putin from his accusations, Khodorkovsky showed no signs of backing down, and continued to be recalcitrant after he too was arrested. That is not the sort of behaviour that can be responded to with leniency.[86] There has been a vindictiveness in the treatment of Khodorkovsky that suggests something of the need for a Russian leader to show who's boss. There is also an element of personal antipathy between the two that is admitted by Khodorkovsky and was evident in the corruption exchange just mentioned.[87]

But is the need to slap down Khodorkovsky, whether for his political activities or his insubordinate attitude, enough to explain the vindictiveness against his company and so many of his colleagues, down to relatively junior levels? Certainly middle level executives currently serving long prison terms had no presidential ambitions and would hardly have had the opportunity to be insubordinate towards the president. Perhaps the antipathy and vindictiveness extends not just to Khodorkovsky, but to all he stands for, including those who work for him. There has indeed been a surprising degree of solidarity among Yukos officials, with even junior staff who did not have the opportunity of their superiors to flee the country steadfastly refusing to admit their guilt.[88]

Lobbying

While personal antipathy and the Russian 'firm hand' cannot be excluded as factors, Yukos's lobbying might be a more powerful 'political' explanation. Although from the time Putin came to power serious efforts were made by the oligarchs to maintain direct institutionalized contacts with the head of state, the oligarchs also felt the need to provide themselves with a locus of representation that had some independent constitutional status, namely the parliament. We have already described the success of Khodorkovsky's parliamentary lobbying, particularly through the efforts of his colleague-turned-parliamentarian, Vladimir Dubov. The evidence suggests that Putin found such parliament-based lobbying unacceptable. It was apparently in response to the so-called Yukos amendment referred to earlier, that Putin said soon after the arrest of Khodorkovsky's associate Platon Lebedev:

> It simply makes me sick. I can't just sit and do nothing any longer ... What business is doing in the chamber transgresses all limits.[89]

He is also quoted as complaining in another interview about people 'receiving billions of dollars through privatization, so that they can spend millions of dollars on politicians and journalists in order to protect those billions'.[90] Although Khodorkovsky was probably the best organized and most persistent of the oligarch lobbyists, they all lobbied to some extent and all benefited from Khodorkovsky's efforts. To that extent the Yukos affair was a lesson for them all, and the articulation and pursuit of oligarch interests in the policy making process has certainly changed considerably since 2003, in a way to be described in more detail in the next chapter.

The Yukos–Sibneft–Exxon deals

Some suggest that Putin felt he had to take action against Khodorkovsky not because of his political activities, whether electoral or lobbying, but because of his growing economic power.[91] The threat came variously from the merger with Sibneft or, it is more usually claimed, the large proposed strategic investment of either ChevronTexaco or Exxon-Mobil in Yukos. In general terms one could imagine that Putin, a nationalistically oriented former KGB employee, might be fearful of foreign investment. However he has never shown particular concerns in that regard, and indeed there are claims that his post-Yukos strategy is to engage foreign investors in partnerships with large state firms. Obviously a partnership with a state firm might be seen by him differently from a partnership with a private firm. Nevertheless the arrest of Lebedev came days after Putin had joyously welcomed the merger of TNK and BP, and he showed no concerns over the purchase of the state's shares in Lukoil by ConocoPhilips not long after. There does not seem to be enough here to explain the Yukos affair.

The merger of Yukos and Sibneft is considerably more mysterious. The merger continued to be negotiated after the arrest of Lebedev and was formally concluded a few days after Khodorkovsky's arrest. It was only near the end of 2003 that Abramovich engineered the circumstances to have it declared null and void by the courts. He was unable to get the Sibneft shareholding back that Yukos had paid $3 billion for in October, since it had been frozen by the courts, but equally Yukos could not get its $3 billion back.

Some insiders have referred mysteriously to anonymous Yukos competitors who were involved in its destruction.[92] But there are those who have bluntly fingered Abramovich. Leonid Nevzlin has spoken most forthrightly. He claims that Abramovich was involved in the Yukos affair from the very beginning, as part of a Kremlin conspiracy. Abramovich told

Khodorkovsky that the merger between Sibneft and Yukos and the subsequent sale of a strategic shareholding to a foreign firm had been fully agreed with Putin. When the head of Exxon told Putin that they were interested in buying a controlling shareholding in the merged entity, Putin decided that he had been misled by Khodorkovsky as to his true intentions, to sell a controlling rather than strategic but minority shareholding. Abramovich made no effort to correct the error, and Putin decided that Yukos would have to be dealt with severely.[93] Tatyana Stanovaya has noted that Abramovich played a useful role for the government in the Yukos affair by taking $3 billion off Yukos (in payment for 34 per cent of Sibneft) at a crucial time.[94] Given that the initial tax claim on Yukos was $3 billion, the company's inability to recover its money, even after the merger was cancelled, certainly made it harder to defend its assets.

Even Nevzlin's somewhat unconvincing claim attributes to Abramovich the role of doing a favour for the Kremlin. It is hard to see how Abramovich could have gained personally from continuing with the merger even after the arrest of Khodorkovsky. So even if Abramovich did play some sort of reprehensible role, that in itself is not an explanation for why the attacks on Yukos were undertaken.

Among other oligarch competitors, it was generally considered that Bogdanov's Surgutneftegaz was a prime candidate to take over Yukos's assets when they became available. But there were no suggestions that Bogdanov set about the destruction of Yukos to get hold of its assets, and when they did become available he showed no interest. Alekperov's Lukoil picked up some of Yukos's contracts, but not enough to suggest an interest in instigating the affair.

Siloviki

The *silovik* explanation, that the affair was designed to give significant economic resources to members of the *silovik* elite, is a strong one, given that in the end it was Bogdanchikov's Rosneft that gained the prize of Yugansk, seemingly stealing it from under the nose of the non-*silovik* Gazprom. As described in Chapter 5, Rosneft had been frustrated earlier in its efforts to obtain Slavneft. On this occasion there is considerable evidence of the involvement of Sechin and Bogdanchikov from early in the piece. Two weeks before the arrest of Lebedev, Bogdanchikov had sent a request to the prosecutor's office that it investigate a 1999 deal under which Yukos had got 19 per cent of Eniseineftegaz.[95] Although this complaint to the prosecutor was not the one that was used against Lebedev and then Khodorkovsky, the intentions were clear.

One of the small mysteries of the Yukos affair is the events around the sale of Yugansk. The situation leading up to the auction was that

Gazprom and Rosneft were about to merge. Indeed one explanation of the Yukos affair was that Rosneft needed a higher capitalization so that when it merged with Gazprom the state could get enough shares out of the share swap to have a comfortable majority shareholding, but with enough shares left to float on the stockmarket. This is a deal described by Chris Weafer of Alfa Bank as a good one ruined by the *siloviki*.[96]

Ruined it was, but how? The first supposition when Baikal Finance Group won the auction against Neftegazprom was that it was a Gazprom front, since – because of the Houston court decision – it was too risky for Gazprom openly to purchase Yugansk and for its Western bankers to finance the purchase. But as it turned out Baikal Finance Group represented Rosneft, dealing on its own account. What would have happened if the Houston court had not made its decision? Presumably there would have been no difference in the outcome. Baikal Finance Group would still have opened the bidding well above the starting price and the Neftegazprom representative would have been just as surprised at the unexpected bid from unknown quarters. Rosneft's surprise attack was not a sudden opportunistic reaction to the Houston court decision. The plan to bid independently had been in place for some time, and it is hard to imagine that Putin did not know about it. He certainly knew the *fizlitsa* (individuals) involved. It is not surprising that Gazprom then had to be paid off with Sibneft, the only question being how voluntarily Abramovich sold out.

A full analysis of the *silovik* coup would need a detailed analysis of why they wanted a piece of the oil industry, and what they intended to do with it. Although Bogdanchikov is the front man, it is universally believed that the real force in the *silovik* camp is Sechin, assisted within the Kremlin by Viktor Ivanov. Once Voloshin, as the last remnant of the Family, had departed, it was as a direct consequence of Khodorkoivsky's arrest that Sechin's sole opponents became the 'liberals', then headed within the presidential administration by Dmitrii Medvedev. Not so much the Yukos affair in itself, but the success that Bogdanchikov had in keeping both Rosneft and Yugansk, at the expense of Gazprom, was an indication of powerful forces at work, since Medvedev was a key proponent of the Gazprom-Rosneft merger.[97] Medvedev has subsequently moved from the Kremlin to a deputy prime ministership.

Is there anything more to the *silovik* struggle for a big part of Yukos than to score points in a Kremlin power struggle? That requires some interpretation of the attitudes of the *siloviki*. One possibility is that they have a strongly ideologically driven view that privatization was a disaster for the Russian state and society, and that it must be reversed. Another is that they are far more pragmatic than that, both in their attitudes to particular oligarchs and their willingness to abandon ideology if they personally and as a group are well enough rewarded financially. On the first possibility, to quote Kryshtanovskaya and White:

> A few oligarchs of the El'tsin period have however maintained their position by establishing good relations with the *siloviki*: these include the heads of such companies as Surgutneftegaz (Vladimir Bogdanov), Severstal (Aleksei Mordashev), Lukoil (Vagit Alekperov) and Interros (Vladimir Potanin). Our interview with an FSB officer suggested that the *siloviki* had at least one guiding principle in their dealings with individual oligarchs: whether or not they were 'nationally oriented'. 'Good oligarchs' were people like Mordashov or Bogdanov ('they're Russians'), but not the others: 'all Jews are traitors, oriented towards the West. That's how it's always been.'[98]

The second would have it that Putin simply wanted or needed to reward some of his *silovik* cronies with a serious economic asset, for their own personal gain and for use in 'political projects'.

In Chapter 5 reference was made to the prediction of Gleb Pavlovsky, the Family ideologist within the Kremlin, that Russia faced a *silovik* coup under the guise of an attack on the oligarchs. Mikhail Delyagin has claimed that that coup has indeed taken place and that Russia is now ruled by a *silovik* oligarchy.[99] While it is too early to come to that conclusion on the basis of one oil company, the evidence is strong that the *siloviki* were closely involved in the Yukos affair from the beginning and were able to continue to take advantage of it throughout. The extent to which their interests were purely personal enrichment and increased political status within the Kremlin, or rather the pursuit of an ideologically driven 'national project' cannot be determined conclusively. Current Kremlin attitudes towards nationalization, however, provide some further food for thought in this regard.

Nationalization

Another popular interpretation of the Yukos affair is that it was the first step in what would be a continuing process of nationalization of Russia's major revenue-earning resource assets. When it seemed that Gazprom would get both Rosneft and Yugansk that interpretation made sense. Gazprom is of course not the same thing as the state. It has a very strong, corporate identity of its own. Nevertheless, as a major global company being subjected to increasing state control, it is the most obvious vehicle for the nationalization of the Russian oil industry. It is also in no way an instrument of the *siloviki*.

The nationalization interpretation fell out of favour when it was revealed that it was Rosneft that had won Yugansk and it became quickly clear that the Gazprom-Yugansk merger would not go ahead. But with the subsequent purchase of Sibneft, Gazprom was back in the game. At the same time a number of assets outside the resource sector also returned to state ownership. Those cases, though, do not clarify whether we are dealing with a nationalization strategy or the granting of economic favours to selected groups, above all the *siloviki*. Major enterprises are returning to state hands, but often those state hands have strong *silovik* connections. The takeover of the car manufacturer AvtoVAZ by a management team from the arms exporter Rosoboroneksport is a clear example.

There are suggestions that Putin is interested in developing links between foreign private capital and a newly strengthened state sector, the reasoning being that foreign capital has more to offer in terms of funding, management skills and technology than domestic oligarchs, and that it is far less threatening to him politically. That makes the reaction of foreign capital to the Yukos affair of critical importance. So far the willingness of Western banks to lend to Rosneft would offer encouragement for such an approach.

We will attempt to bring some more clarity to these matters by way of summary later in the book. But the author will not pretend that the picture is other than opaque. His own feeling is that nationalization is too grand a word for the asset grabbing that is going on.

Taxation

The final explanation of what the Yukos affair was all about is simple and straighforward – it was all about tax. Tax was part of Putin's understanding of the agreement he had with the oligarchs. As long ago as July 2000 he had said in an interview that

> the state has the right to expect entrepreneurs to observe the rules of the game ... The state announced that it would act more vigorously towards the environment in which business operates. I am referring first and foremost to the tax sphere and the restoration of order in the economy.

He then made special reference to domestic offshore zones.[100]

The charges against Khodorkovsky and Lebedev were tax-related, as were those that were brought against Yukos. In October 2004 Igor Shuvalov, a presidential advisor, said that the steps taken against Yukos were 'the beginning of the road in the relationship with other tax payers'. He advised other oil companies 'to examine their credit histories connected with tax payments. ... If it was illegal, then the oil companies would be better off without waiting for the courts to examine their tax history and make extra payments into the budget'.[101] The other oligarchs were quick to swear off the tax minimization schemes that they had all been employing to varying degrees, and tax receipts have increased so dramatically that it is hard to believe that the Yukos affair was not largely about tax. In 2004 3.5 times more tax was collected than in 2003, and then in the first half of 2005 the tax take was $8.4 billion more than expected.[102] In 2005 the oil sector was set to pay 33 per cent more tax than in 2004, and the sector's proportion of total tax revenues continued to rise. In 1999–2001 it had ranged from 14.3 to 14.4 per cent, in 2002–03, 17.1 to 17.8 per cent, and in 2004 reached 22.8 per cent.[103] In terms of individual companies Sibneft significantly increased its rate of payment from the second half of 2003, and by 2004 was paying profits tax at the full 27.5 per cent, when a few years before it had paid 7 per cent. In 2004 Lukoil was paying 24.7 per cent, and Surgutneftegaz 20.[104] We should not forget that substantial arrears also continued to be paid. In 2004, with Yukos payments excluded, the tax office collected $8 billion in arrears, 11 times more than in 2003, and it was predicting continuing high levels of payment in the first half of 2005. It was noted that the main payers of arrears were large companies.[105]

One should not attribute all of these increases to the Yukos effect. With companies swearing off tax minimization schemes in late 2003 and early 2004, by 2005 the effect of their closure should not have been strong. By then the main reason for the increases were very high oil prices and the very high rates of tax – up to 100 per cent – that are payable on high-priced oil.[106] Anatolii Serdyukov, the head of the Federal Tax Service, suggested in mid-2005 that about half the 250 per cent increase in tax revenues since the Yukos affair could be attributed to those events.[107] This is still a major consequence and the rejection of tax minimization schemes by Russian oil companies had a major effect on the Russian budget and on the disposable income of the Russian oil companies. We will devote more attention to the implications of the use made by the political authorities of tax law on Russian political and economic development in the next chapter.

A one-off?

An important aspect of understanding what the Yukos affair was about is determining whether it was a one-off attack on a single individual and his company with, as Putin has insisted, no implications or precedent for other firms, or was it a warning to the other oligarchs? In December 2003 an exhibition was held in Moscow by the artist Oleg Nazarov, to mark the fifth anniversary of the word 'oligarch' in the Russian language (some would say the exhibition was slightly late the word having entered the lexicon a bit before 1998). The exhibition consisted of the heads of the oligarchs made out of chocolate. The message was said to be: 'You can lead a sweet life, but at any moment you might be eaten.'[108] Would the exhibition have been more accurate if only Khodorkovsky's head was on the block? Despite the fact that the other oligarchs also funded political parties and had their deputies in the Duma, the political explanation has generally been seen as directed at Khodorkovsky alone. He was always seen as special in this regard: more ambitious, imaginative and committed in his view of political change, more aggressive in his lobbying, and more willing to be combative in his relationship with political power.

However there is a strong sense in which there was a political message for all the oligarchs. As Aleksei Kudrin put it, the Yukos affair was inevitable 'not in the personal sense, but in the sense of a clarification of the rules of the game'.[109] Initially, in the immediate aftermath of the arrest of Lebedev, business had in something of a panic demanded a firm commitment to new rules of the game. It offered to accept fully its social and ethical responsibilities, including the strict payment of tax and a contribution to the solution of social problems, in return for the guaranteed respect for the results of privatization through a three-year statute of limitations and the greater accountability of the prosecutor's office.[110] At first Putin reacted coolly, but eventually, in April the following year, Finance Minister Kudrin presented a government view of the matter. In a press conference during the Russian Economic Forum he proposed three expectations of business, for which in return the guarantees business wanted might be forthcoming (although he noted that the right moment would have to be chosen for the state to fulfil its side of the bargain, given the state of public opinion on the matter). The expectations of business were: pay tax in full, without taking advantage of minimization schemes even when in formal terms they are legal; engage in charitable activities; and ensure that any political activity undertaken contributes to the development of the country.[111]

Strangely, it was the charity expectation which produced the strongest reaction from such oligarchs as Potanin and Deripaska.[112] Judging by their actions, though, they and the other oligarchs were willing to accept the other two more important components of the offer, although there has never been any suggestion that the two sides have reached an explicit understanding on even an informal basis. There has been much discussion of giving business the security it wants, including the three-year statute of limitations on privatization deals and an amnesty for illegally exported capital. But no firm policy proposals have been forthcoming from the government. Big business has been allowed to lobby its interests reasonably vigorously, including as we will see in the next chapter in the sensitive area of taxation. But Putin in particular continues to be as threateningly ambiguous in his statements regarding business as to suggest a desire not to bring complete clarity to the rules of the game, in order to leave room for arbitrariness.

If Yukos was primarily about giving some resource assets to the *siloviki*, then the threat to the other oligarchs depends on how greedy the *siloviki* are. One suspects that Putin would be reluctant to give them too much, since a *silovik* oligarchy is no more desirable to him than a business oligarchy. If the dispossession of Yukos was the first stage in the nationalization of Russia's resource assets, clearly the remaining oligarchs have a lot to worry about. The state's ambitions though are unlikely to run that far, and there is a limit to how much other claimants on the oligarchs' assets could digest, even if they were allowed to take what they wanted.

The tax explanation clearly has broad implications for the rest of the oligarchs, since they all, to a greater or lesser extent, engaged in tax minimization. This was the sense of Igor Shuvalov's admission that legal pursuit of Yukos was a case of 'exemplary justice'. It is also evident, given the great increase in tax revenues, that this is the way the oligarchs saw the matter.

Almost certainly the Yukos affair was designed to achieve a number of goals. It was not a spontaneous event that got out of hand as prosecutors tried to expand their powers and settle old scores and as judges overcompensated in their second guessing of the wishes of their political superiors. Above all it was designed to put all the oligarchs in their place by making a victim of the most independent-minded of them, and to extract more tax from them. That then allowed Putin to reward his *silovik* colleagues. It was an event that threatened the positions of all the oligarchs in a most serious way. In the next chapter we examine the implications of the Yukos affair in more detail.

8
The Aftermath of Yukos

The Yukos affair is far from over, in the narrow sense that many Yukos officials are still on trial and others avoiding arrest abroad. The ultimate fate of the company is also still unclear, as it faces huge outstanding tax bills and legal proceedings from a range of creditors and other litigants. It is also not over in the sense that it is not yet clear what longer-term changes it is likely to inspire in Russia's political and economic development. While acknowledging that it is not yet over, in this chapter we nevertheless try to come to some conclusions on how the Yukos affair has affected both the oligarchs and Russian society.

In the previous chapter we found that Yukos was probably primarily about politics in the broad sense of setting new rules of the game, rather than Khodorkovsky's personal political interests. It was also about extracting more tax from the resource sector and, perhaps as a side benefit, also about giving Putin's *silovik* colleagues access to the resource sector. What are the consequences for the oligarchs themselves and society as a whole of these events, and what is the verdict of commentators?

The Yukos effect: good or bad?

Four views of the Yukos affair are possible: that it was a thoroughly good thing that did not go far enough; that it has had a positive effect and need go no further; that although the oligarchs needed to be put in their place the practical costs of the Yukos affair outweigh the benefits; and that it was an unmitigated disaster. Not all those who have been cited throughout this book as the 'critics of the oligarchs' have had the opportunity to express their views on the Yukos affair. Discussion of the four views just listed requires some guessing as to what their reactions might have been.

The logic of the harshest critics of the oligarchs suggests that the Yukos affair did not go far enough. For justice to be done and be seen to be done, all the oligarchs have to be dispossessed of economic and political power. Until that is done it is unlikely that Russia's economy will develop to its full potential, and the legitimacy problem that the oligarchs represent at the core of the Russian political transition will continue to hobble Russia's transformation into a true democracy. For those who do not want to abandon the market economy altogether by returning to something like the Soviet approach to economic management, nationalization is the precursor to some sort of new approach to privatization, usually unspecified in detail.[1]

An alternative view is that the Yukos affair has had limited and generally positive implications for the development of Russia into eventually a 'normal' market economy and democratic polity. According to this view, while the logic of the previous view might be undeniable, there are practical difficulties involved in dealing as harshly with all the oligarchs as they deserve. Soviet experience demonstrates that unconstrained 'class warfare' does not bring good results. That means that the judicious use of some 'exemplary justice' directed against one oligarch should be enough. If that were enough to persuade the rest to behave themselves, probably no further action would be required. Exemplary justice is always going to be a bit rough and ready, but if the outcome of the prosecution of Khodorkovsky is that the other oligarchs have begun to pay their taxes and desisted from their attempts to capture the state, then the desired effect has been easily achieved. Paul Klebnikov wrote in November 2003:

> The arrest of the oligarch is indeed an example of selective justice. But that is better than no action at all ... Put yourself in the place of one of the oligarchs. What conclusions will you draw from the Khodorkovsky case? What will you do so as not to find yourself with him behind bars? Obviously, you will prefer always to be on the side of the president, and even better to keep your distance from politics. But you will also direct all your energies to remaining within the boundaries of the law, rejecting get rich quick schemes. Then the prosecutor and the organizers of political campaigns will have no obvious grounds on which to take you on. It is on the basis of such considerations that a law-abiding society is built ... The arrest of Khodorkovsky cannot be called a triumph of legality ... But looking back at these events in the future we will probably be able to declare that they led to the strengthening of the right to property and the Russian market.[2]

Guriev and Rachinsky cite Rajan and Zingales to the effect that Yukos can be seen as a 'political anti-trust' policy, equivalent to the anti-trust policies that were part of building US democracy and its economy early in the twentieth century.[3] This view also focuses on the setting of new 'rules of the game', rules that will bring more certainty to the state-business relationship and thereby encourage investment and growth.

There are some critics of the oligarchs who are uncomfortable even with the judicious use of exemplary justice. They admit that any effort to bring about the complete removal of the oligarchs is difficult to achieve without running the risk of suffering very serious side effects. Buiter warned, well before the Yukos affair began:

A selective policy of restitution and redistribution would run the risk of being pursued in an arbitrary and politically motivated manner and could end up being viewed not as a belated attempt at justice, but as a further degradation of the rule of law. There exists no elegant, efficient and fair solution to this problem. We cannot undo history's earlier throw of the dice, even if we know that those dice were loaded. Probably the best one can hope for is that a combination of sustained growth, efficient and equitable government tax and expenditure programmes and economic reform aimed at eliminating monopoly rents throughout the economy will gradually diminish the significance of the initial distribution of property rights.[4]

This would suggest disapproval of the Yukos affair. Goldman concludes his debate with Anders Åslund on politico-economic developments under Putin, and following the arrests of Lebedev and Khodorkovsky, as follows:

Because the Gaidar–Chubais–Shleifer–Sachs–Åslund reforms were so misguided, sooner or later there was bound to be a correction designed to redress the earlier abuses. Unfortunately the Yukos affair shows that the remedy is likely to be as harmful as the initial prescription.[5]

Goldman makes no suggestions as to what would have been a preferable approach, but the logic of his position suggests sympathy for Buiter's strategy of gradual remediation through tax, anti-trust and developmental policies.[6]

The final view of the Yukos affair is that it has been an unmitigated disaster. It has had serious negative effects on investment, as investors are frightened off by political risk and the increases in taxes that have come out of it. The increase in state interference in the economy, whether in the form of the arbitrary behaviour of tax inspectors and bureaucratic regulators or of increased state ownership of major companies, has the negative effect that state interference always has. The rule of law has been badly damaged, both by persistent procedural irregularities in the legal system and by the creation of dangerous new legal concepts, particularly in tax law. Finally, it has reversed the development of certain institutions, such as parliament, a responsible citizenry and, as just mentioned, the rule of law, that are fundamental to the development of democracy.

We now look in some detail at five of these issues, in order to come to an overall evaluation of the consequences of the Yukos affair: investment and growth, increase in the tax burden, whether justice was done, new concepts in tax law and the development of a democratic state.

Investment and growth

The costs that are claimed by the critics of the state's actions against Yukos are great and multi-faceted. A lot of attention is devoted to the negative effects on the investment climate, both for local and foreign investors. In the case of local investors, the hard-won success in producing in them a longer-term view of investment in Russia was lost by the relative ease with which one such investor, the one who claimed as long a view as anyone else, was dispossessed of his assets. One would therefore expect to see new increases in capital flight. Foreign investors will also be wary, and Russia will continue to perform poorly in the international competition for foreign investment.

The loss of investment through a poor investment climate will have its effects on growth. But the increased tax burden that came out of the Yukos affair will also more directly impact on growth, by so reducing the financial resources of the owners of Russia's resource assets that they will not be able to invest even if they wanted to. If they do invest, they will have to borrow or offer equity in order to do so.[7]

No attempt will be made here to analyze in detail recent trends in investment and growth, or their possible causes. The issues and the debates around them are voluminous and complex. Some sketchy evidence and brief comments are, however, offered with the tax issue examined in more detail in the next section.

Data have been presented to show that there was a major increase in capital flight in the immediate aftermath of the Yukos affair. Private capital outflows increased from $1.9 billion in 2003 to $7.9 billion in 2004; illegal outflows were said to have hit a record $23.7 billion in 2004.[8] There was some improvement in 2005, but Minister of Finance Kudrin has admitted that that was the result of some very large overseas loans taken out by state-owned companies.[9]

However, to counter the disinvestment argument, the remaining oligarchs, and many other big and medium business people who are not the objects of study in this book, remain in Russia, seemingly conducting their businesses with a view to being around in the future. Among the oligarchs there has been a considerable degree of diversified investment within Russia. This might derive from a desire to lay off some of the very high risk involved in the resource sector, although one senses that it is more a matter of restless entrepreneurs seeking new interests and profit opportunities.

The oligarchs have also been involved in legal and open investment abroad, and presumably the capital outflow figures reflect that. Again one senses that this is not capital leaving Russia because of the owner's fear of remaining there, but rather the actions of ambitious entrepreneurs wanting to create truly multinational companies.[10]

Deripaska, through his aluminium company Rusal and Bazel, his structure for non-aluminium assets, represents a good example of all these phenomena. He continues to invest in a major way in the Russian aluminium industry. Admittedly the company has recently stepped back from its strategy of developing a strong aluminium product capacity within Russia, to concentrate on aluminium inputs (bauxite and alumina) and primary aluminium. He has joined the other Russian aluminium producer, Vekselberg's SUAL, in a greenfield bauxite mine and alumina processor in the Komi Republic.[11] At the same time he has major investments in a huge range of Russian industries, including the automobile industry, forestry and agriculture. He also has major overseas investments. These are part of his strategy to transform Rusal into a major company on the world stage. Those investments, including major bauxite and alumina assets in Guinea and a 20 per cent shareholding in Queensland Alumina, the world's biggest alumina producer, are primarily driven by the logic of the aluminium industry, including Russia's poor bauxite endowment, rather than by a fear of investing in Russia.

If the evidence on domestic investment is mixed, analysts are generally sanguine about the effects of the Yukos affair on foreign investment, although one has to keep in mind that many of these analysts are people whose job is to attract investment to Russia. A Barings analyst in November 2003 believed that the Khodorkovsky effect would last no more than six months, although that was premised on Yukos itself being left alone, something that did not happen.[12] Another analyst noted that the Yukos affair itself would have little long-term effect, but high tax rates might.[13] Indeed, as we saw in Chapter 1, the international financial community is not considered to be a friend of the oligarchs and could well be in favour of the diminution of their role.

There were, however, some sour notes. Exxon and Chevron immediately abandoned their merger plans with Yukos; S&P warned there could be consequences for Russia's credit rating;[14] and US investment funds, said to have lost $6 billion in Yukos, warned Putin in harsh terms of the consequences and then sued the Russian state in the US courts.[15] On the other hand ConocoPhillips expanded its investment in Lukoil by buying the state's shareholding when put up for sale in 2004. Alekperov said in an interview how important this deal was for showing that investment was possible despite the Yukos affair. The deal was finally approved after Putin had publicly declared his support for it in June 2004.[16] The situation regarding foreign investment post-Yukos is perhaps best summed up by the position of a major Western oil company which has experienced the full ups and downs of investment in Russia. On 12 April 2005 the chief executive officer of TNK-BP, Robert Dudley, sharply criticised the Russian government at the Russian Economic Forum in London, the day after media reports appeared that the tax office was about to present TNK with a bill for arrears of $1 billion for 2001. He said that 'Russia is becoming inadvertently more difficult to navigate for Russian and foreign investors.' However, despite the worsening business climate the company remained positive about Russia and had big investment plans for the country.[17] Given that BP's previous strategic investment in Russia, in the oil company Sidanko, had ended in tears,[18] clearly the company has a thick skin. Multinational oil companies need to have thick skins, and BP is not the only one that remains positive about Russia despite rough treatment.

In conclusion one could suggest that Russia's investment record is not good, above all for political risk reasons, something that the Yukos affair cannot have helped. There are enough hardy souls, both local and foreign, to keep coming. But the overall level of investment suggests that the less hardy souls, of whom there are very many, still stay away.

Increased tax burden

So far we have discussed the effect of the 'political risk' component of the Yukos effect on investment. To the extent that they can be separated, what might the effect of the increased tax payments that resulted from the Yukos affair have been on investment in the resource sector?

Even Putin claims to recognize that the tax burden on the resource sector should not be such as to kill the Golden Goose.[19] The debate is often expressed in terms of whether Russian resource firms struggle under a greater or lesser tax burden than foreign firms. A quick survey by the *Vedomosti* newspaper in early 2004 revealed a wide range of opinions: Russian firms pay less but they bear higher investment costs; Western firms pay less but they bear higher operating costs; the burden is about the same but Russian firms face higher operating costs.[20] The Ministry of Finance and the Ministry of Economic Development and Trade (MERT) have publicly disagreed over whether the Russian burden was relatively light.[21]

Not surprisingly the oil companies consider themselves to be hard done by. They claim that rates in recent years have been steeply regressive, with each unit of price increase leading to a two-fold increase in the tax burden, with a steep increase in tax as a percentage of revenues in recent years being the result.[22] They claim they are left with insufficient revenue to cover their investment needs, as reflected in the increasing need to borrow.[23] Their opponents point to the relatively low levels of borrowing in the sector.[24]

A feature of the oil sector has been the increasing willingness of companies to look abroad, not only for loans but also for equity investments. This could well be a sign of domestic investors being squeezed for funds through a harsh tax regime. The oligarchs' opponents, however, see it as greedy individuals selling the nation's patrimony and cashing out while the going is good.[25] Another element in the debate is that oil and other resource firms appear, as already mentioned, to have ample funds to invest in non-resource investments.[26] One can respond to this observation from both sides of the argument. On the one hand it could indicate that the resource firms are making returns excessive to their requirements. On the other hand it could be an indicator that oil owners consider the return to be gained in the sector is too depressed by resource taxes and so are looking for a better return elsewhere.

The tax policy debate

What of the policy element to the debate? Initially, as part of the Yukos affair, it became official presidential policy that the resource sector should pay more tax. For a number of years there had been a debate in the government over tax, including on how much extra tax burden the resource sector should be required to bear. The then prime minister, Mikhail Kasyanov, considered to be an ally of the resource oligarchs, used disputes between MERT and the Ministry of Finance to block any increase in resource sector tax rates, and continued to do so even after the arrest of Lebedev and Khodorkovsky.

At the end of 2003 Putin made his position clear when, in an address to the Chamber of Trade and Industry, he declared that he fully supported increasing the resource sector's tax burden through a combination of increases in the export levy and the resource tax known as NDPI. He believed that an extra $3 billion per year could be extracted from the sector without threatening its short or long-term health.[27] The reaction to Putin's intervention was not as immediate as one might have expected, although by February 2004 the Ministry of Finance and MERT had agreed on the split between the export levy and NDPI in achieving the $3 billion goal – $2 billion from the levy and $1 billion from NDPI. After that there were further delays, and in March 2004 Putin was demanding a firm and agreed proposal from the Ministry of Finance and MERT within the month.[28] It took the replacement of Kasyanov as prime minister by the far more compliant Mikhail Fradkov the following month for Putin to get what he wanted. A joint MERT-Finance proposal was then rapidly forthcoming,[29] and a now-amenable Duma quickly passed the requisite legislation. The result was what the oil industry felt to be unsustainably high tax rates.

For a period, however, the industry decided to accept high tax rates, while it pursued reform of the administration of tax in a struggle to be described in the next section. But with tax administration reform legislation before parliament, policy attention turned back to tax rates. There seems to have been something of a reversal of the government's position, and the second half of 2005 saw two proposals from government agencies to cut oil-sector taxes. The first came from the Ministry of Natural Resources, not a natural ally of the oligarchs in recent times. It is concerned that Russian resource tax rates are so high from the very beginning of the life of a field that the development of new fields is being discouraged, at a time when there is increasing concern over the continuation of the West Siberian miracle. The ministry has therefore put forward a proposal for a holiday on NDPI for the early years of a new field. The proposal first surfaced as a leaked document in early September 2005, and then was taken to Putin by the Minister for Industry and Energy, Viktor Khristenko. Putin approved the proposal, on condition that oil companies were not to abuse any privileges they might be given.[30]

These developments were apparently in the context of the deliberations of a special working group within the government that had been considering ways to lighten the tax burden on the resource sector since the beginning of 2005. The group made little progress, and in January 2006 Putin hurried the process along by directing MERT to prepare legislation on changes to NDPI that would include a tax holiday of up to seven years.[31] There was also much talk at this time of how to charge NDPI in such a way as to enable a reduction in the price of petrol on the Russian retail market.[32]

The Yukos affair was undoubtedly an important part of a concerted effort by the state to extract more revenue from the resource sector.[33] While the oil barons have felt that they have no choice but to pay significantly increased levels of tax, their protests that their capacity to invest is being negatively affected seem to be getting some sort of hearing. The Yukos affair has certainly not ended the debate.

Was justice done?

Among the many commentators disquieted by the Yukos affair the greatest concern has been the implications of the approach adopted by the state to the legal proceedings. There is a widespread belief that the Yukos cases fell far short of the appropriate standards of impartiality and due process. In this section some of the concerns raised about the fairness of the legal process as applied in the Yukos affair are briefly examined. Not all areas of concern will be covered, and clearly insufficient information is available to reach reasonable conclusions on all issues. The intention is to give a flavour of the legal process, rather than a detailed examination. We will not deal with the holding of suspects without bail, statute of limitations issues (except in passing), courtroom procedures or the harassment of lawyers.

A feature of many of the cases brought against Yukos and its shareholders and employees was the sudden revival of matters that had apparently been earlier closed through due process. It would be easy to say that no matter relating to the property rights and tax obligations of the oligarchs can be closed, given the current Russian political culture and levels of corruption in the legal system. Nevertheless, the original charges against Lebedev and then Khodorkovsky related to the non-fulfilment of the conditions of a 1994 investment tender for shares in the mineral fertilizer producer Apatit. It was an issue that had been pursued by the relevant government agencies for a number of years, with undenied evidence that not only had the investment funds required by the tender not been provided but that there was a clear intention to hide the fact (by funds being transferred to Apatit one day and returned the next day). When a court in 1998 found that the shares should be returned to the state, it transpired that a few days earlier the Menatep front company holding the shares had sold them on to 'bona fide' buyers from whom they could not be recovered. Whoever the buyers might have been, the share sale had no effect on Menatep's control of Apatit.

After long negotiation, a few months before the arrest of Lebedev, the relevant state agency, the Federal Property Fund, settled the case, with Menatep agreeing to a payment of $15 million. The prosecutor's office had informed the president in April 2003 that all was in order. The arrests then began in July. The justification was presumably that the settlement with the Federal Property Fund was unsound, with the director of the Fund being duly arrested, convicted and given a suspended sentence for 'exceeding his powers' in allowing the settlement. The implication was that the settlement had been reached because of corruption, although a Fund employee suggested in evidence that they had decided to settle out of a realization that they would make no progress any other way, not least because they could get no assistance from the prosecutor's office.[34] The defence was based on the argument that if there were any loss in the failure to fulfil the investment conditions, then it was incurred, not by the state, but by a firm which was now thriving and with no complaints. The firm was thriving because Menatep had invested in it more money and in more sensible ways than the investment tender required. Brief data on the performance of Apatit under Yukos was provided in Chapter 4.

The issues here are as murky and complex as one might expect (and we have not even touched upon the possible involvement of regional politicians and business competitors in stirring up the issue). Menatep was clearly pushing the letter of the law to its absolute limits. Any 'reasonable' opponent of the oligarchs might say that Menatep was obviously behaving in an unacceptable way, and should be treated accordingly regardless of the letter of the law. A 'reasonable' supporter of the oligarchs might say that Menatep did such a good job at Apatit that any technical breaches of the law should be ignored. In terms of the specific issue which introduced this section, whether it was reasonable to reopen the case so soon after an out-of-court settlement had been reached, this author would suggest that it was a case in which the settlement, even if there some doubts about it, should have been enough to close the matter.

The closure issue is also relevant to the other major aspect of the Yukos affair, tax. In April 2003 the prosecutor's office issued an instruction calling on the tax authorities to obey the law scrupulously. It raised the question of the legality of criminal cases and arrests in custody for the non-payment of tax.[35] Within a few months it was doing precisely what it had just called into question. The aspect of the legality of the actions of the tax office against Yukos that has remained as one of the business community's most serious unresolved issues is its right to undertake review audits of completed tax audits. Under the law the tax office cannot review a signed-off audit; this is to give taxpayers some sense of security that once the tax office has signed off on an audit the matter is closed. In the Yukos cases the tax office got around the problem by carrying out so-called review (*povtornye*) audits, reviewing not Yukos's tax affairs but the work of the subordinate tax offices that did the original audits.[36] In doing so errors were found, errors to the tune in total of something over $30 billion. There have been no suggestions in these cases that the errors were errors of commission induced by corruption. The errors discovered were clearly that tax arrangements that were accepted as legal in the original audits were considered to be illegal when reviewed. The legality of the arrangements had been upheld in many courts over the preceding years. This might have been only, as some claimed, because the oil companies had better lawyers than the tax authorities.[37] Nevertheless as a consequence not only had the lower-level tax offices carrying out the audits accepted the schemes, but so had, albeit with considerable distaste, the prosecutor's office and the Accounting Chamber (the government's independent financial watchdog).[38] The schemes were schemes that would not be valid in most domestic jurisdictions outside Russia, although their tax haven and transfer pricing elements remain problems in the international jurisdiction. But the reopening of cases in the way that it was done is not conducive to the strengthening of the rule of law, and cannot be welcomed. The inconclusive and continuing policy debate about review audits will be considered in the next section.

If there were doubts about the appropriateness and fairness of resurrecting cases when the defendants had reasonable expectations that they were closed, particularly when Russian law holds that any uncertainties in the law should be allowed to favour the taxpayer,[39] then one might at least expect some leniency in terms of penalties. We will return to criminal penalties imposed on individuals in a moment, but one of the most striking features of the tax claims against Yukos is their staggering size. The reason is that penalties (*peni*) and fines (*shtrafy*) make up the great bulk of the tax arrears levied. For example, the judgement against Yukos for its 2002 accounts consisted of unpaid profits tax of R50.4 billion, unpaid VAT R35.5 billion,[40] penalties R30.5 billion and fines R72 billion. Fines in particular are levied at very high rates if it is found that the taxpayer wantonly avoided tax and if it is not a first offence, which is what Yukos was found guilty of on both counts.[41] While there might be legal logic to that argument, to claim fines on taxes unpaid over long periods during which the tax arrangements, as dubious as they might have been, were nevertheless recognized at all levels as legal, does not reflect well on the legal system. Neither does the argument that it is not a first offence when the verdict on the previous offence was arrived at after the alleged second offence took place.

One of the features of the Yukos affair was the way in which the net of those affected was spread ever wider. What many took initially to be an attack on Khodorkovsky personally, with Lebedev a piece of unfortunate collateral damage, spread to the company itself, its other shareholders, and then to its senior executives, lower level officials with technical functions, and outside consultants. While the culpability of those carrying out the orders of their superiors has always been a complex legal and moral issue, in this case the matter is complicated by claims that junior officials have been held as hostages for their superiors who had managed to escape abroad. Those claims have been made particularly strongly with regard to the arrest and trial of Svetlana Bakhmina, arrested in late 2004 and held in custody on charges of tax evasion on her personal income and, as part of an organized crime group, the embezzlement of the assets of the Yukos subsidiary Tomskneft. It is claimed that she was arrested because her superior had fled to London. A Yukos tax consultant, Elena Agranovskaya, is said to have been arrested for the same reason.[42] Both were involved in working out the legal details of tax minimization schemes. Bakhmina, the deputy head of Yukos's legal department and a member of Tomskneft's board of directors, was accused by the prosecution of forcing the board members to agree to the transfer of their company's assets to front companies at fraudulently low prices. The defence argument, supported even by Tomskneft officials presented as witnesses for the prosecution, was that she was a junior manager in no position to impose anything on anyone and that the arrangements brought no harm to Tomskneft anyway. The income tax accusations related to her being paid by Yukos in the form of annuity payments from an insurance policy, payments which did not attract an income tax liability. It was a scheme which was used by hundreds of thousands of employees. The amount of tax the prosecution claimed was avoided suggested an income of at most $5,000 per month (the size of the policy suggested rather less). The prosecutor asked for a nine-year sentence, more than that received by Khodorkovsky and Lebedev. She was found guilty in April 2006 and sentenced to seven years imprisonment. If the sentence had been six years, she would have been immediately released, under a blanket amnesty for the mothers of small chidren.[43]

Another case involving someone who appears to be a relatively junior Yukos official is that of the 'charity' tax minimization schemes run by Mikhail Trushin, a senior vice-president of Yukos-Moskva. Since Trushin fled abroad, it was Aleksei Kurtsin, the acting office manager of Yukos-Moskva, who was the main defendant. The prosecutor's claims were that the so-called charities were simply fronts for the claiming of tax relief. Kurtsin received the extraordinarily harsh sentence of 14 years hard labour. The couriers involved who had cooperated with the prosecution received seven years. Even the prosecution found the latter sentences harsh and appealed against them, but no similar feelings were expressed on behalf of Kurtsin.[44]

The prosecutor's office has responded to comments about the arrests of Yukos employees with very strong words as to the responsibility of all those involved in 'dirty theft, the naked and shameless theft of billions of rubles and dollars', 'whether they be executives, managers or other staff'.[45] With long sentences handed down for managerial staff in some Enron cases in the United States, clearly the culpability and appropriate penalties for non-executives is a matter of debate not only in Russia. In the Russian case the element of arbitrariness in who is arrested and the penalties they attract leads commentators, and even Putin himself on one occasion, to use the phrase 'tax terror', with all its Stalinist overtones.[46] The effect presumably will be, as intended, that Russian business people will strike resistance among their staff when asked to do anything that might be seen as possibly irritating the authorities, perhaps at some time in the future and regardless of current attitudes. There are surely implications for what is already seen as an excessively 'top-down' management style in Russian business.

The Yukos case is described as a case of both selective justice and exemplary justice. It is selective justice if Yukos is being judged for crimes which other taxpayers have been allowed to commit with impunity. All the big oil and metal firms have used the schemes for which Yukos has been prosecuted, some to no less degree. Few investment tenders were followed by the required investment in the required form. Literally millions of entrepreneurs used the personal income tax schemes of which Lebedev and Khodorkovsky were convicted. Although many other companies and individuals have indeed been pursued in the courts for the same alleged crimes, the persistence in the pursuit of Yukos and the harshness of the penalties clearly mark it out. There are two approaches to redressing the inequity of selective justice. One, and the logically most compelling, is clearly undesirable in practice. That is to subject everyone else to the same legal process and penalties as Yukos. The other is, if not to let Yukos off altogether, then at least treat it with considerably more leniency than has been evident.

The Yukos affair is not in fact primarily a case of selective justice. It is, rather, as Kremlin aide Igor Shuvalov admitted in an address to the US Chamber of Commerce in March 2005, a case of exemplary (*pokazatel'nyi*) justice.[47] Despite the shock that Shuvalov's statement caused, because of its Stalinist overtones in the Russian context, all justice is in some way exemplary. Justice is meted out to some, to provide a lesson to the rest. It is that aspect of the Yukos affair that leads some to regard it as likely to have a beneficial effect – one is punished in order to persuade the rest to behave themselves. Clearly, though, a careful balance has to be struck here. The example made of the one prosecuted cannot be so severe as to suggest a lack of proportionality between the crime and the exemplary effect on society that is desired. In the Yukos case whether one believes proportionality was violated or not depends on how serious one regards Yukos's transgressions to have been, and how one rates the chances of getting the oligarchs to behave themselves with a less draconian example.

The final aspect of the Yukos affair to be discussed here is the conviction of Aleksandr Pichugin, the head of one of Yukos's security units, for murder and attempted murder. While one might debate the degree of culpability for economic crimes, particularly in the circumstances of transition Russia, clearly having a contract murder unit in one's firm cannot be condoned in any circumstances. In what follows the author is relying on newspaper reports, generally from newspapers more inclined to support the oligarchs than oppose them.

The case against Pichugin was that in 1998 a senior Yukos executive and shareholder, subsequently in exile in Israel, Leonid Nevzlin, was upset when a member of his staff, Olga Kostina, left the company to work for the mayor of Moscow. When she refused to return to Yukos, Nevzlin ordered Pichugin to arrange her murder.[48] Through a couple called Gorin, a contract was arranged. The murder attempt failed, but when the Gorins attempted to blackmail Pichugin he had them disposed of. (They disappeared in November 2002 and their bodies have never been found.) The evidence against Pichugin in the Kostina case is based on the testimony of the person alleged to have carried out the attempt on her life, a multiple offender already serving a life sentence for other offences when he informed on Pichugin. (He also provided the testimony against Nevzlin, for whom an arrest warrant has been issued.)[49] The forensic evidence in the Gorin case consists of a cigarette butt and human tissue found in the car park of their block of flats several months after they disappeared and after the Yukos affair was underway.[50]

Pichugin was arrested for these crimes two weeks before the arrest of Lebedev, and after being found guilty by a jury was sentenced to 20 years hard labour. He has subsequently been further charged with the 1998 murder of the mayor of Nefteyugansk, the centre of Yuganskneftegaz's production operations. It has always been considered that, since he was causing Yukos problems at the time, the murder of the mayor was most convenient for the company.[51] Without access to the evidence no further comment can be made, except to point out that since the takeover of Yugansk by Rosneft the mayor of Nefteyugansk has been murdered and the deputy mayor wounded in an assassination attempt. The deputy general director of Yuganskneftegaz has also been the victim of an assassination attempt.[52] Nefteyugansk is clearly a violent place, with the impression being given in press reports that these cases were the result of local conflicts.[53]

One's attitude to all these matters is unavoidably coloured by one's attitudes towards Yukos in particular and the oligarchs in general. The 'letter of the law' approach will not resolve the issue of whether the treatment of Yukos was reasonable, since clearly both Yukos, on the one hand, and the prosecutors, judges and political figures behind them on the other hand have pushed the law to its very limits. These are circumstances in which one might expect a degree of restraint on the part of the state that has been conspicuously lacking. On those grounds the author finds the state's actions to have been unreasonable.

New concepts in tax law

The Yukos affair has brought to the fore some specific issues relating to tax and a major policy debate regarding the powers of the tax office and tax administration in general. As already mentioned, the circumstances under which the tax office carried out review audits was controversial at the time and continues to be a topic of discussion. Since the Yukos audits business interests have endeavoured to have the approach adopted by the tax office banned, or at least to allow review audits only in specified circumstances. One proposal was that they be allowed only when criminal charges or allegations of collusion with the taxpayer have been brought against the lower-level tax office.[54] Other suggestions were that review audits only be allowed when signed off by the head of the Federal Tax Service or the Minister of Finance.[55] The Minister for Economic Development and Trade, German Gref, suggested that firms be allowed to demand a 'final' audit, on which resolution has been most elusive which could not then be reviewed.[56] It is the matter of review audits on which resolution has been most elusive in negotiations between the government and business.

Much attention has been devoted to the statute of limitations for tax crimes. That has been closely tied to another concept that has received the greatest attention and is seen as the most dangerous for the rule of law in Russia: the concept of the bona fide (*dobrosovestnyi*) taxpayer. The concept was first mentioned by the Constitutional Court in 2001. In July of that year the tax ministry had asked the court to rule on the legality of tax payments deliberately made through banks which after the 1998 financial crisis were unable meet their obligations, including to the tax authorities.[57] The court ruled that such payments were not bona fide tax payments, and introduced the concept of the 'bona fide taxpayer'. This suggested that actions taken purely to avoid tax were not legal, regardless of their correspondence to the letter of the law.[58] The concept has been applied more widely since then, particularly in cases related to the statute of limitations on tax crimes. The courts have suggested, with what some see as confusing logic, that only bona fide taxpayers are covered by the statute of limitations.[59] The terms of the debate are in a sense straightforward. There are those who say that if tax arrangements abide by the letter of the law, then they are legal and those entering into them cannot be held accountable. It does not matter whether the arrangements are purely to avoid tax. If there is no specification of what content the arrangement must have beyond the avoidance of tax, for example, if the law does not specify whether any or how much investment, charity work, or employment of the disabled has to be carried out to justify claims for tax deductions, then no legal claims can be made against those arrangements, no matter how clear it is what their ulterior purpose may be.

The opposing view is that to be legal an arrangement has to not only abide by the letter of the law, but must also be 'bona fide'. The narrowest interpretation of the phrase's meaning is that there must be some business or commercial purpose to the deal beyond pure tax minimization. The Minister of Finance, Aleksei Kudrin, has stated with reference to 'offshore' schemes that

> our laws suggest that an arrangement which is correctly documented on the surface can be considered null (*nichtozhnyi*) in essence. That is, it was put in place not in the interests of the arrangement itself, but in the interests of tax avoidance (*uklonenie*) . . . The Ministry of Taxation considers that it can prove in court that these arrangements were not in the interests of commerce and the company, but purely in the interests of avoiding tax . . . Such precedents, in which it has been recognized that a correctly documented arrangement from the formal point of view is in certain circumstances null, exist in Russia.[60]

A broader interpretation is that the tax benefits gained from the arrangement must be proportional to the other commercial purposes of the arrangement.[61] A further much broader interpretation holds that tax arrangements are legal, regardless of their consistency with the letter of the law, only if commonsense, social morality and other such concepts are not outraged by the tax minimization aspects of the arrangement. In a case brought against Lukoil over its use of the Baikonur offshore zone, a lower-level court had used Article 169 of the Civil Code to declare null any arrangement entered into with the deliberate intention of transgressing order and morality.[62] Aleksei Kudrin saw things as follows:

> Business must not aggressively take advantage of the shortcomings in our legislation. I stress 'aggressively', that is, when billions of dollars are deliberately removed from being subject to tax.[63]

He is suggesting, presumably, that one must have a sense of proportion that will, in terms of other statements he has made on the subject, be determined by one's sense of social responsibility. The difficulties that such an approach to the payment of tax bring are evident in the verbal contortions that Sergei Shatalov, the deputy Minister of Finance with responsibility for taxation, got himself into in discussion of the matter in mid-2004:

> The main criterion is for what purpose the arrangement or sequence of arrangements are made and their economic content. If they have business goals, and not saving tax, it is legal and free from suspicion. In the reverse case the state must prevent such behaviour.

He went on with what can only be described as a somewhat confusing qualification:

> If the arrangement has no economic content but the minimization of tax, then such an arrangement is seen as not so much illegal as 'incorrect'. In such a case the state must demand full payment of all taxes.

When further questioned on the actual illegality of taking advantage of loopholes, he agreed that taxpayers cannot be reproached for that, but then referred to the ethical aspects of the matter:

> I worked in a large auditing firm and would see our consultants advising clients: in principle the scheme is permissible and one cannot be held responsible, but it smells bad. So big companies, even when they see loopholes in the law, refrain from using them.[64]

Even when Putin's assistant, Igor Shuvalov, made his famous admission that the Yukos affair was all about getting Yukos and other companies to pay their taxes, he could not help noting that some companies had used legal tax minimization schemes, and that he had no complaints about them. However, even loopholes used by bona fide tax payers would be closed.[65]

The Constitutional Court was unable to avoid such contortions as well in a well-known 2003 judgement. The court stated that prosecutions for actions were not justified where, 'although a consequence [of those actions] is the non-payment of tax or a decrease in its amount, [those actions] proceed from the use of rights offered the taxpayer in relation to the freedom not to pay tax or to the choice of the most beneficial form of entrepreneurial activity and consequently most optimal form of payment', and that 'the choice by a taxpayer of an optimal form of tax payment cannot be considered as a means of tax avoidance (*uklonenie*)'. However, the court then went on to say:

> An action can be considered to be *prima facie* a crime which is carried out with intent (*s umyslom*) and is intended for the avoidance (*izbezhanie*) of tax in contravention of the rules established by tax legislation.[66]

Through all the contortions the suggestion seems to be that minimizing tax deliberately is a crime.

In May 2005, in the hope of resolving the issues raised by these contortions, the Ministry of Finance announced a competition, to arrive at the best definition of the differences between tax optimization (presumably legal) and tax avoidance (presumably illegal). The two intending contestants, as of June 2005, were both inclining to the principle that the arrangement must have some purpose other than just the minimization of tax. That was the principle that Kudrin was trying to claim above as already being a valid legal principle, and which was foreseen in the Ministry's policy planning document for 2005, prepared in September 2004, as being the basis for future legislation.[67] In a 2005 case dealing with the application of the 'bona fide' tax payer argument to the statute of limitations, the Constitutional Court's ruling on the matter weakened the 'bona fide' argument, by finding that the statute of limitations on tax crimes does not apply only if the tax authorities were prevented from carrying out tax audits in good time. It leaves it to the lower courts to determine in what circumstances the tax office might reasonably be considered to have been prevented from carrying out an audit within the statute of limitations period. The business community is not happy with the ruling, since it leaves plenty of room for audits to be carried out beyond the statute of limitations on the basis that firms did not go out of their way to help the tax office. But at least the principle that only taxpayers who try to pay their taxes to the degree expected by the state, including *retrospective* expectations, are protected by the law has been weakened.[68]

All the issues mentioned here continue to be keenly debated, including within an important policy-making process.[69] It is a process in which the business community has been closely involved. In January 2005, at a meeting of the government–business Council for Competitiveness, the big business representatives present complained to prime minister Fradkov, not seen as their natural ally and a previous head of the tax police, about the excessive zeal of the tax authorities in claiming tax arrears in the preceding years. Fradkov suggested they give a proposal to deputy prime minister Aleksandr Zhukov and finance minister Kudrin, who then suggested to Putin that measures be taken to impose some controls on the auditing powers of the tax office.[70] Putin accepted their proposals in principle, and a working party was set up to prepare legislation. By March 2005 a draft document had been prepared and it was discussed by Putin with cabinet ministers later that month.[71] Putin, while sounding sympathetic about the concerns of business and indeed calling on the tax authorities not to 'terrorize' business and to adopt a more constructive approach to tax arrears,[72] with characteristic ambiguity also assured them that the role of the tax service in controlling business would remain considerable.[73] After that, it was not surprising that matters did not go smoothly. In mid-April the matter was removed at the last moment from the agenda of a cabinet meeting. A meeting of the working group the night before had not been able to overcome strong business opposition to what it believed to be a strengthening of the powers of the tax office, not their weakening.[74] The further negotiations which led to a draft finally going to cabinet at the end of April did not allay business's concerns. The major issue of review audits was left unresolved.[75] Cabinet accepted the draft, subject to some amendments required so as 'not to remove the necessary levers from the tax office' to enable it to carry out its work, to quote Fradkov.[76] Not surprisingly business was even less happy.

Nevertheless the legislation went to the Duma, where in October 2005 it was passed at the first reading, essentially unchanged. In the words of *Kommersant*, the law 'did not end, but rather formalized tax terror'. There were many negative comments from deputies themselves, who promised to improve the legislation at the second reading.[77] Many amendments meeting most of the concerns of business were indeed proposed for inclusion at the second reading, including a strengthening of the presumption of innocence and controls on review audits, to the disgust of the government. By the time the legislation was passed at the second reading in June 2006, after a vigorous period of negotiation between government, business and Duma deputies sympathetic to the latter, all sides were claiming to be reasonably satisfied.[78]

With legislation pending, it is hard to come to a firm conclusion on the tax administration reform. Business was certainly listened to during the process, but was increasingly unhappy with the direction things were taking. The tax authorities were clearly fighting hard to maintain if not actually strengthen their role, and the government as a whole was not prepared to give up its capacity to keep business in a state of uncertainty and fear. Eventually business had to rely on the Duma, an unreliable ally in current political circumstances, to push their interests against the opposition of the government.

Yukos, tax and democracy

We will conclude this chapter by discussing far more broadly and speculatively the effect of the Yukos affair on the development of the Russian political system.

Many commentators have expressed concern over the effects of the affair on the general development of a democratic society. There are the direct negative effects on the sense of security that citizens should feel from the protection of the law and the enjoyment of private property rights, seen as fundamental pillars of liberal democracy. There are also the broader implications of the persistently Stalinist overtones of the anti-oligarch campaign – destruction of a class, exemplary justice, terror and enemies.[79] There are clear dangers of exaggeration here – the Putin state is not a Stalinist state. Perhaps the concerns can be put in more cool-headed terms by making use of tax state theory. The treatment of that complex and controversial theory will be cursory in the extreme, but some useful insights, even if of a highly speculative nature, might come out of it.

The basic principles of tax state theory are: those in society who provide the state with revenue expect the state to be accountable to them as to how the revenue is spent, that is, to use one of the best known of all political slogans, 'no taxation without representation'; in early and transitional stages of capitalist development those in a position to provide the state with substantial revenue and to demand in return representation are likely to be a small elite, what could be called in terms of this book an oligarchy; with diversification of the economy and the spreading of prosperity an ever-greater proportion of society provides revenue and in return has the right and opportunity to keep the government accountable. The result is a broadly based democracy.[80]

It could be argued that in the lead up to the Yukos affair Russia was at the early oligarchical stage of the development of a tax state. The narrow economic elite that one would expect of such a stage of capitalist development demanded and received a high level of representation in return for the provision of revenue. There are those, of course, who claim that the oligarchs demanded and used representation in order *not* to pay tax. One cannot deny the force of the argument, but can counter on two grounds. Firstly, even at the height of tax minimization schemes the oligarchs were still providing a considerable share of the state's revenues. Secondly, they were increasingly frustrated at what they considered to be the failure of the Putin government to take their concerns into account, particularly concerns about corruption and incompetent bureaucratic interference in their affairs. That is, they were dissatisfied over the level of service they were getting in return for their taxes. Khodorkovsky's famous exchange with Putin over corruption in early 2003 was an expression of the frustration. This was not an isolated complaint. It came at a time when the oligarchs were pursuing a concerted campaign for a more efficient, honest and ethical state apparatus, and in particular were demanding that the prosecutor's office and other *siloviki* keep out of business.[81] As described in Chapter 6, they also claimed to have felt cheated over Putin's tax reform early in the decade. They had been led to believe that it would result in lower overall tax rates, but because of the removal of some investment tax credits the overall result for big business was an increase in tax payments.

In terms of tax state theory it was particularly important that the oligarchs turned to parliament to advance their interests, rather than relying as in the past on special deals worked out in the corridors of power. The result might have had the appearance, common enough in early capitalist parliaments, of a body corruptly pursuing narrow interests. But democracy needs a body which represents the interests of sectors of society other than the state. With time and economic development broader sectors of society will come to be represented.

As relations between Putin and the oligarchs worsened in early 2003, the president faced a choice. He could continue to accept the challenge of negotiating with the oligarchs an arrangement which balanced his expectations of revenue with their expectations of representation; or he could step back from the negotiations, denying the oligarchs the right of representation at the same time as extracting revenue, rather than receiving it as part of a tax state deal.

It is possible to interpret the Yukos affair in terms of the first choice. Tax state negotiations in the early stages of capitalist development are rough-and-ready affairs. In one, albeit far from consensual view of English history, a king lost his head in an episode in such negotiations. In the Russian case the oligarchs were indeed trying to enforce a deal under which they used representation in order not to pay tax. Putin has redressed the balance, by presenting to business a new pact, or perhaps by offering again the original *shashlychnoe soglashenie*.[82] As we saw in the preceding section, the demands of business regarding guarantees of the outcomes of privatization are widely discussed and it is allowed representation of its more specific interests, including in parliament. But business no longer dominates in the way it did; it can no longer be said to have 'captured' or 'privatized' the state.[83] Certainly it is no longer allowed to 'buy' policy outcomes, least of all policy which removes from the state its right to levy taxes. This provides an opportunity for other sectors of society to share in the nation's resource wealth, and in doing so contributes to the broader prosperity of society. Business has to treat Putin with the respect and even subservience due to a Russian leader, but in return he will treat it with respect. In doing so he encourages the population to do so as well, thereby allowing business to win popular legitimacy, the lack of which is one of the great stumbling blocks in Russia's movement to 'normality'. The combination of greater and broader prosperity and business legitimacy will eventually bring beneficial political developments.

Putin is prepared to do all this because he recognizes the unavoidable need for Russia to nurture a globally competitive economy, something which can be done only with a predominantly privately owned business sector and private sources of investment. The post-Yukos decline in both domestic and foreign investment – business's threat of the 'investment veto' – has reinforced him in his belief that not only must private enterprise be allowed to exist but that it must also be treated with some respect.[84]

A strong and more pessimistic argument can be made that Putin in fact adopted the second choice. The oligarchs, and by implication anyone else with property and a desire to provide the state revenue only in exchange for representation, have been rudely reminded that they exist only by the favour and at the whim of the state. They have no rights of representation; the state has unlimited rights of expropriation. The Putin government might choose at times to listen to them, and might choose at times to reduce the tax burden on them. But these choices by the state imply no political rights for its subjects.

This can be seen in the carefully cultivated threatening ambiguity in everything he has to say about business. He has no desire to encourage the general population to grant legitimacy to business, since to do so would remove one of the pillars of his populist appeal. Although he is prepared to allow business an 'informational' role in policy making, he feels no need to guarantee anything more. The 'investment veto' has proven to be a sham, as investors continue to scramble for Russia's resources. He is perfectly prepared to fill any private gaps with state capital, including that extracted from an emasculated private sector, as well as with private foreign capital.

If this is the choice Putin has made, it is destructive not only because it removes the beginnings of autonomous political power, but also because it has a highly negative effect on any sense of citizenship among the general population. Citizenship here is defined in controversial terms as having the right to pay tax and in return to keep the government accountable.[85] Those with a negative view of Putin's actions against Yukos see them, rather than encouraging the development of such a form of citizenship, as having the opposite effect. The Russian population has been encouraged to believe that those having wealth have no rights of representation and deserve to be expropriated. The people themselves expect to pay no tax, but as a consequence they are not encouraged to feel that they have the right to keep the government accountable. Their relation with the state remains either a sullen one or a populist enthusiasm for a president willing to 'expropriate the expropriators'. As Ella Paneyakh pointed out after the post-Khodorkovsky Duma elections in December 2003, 'Active taxpayers are no longer represented in parliament'. Tax recipients are well represented, and while they might disagree on how best to expropriate the taxpayers, there is no one to oppose the expropriation.[86] In these circumstances parliament exists to assist in expropriation, not to keep the government accountable.

In early 2006 it is still too soon to determine which choice Putin actually made. The author will admit to strong fears that it was the second, in which case he can only conclude that an opportunity to contribute in a positive way to the political development of Russia has been sadly missed. That, added to the echoes of the traditional Russian 'firm hand', some specifically Stalinist symbolism, and a vindictively corrupted legal system, all lead one to the conclusion that the Yukos affair did more damage to Russia than the oligarchs ever did. In the final chapter a summary of the contribution of the oligarchs to the Russian transition, whether it be positive or negative, will be provided, as well as some speculation on the future development of Russian society, with or without the oligarchs.

9
Conclusion

The critics of the oligarchs – and their critics almost certainly outnumber their supporters by a considerable margin – describe them as having shady backgrounds, backgrounds which are reflected in their continuing willingness to behave in corrupt ways. They have always used the state to serve their own interests, and as they became richer and more powerful were able to ensure that the state had no option but to continue to do so. At worst they were cynical asset strippers, at best incompetent managers. Their activities had catastrophic political and economic consequences. In economic terms they created an over-concentrated and inefficient resource sector; in political terms they contributed to the complete de-legitimization of capitalism and the market. Those seeing things in such terms have had little choice but to welcome Putin's approach to the oligarchs, regretting only that it has not gone further, or to be resigned to accepting its inevitability.

It is a view which tends to see the Russian experience as unique, not to be compared to Robber Barons, South Korean *chaebols*, and so on, since Russia's experiences at the hands of the oligarchs have been far worse and with far more serious long-term consequences than the experiences of those other countries. Generally the blame for their depredations is attributed to the follies of shock therapy, although with some recognition granted to the Soviet legacy.

The historical record since the early 1990s contains enough that is disturbing and even shocking that one disputes these critics' views with some sense of discomfort. Nevertheless, the author wishes to offer the following counter-views. The origins of the oligarchs were in fact very varied. What they had in common were highly developed entrepreneurial instincts and a willingness to take risks, both political and economic. Although never unimportant, the importance of Soviet-era connections in the development of their careers has been overestimated in the literature. As they moved into the post-Soviet period they did all try, to varying degrees, to use the state to further their own interests. Even a state as weak and radically market-oriented as Yeltsin's, in circumstances of dismantling the centrally planned economy, had a lot of patronage and assets in its gift.

The most important feature of the state as far as the oligarchs were concerned was that it was a state, influential elements of which adopted a strategy of developing powerful private firms able to compete on a global scale. It is unclear whether they rejected foreign ownership of these firms as a matter of personal belief or out of recognition of the infeasibility of foreign ownership in Russian circumstances. The rejection, though, made a Central European-style transition impossible, with considerable consequences for Russia.

The strategy having been implemented, in economic terms it has not been as catastrophic as the critics suggest. The evidence suggests that the asset-stripping accusations against the oligarchs are overstated if not entirely baseless. These are clever, adaptable people who have at the very least restored to health and at most transformed the sectors they are involved in. As time has passed they have increasingly run their businesses in what we might call a 'normal' way. It is true that they have not built their resource businesses from scratch, but this hardly seems reason to dismiss and damn their efforts. They have been prepared to invest, and although they have expected high rewards, these are not clearly excessive in the circumstances.

Politically, they were never a true oligarchy, since they never even tried to govern, that is, take for themselves the formal reins of government. They did perhaps try to rule, and indeed at times they were able to pursue their interests almost unopposed, to a degree that exasperated even Chubais. But to the extent that that is true, they demonstrated how hard it is to rule without governing, that is, how hard it is to run the affairs of state without holding formal positions of power.

The collective action problem has been overstated as an explanation for their inability to rule as an oligarchy, or even easily to pursue their interests as a group of individual oligarchs. While it is true that they were too ready to use non-business methods in their business rivalries, when they really needed to they were able to cooperate. In practice it was not always necessary that their interests be pursued collectively in order to be represented.

The problem they face that has perhaps received inadequate attention is their complete lack of legitimacy in the eyes of the general population.

Any efforts to present a more respectable face, through commitments to transparent corporate governance and to social responsibility, have done them no good at all. It is difficult to imagine how that problem might be turned around, short of complete dispossession. If that option is rejected as another revolution that Russia does not need, one has to rely on the processes of time, in a form to be described below. One suspects that a truly legitimate government would help, if such a thing could be devised that was not based on dispossession of the oligarchs.

What position do the oligarchs find themselves in at the moment, in early 2006? One possibility is that Putin, although determined to exercise strong state authority, recognizes the need for a globally competitive private sector. He sets the rules of the game, but there is room for negotiation at the margins, and the margins are set wide enough to allow oligarch businesses to continue to operate and enjoy reasonable rates of return. The Yukos affair was just a normal part of the hurly burly of early capitalism, of the negotiations of the early tax state. While justice is selective, it is recognisably justice and has had a salutary, exemplary effect. Putin could perhaps be seen as Russia's Teddy Roosevelt.

Another possibility is that Putin regards the oligarchs far less benignly. His intention is to pick them off one by one, through arrests, exile and encouragement to sell out. He is doing this either to ensure that there is no one even remotely capable of opposing him, to look after his *silovik* cronies, or to renationalize the economy. Given the 'statist' orientations of the *siloviki*, there is not much difference between the last two.

Even if his intention is not literally to drive all the oligarchs out of business, it is to shift the balance of the economy decisively away from big private capital, with their political emasculation as part of the process. Some suggest that this is a strategy that does not exclude openness to the global economy and foreign investment. Putin is attempting to produce some sort of alliance with big Western firms in order to obtain the extra funding and management expertise that his *silovik* friends do not have. He is adamant, however, that foreign capital will not be given controlling shareholdings of any strategic resource firms. To find a balance between being welcoming, not upsetting nationalist sentiment, and maintaining the state's control over foreign investors will not be easy.

The alternative is that he takes Russia into something like a Latin American populist dead end, based on a semi-authoritarian state enjoying the populist support of the population by appealing to the politics of dispossession.[1] A Latin American sort of circulation of power could even be possible: the semi-authoritarian who drives out the oligarchs is unable to provide competent and honest government, and is then abandoned by the people in favour of anti-authoritarian democratic movements with the backing of private big business. That becomes an oligarch government, which is eventually driven out by a new anti-oligarch populist.

The populist politics of dispossession provides poor opportunities for development. As an alternative, if the inequalities of power and wealth that make oligarchy politically and even economically unsustainable can be removed, there is hope that oligarch capitalism can be transformed into a democratic and socially responsible capitalism. In terms of the first scenario outlined above, that the Yukos affair is just an adjustment in the business–state relationship, Putin might yet assist in such a process. Alternatively a new government that is not anti-oligarch might be required, as unlikely as that sounds. The de-concentration of economic power is then needed, so that the increasing prosperity of the rest of society and the strengthening of new institutions can lead to the tax state outcomes described in the previous chapter. As any good gradualist will tell you, this is something which should not be rushed. A judicious Russian state now has more time available to it than Yeltsin's shock therapy government had, since the economic and social circumstances in which it is operating are less dire.

It is recognised that Russia faces some particular difficulties in this regard. It is very easy to make the populist argument in Russia because of the privatization component of the oligarchs' rise. The Robber Barons might have been given wealth by the state, in terms of railway concessions and land. But they were less obviously receiving an existing asset. There is also the resource curse aspect to Russia's situation. Most of Russia's wealth is in resources, and there is by now a large literature showing how hard it is to achieve a balanced distribution of political power and economic prosperity in those circumstances.[2] Finally, because of the unusual circumstances of Russia's modernization, the country has a middle class large sections of which are deeply alienated from the market and wealth. While not universally accepted, there is a widespread general consensus that a pro-market middle class is an essential component of the development of liberal democracy.

Keeping the above difficulties in mind, how might the de-concentration of economic power that could lead to movement away from oligarch capitalism without a reliant populism come about?

One way it cannot be done, if the principles of the tax state are to be observed, is through a highly redistributive tax system. In the Russian case, a highly confiscatory tax approach would be needed to bring about serious change in the concentration of wealth through the tax system.

We have seen something of this approach in the Yukos affair. It is theoretically possible that those possessing wealth would agree to the confiscation, and so it could be carried out without denying them political representation commensurate with the level of tax they pay. It is more likely, though, that in order for such a policy to be implemented, those having the wealth confiscated would have to be denied political representation, quite possibly in a vigorous way. Very probably the state would appeal to populist support to bring about the confiscation, an outcome we are trying to avoid.

The idea of a one-off compensation payment from the wealthy beneficiaries of privatization has become popular, in order to draw a line under privatization in a way that might reconcile the population to the oligarchs.[3] One fears that no one-off compensation would be enough to satisfy the population, nor in itself provide the spread of prosperity that is needed.

If major wealth redistribution through the tax system is undesirable and a one-off compensation payment inadequate, what other approaches to de-concentration can be adopted? Leaving aside the complexities of competition policy, the feasible scenarios all seem to involve a considerable degree of reliance on 'organic' change. This could be a change in economic and technological circumstances that brings about shifts in who possesses wealth and so who pays tax. The most dramatic in Russian circumstances would be the depletion of natural resources or technological changes that render oil redundant. While ultimately inevitable, such developments are unlikely in anything other than the long term.

The classic route would be a gradual increase in national prosperity leading to a broadly prosperous wage and salary class. That requires dealing with the resource curse problem, as well as finding the balance between the concentration of economic assets needed for global competitiveness and the broader ownership needed to promote social and political change.[4]

We could look to non-directed diversification by the current holders of wealth into new areas of economic activity. Such diversification is going on in Russia on a major scale. It is a process that some observe with horror, seeing it as a further tightening of the grip of a small elite over the economy. It does nevertheless have the effect of members of the elite coming to have different economic interests. The beginnings of such a process can be seen, for example, in the increasingly ambiguous policy interests of a metal magnate such as Deripaska after he diversified into vehicle manufacturing. In order to protect his vehicle interests he came to oppose Russian entry into the WTO.[5] That is a process one could well imagine continuing and, if allowed to run its 'organic' course, strengthening the place in parliament of the lobbying of different interests.

An 'organic' de-concentration of economic power will come about eventually through generational change, when the current elite, if they are allowed to experience such a natural change, will for biological reasons be forced to transfer their assets to other hands. The Russian economic elite is a young one, and there are few signs as yet of how generational change might be handled.[6] In recent times Russian elite culture has not been particularly nepotistic, and perhaps the oligarchs will not work to create family dynasties. If they do, we have no way of knowing whether they will adopt a primogeniture approach or the far more de-concentrating equal distribution of assets among their offspring. Either way, experience suggests that generational change has de-concentrating effects on economic power.

The oligarchs might choose simply to sell out. Abramovich has done so already, although under what degree and form of pressure is hard to tell. Others talk of preparing their companies for stock market listings, but with few suggestions at this stage of selling controlling stakes. One doubts that the suggestion of Guriev and Rachinsky, selling out to foreign investors, would help them solve their legitimacy problem.[7] One of the reasons the oligarchs were created is that foreign ownership was too hard to justify ideologically and culturally.

For the moment the oligarchs have tended to respond to the increasing complexity and size of their empires by increasingly relying on professional managers.[8] There is no reason to believe this process will not strengthen as generational change approaches. It is indeed likely to be more important than family succession as a force for the transformation of oligarchic capitalism. One might particularly expect this to be the case if the oligarchs had been forced to bring in outside investors as equity partners, something which in fact we are already seeing. The consequent 'depersonalization' of economic power has considerable implications for the nature of tax paying and political representation.

If these changes were to occur, we would have an economy transformed once again, and in a way that might have increased the legitimacy of big business among the population and decreased the opportunity for politicians to pander to populism. To adopt the sentiments of the gradualist opponents of shock therapy, these might be circumstances in which the slow adjustment of culture and institutions might be effective.

That suggests that the story of the oligarchs is not as bad as their critics have made out. Indeed a happy ending is possible. But that depends on a government prepared to recognize the right of the oligarchs to exist and evolve, and in such a way that the population will come to do so as well. Whether Russia has such a government remains to be seen.

Notes

Preface

1. Hans-Henning Schröder, 'The "Oligarchs": a Force to be Reckoned With?', in Stefanie Harter and Gerald Easter (eds), *Shaping the Economic Space in Russia. Decision making processes, institutions and adjustment to change in the El'tsin era*, Ashgate, Aldershot, 2000, p.50.
2. 'Ot redaktsii: peredelai oligarkha', *Vedomosti*, 10 October 2005, *http://www.vedomosti.ru/newspaper/print.shtml?2005/10/10/98032*.
3. Sergei Guriev and Andrei Rachinsky, 'The Role of Oligarchs in Russian Capitalism', *Journal of Economic Perspectives*, vol. 19, no. 1, Winter 2005, pp.131–2.

1 Introduction

1. Paul Klebnikov, *Godfather of the Kremlin. Boris Berezovsky and the looting of Russia*, Harcourt, New York, 2000; Chrystia Freeland, *Sale of the Century. Russia's wild ride from communism to capitalism*, Crown, New York, 2000; Matthew Brzezinski, *Casino Moscow. A tale of greed and adventure on capitalism's wildest frontier*, Free, New York, 2002. See also David Satter, *Darkness at Dawn. The rise of the Russian criminal state*, Yale University Press, New Haven, 2003; David Hoffman, *The Oligarchs. Wealth and power in the new Russia*, Perseus, Cambridge MA, 2002.
2. A statement made just before Putin was elected president in March 2000, quoted in 'Putin Versus the Oligarchs?', *The Economist*, 17 June 2000, p.55.
3. From a 26 October 2000 interview in the French newspaper *Le Figaro*, quoted in 'Putin Warns the Oligarchs that the State Carries a Big Stick', *Jamestown Foundation Monitor*, vol. 6, issue 201, 27 October 2000.
4. Chris Ward (ed.), *The Stalin Years. A reader*, Palgrave, Basingstoke, 2003, p.83.
5. Plato defined an oligarchy in *Politeia* as 'such a constitution based on wealth, where the rich rule while the poor have no part in government'. Quoted in Hans-Henning Schröder, 'The "Oligarchs": a Force to be Reckoned With?', in Stefanie Harter and Gerald Easter (eds), *Shaping the Economic Space in Russia. Decision making processes, institutions and adjustment to change in the El'tsin era*, Ashgate, Aldershot, 2000, pp.61–2. For Aristotle an oligarchy was an aristocracy gone wrong, a small ruling elite that had chosen to serve its own interests rather than those of society. *Politics*, Book 3, Para.8, from Abraham Edel (ed.), *Aristotle*, Dell, New York, 1967, p.461.
6. On the *nomenklatura* synonym, see Aleksei Iu. Zudin, 'Oligarchy as a Political Problem of Russian Postcommunism', *Russian Social Science Review* , vol. 41, no. 6, November–December 2000, p.4. On the Mafia synonym, see Hans-Henning Schröder, 'El'tsin and the Oligarchs: the role of financial groups in Russian politics between 1993 and July 1998', *Europe-Asia Studies*, vol. 51, no. 6, 1999, p.957.

7. I have made considerable use of Graeme Gill's work-in-progress manuscript on the rise of the bourgeoisie in Britain, France, Germany, the United States and Russia. I look forward to the publication of that study so that Gill can lay proper claim to those of his ideas that are contained here.

8. For studies of these relationships, see among a very large literature Barrington Moore, *Social Origins of Dictatorship and Democracy. Lord and peasants in the making of the modern world*, Penguin, Harmondsworth, 1969; Dietrich Rueschmeyer, Evelyne Huber Stephens and John D. Stephens, *Capitalist Development and Democracy*, University of Chicago Press, Chicago, 1992.

9. For a useful recent summary of tax state theory, see Mick Moore, 'Revenues, State Formation, and the Quality of Governance in Developing Countries', *International Political Science Review*, vol. 25, no. 3, 2004, pp.297–319.

10. Michael Useem, *The Inner Circle. Large corporations and the rise of business political activity*, Oxford University Press, Oxford, 1984.

11. Michael L. Ross, 'The Political Economy of the Resource Curse', *World Politics*, vol. 51, no. 2, January 1999, pp.297–322.

12. Paul J. Dosal, *Power in Transition. The rise of Guatemala's industrial oligarchy, 1871–1994*, Praeger, New York, 1995.

13. Schröder, 'El'tsin and the oligarchs p.50.

14. Aleksandr Privalov and Valerii Fadeev, 'Pora sosredotochit'sia', *Ekspert*, 24 November 2003, *http://www.amicable/ru/polit/expert*.

15. 'Taxman in a tank', *The Economist*, 13 June 1998, p.82. For more on the anti-big business tax campaign of Fedorov, see Gerald Easter, 'Institutional Legacy of the Old Regime as a Constraint to Reform: the case of fiscal policy', in Stefanie Harter and Gerald Easter (eds), *Shaping the Economic Space in Russia. Decision making processes, institutions and adjustment to change in the El'tsin era*, Ashgate, Aldershot, 2000, pp.312–14.

16. Quoted in Merritt B. Fox and Michael A. Heller, 'Corporate Governance Lessons from Russian Enterprise Fiascoes', *New York University Law Review*, vol. 75, no. 6, December 2000, p.1776.

17. Quoted in William Tompson, 'Nothing Learned, Nothing Forgotten: restructuring without reform in Russia's banking sector', in Stefanie Harter and Gerald Easter (eds), *Shaping the Economic Space in Russia. Decision making processes, institutions and adjustment to change in the El'tsin era*, Ashgate, Aldershot, 2000, p.65.

18. *Silovik* refers to someone with a background in or connections to the 'power ministries', those that have at their disposal the forces of coercion, including the post-Soviet incarnation of the KGB, the FSB; the military; the Ministry of Internal Affairs (controlling the police and domestic security forces); and the Prosecutor General's Office. Putin made his Soviet career in the KGB and served as head of the FSB before becoming prime minister under Yeltsin.

19. Aleksei Zudin, *Rezhim Vladimira Putina: kontury novoi politicheskoi sistemy*, Moskovskii tsentr Karnegi, Moscow, April 2002.

20. 'President Calls for Tax Increases on Oil Sector's "Super Profits" ', *RFE/RL Newsline*, vol. 7, no. 238, Part 1, 19 December 2003; Svetlana Ivanova, Boris Grozovskii 'Sdavaite litsenzii' *Vedomosti*, 23 December 2003, *http://www. vedomosti.ru/stories/2003/12/23-55-02.html*.

21. Not surprisingly politicians and parties on the left are unfriendly in their views of the oligarchs. For examples of policy statements from the 'Rodina' party and Zhirinovsky's Liberal Democratic Party, see 'While Nationalists Create "National Liberation Movement" ', *RFE/RL Newsline*, vol. 8, no. 232, Part 1, 13 December 2004; 'As Nationalist Leader Unveils his Plans for Achieving Economic Growth', *RFE/RL Newsline*, vol. 7, no. 158, Part 1, 20 August 2003.

22. Vitalii Ivanov, 'Rossiiane ne schitaiut biznes grekhom', *Vedomosti*, 29 July 2003, *http://www.vedomosti.ru/stories/2003/07/29-67-02.html*; A. Zudin, ' "Punish but don't Destroy". The oligarchs and the state in public opinion', 2002, unpublished paper; 'The Radical Authoritarian Syndrome in Russian Mass Consciousness', report on survey research done by the 'Ekspertiza' Fund for Analytical Programs, *Politcom.ru*, 23 March 2004.

23. 'Ot redaktsii: ikh ne liubiat', *Vedomosti*, 18 July 2003, *http://www.vedomosti.ru/newspaper/article.shtml?2003/07/18*.

24. Manfred F. R. Kets de Vries, Stanislav Shekshnia, Konstantin Korotov and Elizabeth Florent-Treacy, *The New Russian Business Leaders*, Edward Elgar, Cheltenham UK and Northampton MA, 2004, p.174.

25. 'Plurality of Russians Think Country Heading into Dead End', *RFE/RL Newsline*, vol. 9, no. 7, Part 1, 12 January 2005.

26. Igor' Bunin, 'Vlast' i biznes v novoi Rossii', *Politcom.ru*, 11 June 2004, *http://www.politcom.ru/print.php*.

27. Letitia Rydjeski claims that 'the old established Soviet industrial elite was in a position to maintain much of its position and ... the newcomers would maintain many of the practices of the old *nomenklatura*'. 'The Russian Crisis: what the Russian analysts "missed", 1990–8', in Peter Westin, *The Wild East. Negotiating the Russian financial frontier*, Reuters/Pearson Education, Harlow, 2001, p.64. See also Donald N. Jensen, 'How Russia is Ruled', in Peter Rutland (ed.), *Business and the State in Contemporary Russia*, Westview, Boulder, 2001, p.38. The claimed origins and status of at least one oligarch, Boris Berezovsky, are clear from the title of Paul Klebnikov's book, *The Godfather of the Kremlin*. For the *tolkach* reference, see Bernard Black, Rainier Kraakman, Anna Tarassova, 'Russian Privatization and Corporate Governance: what went wrong?', *Stanford Law Review*, vol. 52, 1999–2000, p.1753, a *tolkach* being those in Soviet enterprises responsible for obtaining scarce inputs through informal means. As we will see in the next chapter, none of those included in the oligarchy in this book, with the possible exception of Aleksandr Smolensky, had *tolkach* experience.

28. Marshall I. Goldman, 'Anders in Wonderland: comments on Russia's economic transformation under Putin', *Eurasian Geography and Economics*, vol. 45, no. 6, 2004, p.433.

29. Joseph E. Stiglitz, *Globalization and Its Discontents*, Penguin, London, 2002, p.160.

30. Andrew Barnes, 'Comparative Theft: context and choice in the Hungarian, Czech, and Russian transformations, 1989–2000', *East European Politics and Societies*, vol. 17, no. 3, 2003, pp.533–65.

31. Black, Kraakman, Tarassova, 'Russian Privatization'.

32. Schröder, 'El'tsin and the Oligarchs', p.957.

33. Black, Kraakman, Tarassova, 'Russian Privatization', p.1799.

34. Anders Åslund, 'Russia's Economic Transformation under Putin', *Eurasian Geography and Economics*, vol. 45, no. 6, 2004, pp.397–420.

35. Quoted in Black, Kraakman, Tarassova, 'Russian Privatization', p.1777.

36. R. S. Dzarasov and D. V. Novozhenov, *Krupnyi biznes i nakoplenie kapitala v sovremennoi Rossii*, URCC, Moscow, 2005, pp.183, 191.

37. *From Transition to Development. A country economic memorandum for the Russian Federation*, World Bank, Washington DC, Report No. 32308-RU, March 2005, pp.v–vi.

38. *From Transition*, p.3. It is interesting to note that the authors of the part of the report dealing with big business, Sergei Guriev and Andrei Rachinsky, two Moscow-based Russian academic researchers, in presenting the same data that they collected for the World Bank report have written far more positively of the oligarchs in an academic article. One wonders to what extent it was World Bank editorial influence that produced the more anti-oligarch tone, as restrained as it might be, in the report. One notes the near satisfaction with which Christof Ruehl, the then head of the World Bank's Moscow office, greeted the arrest of Lebedev. Anastasiia Onegina, 'Amnistiia vredna', *Vedomosti*, 5 August 2003, *http://www.vedomosti/ru/stories/2003/08/05-55-02.html*; Kristof Riul' [Christof Ruehl], 'Delo "IuKOSA": poverkh skandalov', *Vedomosti*, 6 August 2003, *http://www.vedomosti.ru/stories/2003/08/06-47-05. html*; S. Guriev and A. Rachinsky, 'The Role of Oligarchs in Russian Capitalism', *The Journal of Economic Perspectives*, vol. 19, no. 1, Winter 2005, pp.131–50.

39. As reported in 'Report: oligarchs are blocking economic development', *RFE/RL Newsline*, vol. 6, no. 223, Part 1, 27 November 2002; Boris Grozovskii, Mikhail Overchenko and Dmitrii Simakov, 'Vrag biznesa – krupnyi biznes', *Vedomosti*, 26 November 2002, *http://www.kapital.ru/stories/2002/11/26-55-02.html*.

40. Willem Buiter, 'From Predation to Accumulation? The second transition decade in Russia', *Economics of Transition*, vol. 8, no. 3, 2000, p.604.

41. Raghuram Rajan and Luigi Zingales, *Saving Capitalism from the Capitalists. Unleashing the power of financial markets to create wealth and spread opportunity*, Crown, New York, 2003, p.155. A summary is available in 'The Road to Prosperity: saving capitalism from capitalists', *Transition*, vol. 14, no. 7–9, July/August/September 2003, pp.1–3.

42. *From Transition*, p.iv.

43. *Russian Economic Report*, no. 9, November 2004, p.6.

44. *Strategy for the Russian Federation*, European Bank for Reconstruction and Development, London, 16 November 2004, p.18.

45. *Strategy for the Russian Federation*, p.44. Given his comments in 2000, that 'a selective policy of restitution and retribution would run the risk of being pursued in an arbitrary, selective and politically motivated manner and could end up being viewed not as a belated attempt at justice, but as a further degradation of the rule of law', one assumes that Buiter of the EBRD would not approve of the proceedings against Khodorkovsky and Yukos. Buiter, 'From Predation', p.607. Also given that at the time the EBRD was suing the apparently untouchable Abramovich for corporate governance abuses, the selectiveness of the Russian legal system would have been particularly evident to the EBRD authors. Svetlana Petrova *et al.*, 'Zasudit' Abramovicha',

20 January 2005, *http://www.vedomosti.ru/newspaper/print.shtml?2005/01/20/ 85907.*

46. *Strategy for the Russian Federation*, p.20.

47. Mikhail Overchenko, 'Interv'iu: Piter Voike, ispolnitel'nyi vitse-prezident Mezhdunarodnoi finansovoi korporatsii', *Vedomosti*, 18 July 2004, *http://www. vedomosti.ru/newspaper/print.shtml?2004/07/18/78533.*

48. Quoted in Maksim Shilov, 'Minoritariev unichtozhaet kak klopov', *Politcom.ru*, 28 September 2004, url not available. In March 2006 Browder, manager of one of the biggest investment funds in Russia and a keen supporter of Putin, was unexpectedly and mysteriously refused entry to the country at Moscow airport. 'An enemy of the people', *The Economist*, 25 March 2006, p. 70; 'Uil'iam Brauder: my nikogada ne byli sviazany s "Rosneft'iu"', *Kommersant*, 3 April 2006, *http://www.Kommersant.ru/ doc.html?DocId=662992&IssueId=30058.*

49. Hoffman, *Oligarchs*, p.476; 'Iakov Pappe: "Oligarkhicheskii period zakonchen. Zabud'te" ', *Politcom.ru*, 7 October 2005, *http://www.politcom.ru/ 2005/business8. php.* See also Dmitrii Butrin, 'Siuzhet dlia nebol'shogo otkaza', *Kommersant*, 10 November 2003, *http://www.kommersant.ru/k-money/get_page.asp? page_id=28788334.htm&ws=1.*

50. Ol'ga Proskurnina, Igor' Fediukhin, 'Deripaska predosteregaet', *Vedomosti*, 11 February 2004, *http://www.vedomosti.ru/stories/2004/02/11-68-02.html.* See one Russian financial analyst's claim that foreign investors cannot understand why Putin should be expected to negotiate with the oligarchs to resolve issues coming out of the Yukos affair. Anastasiia Onegina et al., 'Ne o chem govorit'', *Vedomosti*, 28 October 2003, *http://www.vedomosti.ru/ 2003/10/28-55-01.html.*

51. Anders Åslund, 'Comparative Oligarchy: Russia, Ukraine and the United States', paper presented to the CASE conference, 'Europe after the Enlargement', Warsaw, 8–9 April 2005, pp.7–8.

52. Andrei Shleifer and Daniel Treisman, 'A Normal Country: Russia after communism', *Journal of Economic Perspectives*, vol. 19, no. 1, Winter 2005, p.161.

53. Guriev and Rachinsky, 'Role of Oligarchs', p.131.

2   Who are the Barons and Magnates?

1. *Biznesmeny Rossii. 40 istorii uspekha*, 'OKO', Moscow, 1994, p.367.

2. O. Kryshtanovskaya and S. White find that only 15 per cent of the 1993 business elite was still in that category by 2001. 'The Rise of the Russian Business Elite', *Communist and Post-Communist Studies*, vol. 38, 2005, p.299.

3. The historical allusion is to the *semiboyarshchina*, or rule of the seven boyars. The boyars, the early Russian aristocracy, dominated Russian politics in the Time of Troubles, the period of chaos between the death of Ivan the Terrible and the ascension to the throne of the first Romanovs. George Vernadsky, *A History of Russia*, Yale University Press, New Haven, 1961, pp.113–20. According to Andrei Zorin, part of the symbolism of the recently instituted new November public holiday, commemorating the driving of the Poles out of Moscow and thereby the end of the boyar-induced Time of Troubles, is that Putin's attack on the oligarchs signals the end of Russia's most recent Time of Troubles. 'As Analysts Say New Holiday Marks Rise of New Nationalism', *RFE/RL Newsline*, vol. 9, no. 208, Part 1, 4 November 2005.

4. The first reference to the 'Gang of Seven' was by Berezovsky in a November 1996 *Financial Times* interview. He excluded Vinogradov from his seven, making up the numbers by including Mikhail Fridman's partner at Alfa Bank, Petr Aven. On Berezovsky's and other samples, see Hans-Henning Schröder, 'El'tsin and the Oligarchs. The role of financial groups in Russian politics between 1993 and July 1998', *Europe-Asia Studies*, vol. 51, no. 6, 1999, p.970. Here a direct transliteration of Fridman's name in Russian is used. He is sometimes identified in English-language sources as Friedman.

5. Vinogradov had invested in the metals sector, but was apparently excluded from the most lucrative deals by the other bankers. His resource presence was inadequate to get him through the 1998 crisis, especially as the Central Bank took a far harder line against him post-1998 than against some other banks. David E. Hoffman, *The Oligarchs. Wealth and power in the new Russia*, Public Affairs, New York, 2002, pp.315–17,434; William Tompson, 'Nothing Learned, Nothing Forgotten: restructuring without reform in Russia's banking sector', in Stefanie Harter and Gerald Easter (eds), *Shaping the Economic Space in Russia. Decision making processes, institutions and adjustment to change in the El'tsin era*, Ashgate, Aldershot, 2000, p.71.

6. Anders Åslund, 'Russia's Economic Transformation under Putin', *Eurasion Geography and Economics*, vol. 45, no. 6, 2004, p.413.

7. Russia is not a big exporter of unprocessed minerals. However, through transition its metals industry has been transformed from the producer of a wide range of metals for domestic producers into a commodity metal exporter. As such, it has come to resemble closely the oil sector.

8. In 2004 the World Bank compiled a list of 23 large private firms and their owners. As ranked by sales, our sample of 11, plus Potanin and Fridman, are in the top 17 of the World Bank's 23. Those in the top 17 not included here are: Khodorkovsky, for obvious reasons; Kadannikov, until recently of the car manufacturer AvtoVAZ; Blavatnik, of the oil firm Renova, who is not a Russian resident; and Takhautdinov of Tatneft, the Tatar oil company that could barely be described as independent of the Tatar regional government. Renova could be said to be represented in our sample by Vekselberg, a longtime partner of Blavatnik. Blavatnik left the Soviet Union in 1978 while a student. He completed his studies at Harvard in 1986, and then set up an investment firm Access Industries. Some time later he renewed contact with Vekselberg, with whom he had studied in the Soviet Union. In 1989 they went into business together. *From Transition to Development, A country economic memorandum for the Russian Federation*, World Bank, Washington DC, Report No. 32308-RU, March 2005, p.96; Mariia Rozhkova, Anastasiia Bokova and Nikolai Borisov, 'Glavnaia sdelka Blavatnika', *Vedomosti*, 6 May 2005, *http://www.vedomosti.ru/newspaper/article.shtml?2005/05/06*.

9. Stephen Fortescue, 'The Russian Aluminum Industry in Transition', *Eurasian Geography and Economics*, vol. 47, no. 1, 2006, p.79.

10. Iuliia Fedorinova and Mariia Rozhkova, 'Tikhii Millhouse', *Vedomosti*, 19 July 2006, *http://www.vedomusti.ru/newspaper/article.shtml?2006/07/19/109742*.

11. Iuliia Fedorinova and Mariia Rozhkova, 'Usmanov sobiraet aktivy', *Vedomosti*, 14 November 2005, *http://www.vedomosti.ru/newspaper/print.shtml?2005/11/14/99419*. For biographical details, see *http://www.ippnou.ru/biography.php?idarticle=001390*, accessed 6 March 2006.

12. *Vozrozhdennaia elita rossiiskogo biznesa*, Institut izucheniia reformy, Moscow, 1994, pp.214–15; Manfred F. R. Kets de Vries, Stanislav Shekshnia, Konstantin Korotov and Elizabeth Florent-Treacy, *The New Russian Business Leaders*, Edward Elgar, Cheltenham UK and Northampton MA, 2004, p.149.
13. It is usually stated that his father worked as Soviet trade representative in New Zealand in Potanin's teens. Hoffman, *Oligarchs*, p.303; Chrystia Freeland, *Sale of the Century. Russia's wild ride from communism to capitalism*, Crown, 2000, p.128. Anvar Amirov and Vladimir Pribylovskii say Indonesia in *Rossiiskie biznesmeny i menedzhery. Biograficheskii spravochnik*, Informatsionno-ekspertnaia gruppa 'Panorama', Moscow, February 1997, pp.121–2.
14. Hoffman, *Oligarchs*, p.130.
15. Paul Klebnikov, *Godfather of the Kremlin. Boris Berezovsky and the looting of Russia*, Harcourt, New York, 2000, p.52; Freeland, *Sale*, p.138.
16. *Vozrozhdennaia elita*, pp.62–3; *Rossiiskie biznesmeny*, pp.51–4; Hoffman, *Oligarchs*, chapter 7.
17. *Vozrozhdennaia elita*, pp.177–8; Hoffman, *Oligarchs*, chapter 2.
18. Freeland, *Sale*, p.113.
19. Extract from Igor Svinarenko's book, *Nashi liudi (vybrannye mesta iz besed s velikimi)*, *Moskovskie novosti*, no. 36, September 2000, pp.12–13.
20. *Rossiiskie biznesmeny*, p.56; Freeland, *Sale*, pp.114–17.
21. On involvement in the second economy as a typical background of entrepreneurs, see also Thane Gustafson, *Capitalism Russian Style*, Cambridge University Press, Cambridge, 1994, pp.114–15.
22. One source has Khodorkovsky as a member of the Sverdlovsk district Komsomol committee, another as deputy secretary of the Frunze district committee. The first states he was never a member of the party, the second that he was. *Vozrozhdennaia elita*, pp.214–15; *Rossiiskie biznesmeny*, pp.181–3. See also *Komu prinadlezhit Rossiia*, Vagrius, Moscow, 2003, p.396. Even these unconfirmed claims are not enough to justify Klebnikov's claim that he was a 'top leader of the Moscow Komsomol'. Klebnikov, *Godfather*, p.202.
23. Hoffman, *Oligarchs*, p.106.
24. Hoffman, *Oligarchs*, p.107.
25. Klebnikov, *Godfather*, p.203. For a detailed study of the Komsomol and its business activities under Gorbachev, see Steven L. Solnick, *Stealing the State. Control and collapse in Soviet institutions*, Harvard University Press, Cambridge MA, 1998.
26. *Biznesmeny Rossii*, p.174.
27. Hoffman, *Oligarchs*, pp.109–14
28. *Biznesmeny Rossii*, pp.169–71.
29. Hoffman, *Oligarchs*, pp.46,124.
30. *Rossiiskie biznesmeny*, pp.35–7. Note that Freinkman claims that Inkombank was started from scratch, 'without the participation of any well-known and financially powerful state enterprises'. Lev Freinkman, 'Financial-industrial Groups in Russia: emergence of large diversified private companies', *Communist Economies and Economic Transformation*, vol. 7, no. 1, 1995, p.59.
31. *Rossiiskie biznesmeny*, pp.35–7; persona.rin.ru/cgi-bin/rus/view.pl?id=16022&a=f&idr=11, downloaded 28 May 2004.
32. *Rossiiskie Biznesmeny*, pp.121–2.

33. Valery Kryukov and Arild Moe, 'Banks and the Financial Sector', in David Lane (ed.), *The Political Economy of Russian Oil*, Rowman & Littlefield, Lanham MD, 1999, p.52. On ONEKSIMbank and Interros, see also William Tompson, 'The Present and Future of Banking Reform', in David Lane (ed.), *Russian Banking. Evolution, problems and prospects*, Edward Elgar, Cheltenham and Northampton, MA, 2002, pp.87–99.

34. A *nomenklatura* background is considered widespread among the broader business elite. Lapina, in a 1994 study, finds that 33 per cent got their start through the Komsomol or communist party. N. Iu. Lapina, *Formirovanie sovremennoi rossiiskoi elity (Problemy perekhodnogo perioda)*, Institut nauchnoi informatsii po obshchestevennym naukam, Moscow, 1995, pp.30–1.

35. *www.compromat.ru/main/fridman/a.htm*.

36. According to Klebnikov, the institute had nothing to do with forestry, but was rather involved in the space programme. *Godfather*, p.52. No corroboration of this statement has been found.

37. In 1991 Berezovsky was elected a corresponding member of the Academy. Although the 1991 Academy elections were highly controversial, because of the election of such political figures as Khasbulatov, no obvious scandal surrounded the election of the then unknown Berezovsky. 'Novaia Akademiia – novye liudi', *Poisk*, 6–12 December 1991, p.3.

38. *Rossiiskie biznesmeny*, p.15.

39. The economist A. Bunich combines the two, claiming that 'shadow economy entrepreneurs were not honest, capable businessmen who had been victims of the old system. Their ability to operate in the 'shadows' did not depend on their business capabilities, but on their links with the party-bureaucratic apparatus'. 'Tenevaia – chast' biurokraticheskogo aisberga', *Ekonomika i zhizn'*, no. 3, 1992, p.15.

40. Mordashov's father was an electrician and his mother an office worker at the mill. He describes the family as typically 'Soviet middle class', with 'a two-room flat, a "Moskvich" car, a dacha with a stove. Two big bookshelves. And summers in the south, by the sea.' While saying something about the self-identification of aspirational workers in the Brezhnev period, this is a different background from that of a Muscovite intellectual, even of the technical variety. 'Vremia', *Ekspert*, 5 February 2001, p.32. The sense that a 'middle class' worker family such as Mordashov's could be materially better off than a middle class 'intelligentsia' family, such as Khodorkovsky's, fits the claimed anti-intelligentsia policies of the Brezhnev era.

41. *www.kompromat.ru/main/melnichenko/a.htm*, downloaded 18 June 2004 (reprint from satcor.ru, 16 January 2003).

42. *www.nccg.ru/site.xp/050052056124.html*, downloaded 5 March 2004.

43. For a hint at the rough methods used, see Tat'iana Sorokina, 'O pol'ze arestovannykh aktsii', *Ekspert*, 25 January 1999, p.39.

44. *Rossiiskie biznesmeny*, pp.17–18.

45. *Rossiiskie biznesmeny*, p.8; *Vozrozhdennaia elita*, pp.7–8.

46. *Kompaniia*, no. 123, 18 July 2000, *www.ko.ru/document.asp?d_no=1941&p=1*, downloaded 5 March 2004.

47. Whether Mordashov 'did the dirty' on Lipukhin in the privatization of the plant is not entirely clear. 'Vremia', *Ekspert*, 5 February 2001, p.34.

48. *www.nccg.ru/site.xp/050050048124.html*, downloaded 5 March 2004.
49. *www.nccg.ru/site.xp/050051048124.html*, downloaded 5 March 2004.
50. Andrew Barnes, 'Russia's New Business Groups and State Power', *Post-Soviet Affairs*, vol. 19, no. 2, 2003, pp.166–7.
51. Abramovich Roman Arkad'evich', *newlist.ru*, no date, *http://Newlist.ru/Detailed/ 3390.html*, downloaded 22 June 2004; Aleksei Roshchin, 'Protivogaz Abramovicha', *Politcom.ru*, 20 January 2006, *http://www.politcom.ru/ print.php?id=2063*.
52. The offence was to buy oil at a subsidized price ostensibly for a local consumer, and then sell it through the Baltics on the open market and at a market price. *www.kompromat.ru/main/abramovich/a.htm*, downloaded 22 June 2004 (claiming to be excerpts from an English-language article published by the International Bureau of East European Research, vol. 7, no. 3, Spring 1999).
53. Iana Galukhina and Maksim Rubchenko, 'Podrok prezidentu', *Ekspert*, 8 December 2003, *http://www.expert.ru/expert/current/data/tema1 4.shtml*.
54. One source describes Makhmudor as a military interpreter. Ekaterina Derbilova, Mariia Rozhkova and Mikhail Overchenko, 'Izdatel' Makhmudova', *Vedomosti*, 8 June 2005, *http://www.vedomosti.ru/newspaper/ print.shtml?2005/06/08/93100*.
55. Ia.Sh. Pappe, 'Rossiiskii krupnyi biznes kak ekonomicheskii fenomen: osobennosti stanovleniia i sovremennogo etapa razvitiia', *Problemy prognozirovaniia*, no. 1, 2002, p.39.
56. 'Mel'nichenko Andrei Igorevich', *Skandaly.ru*, no date, *http:// www.scandaly.ru/ print/news590.html*, downloaded 18 June 2004.
57. Some sources have Deripaska born as well as spending his childhood in a village in the Ust'-Lebinsk district of Krasnodar region. He has certainly shown a keen interest in the area, both commercially and philanthropically, in recent years, including extensive agricultural holdings and football and other investments.
58. 'Gonka na vyzhivanie', *Ekspert*, 13 September 1999, pp.56–7.
59. 'Biografiia Olega Deripaska', *tema dnia*, 24 September 2003, *http://www. temadnya.ru/spravka/24sep2003/3161.html*.
60. There is a rough similarity in the differences between our G7 and new oligarchs, and David Lane's financial and oil elites, the latter in his analysis being older, more regional by origin, and with less evident party-Komsomol background. David Lane, 'The Russian Oil Elite: background and outlook', in David Lane (ed.), *The Political Economy of Russian Oil*, Rowman & Littlefield, Lanham MD, 1999, pp.77–9. See also Kryshtanovskaya and White, 'Rise of the Russian Business Elite', pp.293–307.
61. *Rossiiskie biznesmeny*, p.367.
62. Donald N. Jensen, 'How Russia is ruled', in P. Rutland (ed.), *Business and State in Contemporary Russia*, Westview, 2001, p.38; Jerry F. Hough, *The Logic of Economic Reform in Russia*, Brookings Institution Press, Washington DC, 2001, pp.31–6.
63. In the early 1990s the author interviewed a deputy minister of the then Ministry of Metallurgy. He was receiving considerable publicity at the time for his involvement in the 'commercialization' of the ministry's structures. He described those changes, and his recent trip to European steel mills, with

considerable enthusiasm. But there was always a hint of uncertainty in his voice, and as he concluded the interview he suddenly declared, with the uncertainty now more like desperation: 'That's all very well, but to be honest, what can be done here, in Russia, I have no idea.' The would-be oligarchs of the time were presumably not wracked by such doubts. My interviewee quickly disappeared from the scene.

64. Klebnikov, *Godfather*, pp.58–60.
65. *Rossiiskie biznesmeny*, p.373.
66. Peter Maass, 'The Triumph of the Quiet Tycoon', *NYTimes.com*, 1 August 2004.
67. Hoffman, *Oligarchs*, p.172.
68. 'Vladimir Gusarov, predsedatel' soveta direktorov banka "Derzhava": "Rabota prinosit nezavisimost' " ', *Politcom.ru*, 1 December 2005, *http://www. politcom.ru/print.php*; 'Sergei Shapiguzov, prezident kompanii FBK: "Sotrudniki kompanii dolzhny stat' tvoimi partnerami" ', *Vedomosti*, 15 December 2005, *http://www.politcom.ru/print/php*.
69. Willem Buiter, 'From Predation to Accumulation? The second transition decade in Russia', *Economics of Transition*, vol. 8, no. 3, 2000, p.609.

3 How Did They Get Rich?

1. Willem Buiter, 'From Predation to Accumulation? The second transition decade in Russia', *Economics of Transition*, vol. 8, no. 3, 2000, p.607.
2. Anatolii Chubais, the architect of Russian privatization, in 2004 admitted to having 'underestimated the deep feeling of injustice' that it would create, although he still maintained that given the choice between bandit communism and bandit capitalism, then the choice he made in favour of the latter was the right one. *Financial Times*, 15 November 2004, cited in 'Chubais Defends Privatisation Plan', *RFE/RL Newsline*, vol. 8, no. 216, Part 1, 16 November 2004. While it might have seemed to him in 2004 that he had underestimated the reaction to privatization, he is also reported as having said to Gaidar when the latter asked him to take on the task in 1992: 'Do you understand that regardless of what the result will be, I will be hated for the rest of my life because I was the person who sold off Russia.' David Hoffman, *The Oligarchs. Wealth and power in the new Russia*, Perseus, Cambridge MA, 2002, p.185.
3. This was the time when entrepreneurial Moscow lawyers were looking for people about to die, so that they could arrange for an 'heir' to be found outside the country. An 'estate' funded in black market rubles could then be sent abroad at the official exchange rate.
4. Lev Freinkman, 'Financial-industrial Groups in Russia: emergence of large diversified private companies', *Communist Economies and Economic Transformation*, vol. 7, no. 1, 1995, p.56.
5. Valery Kryukov and Arild Moe, 'Banks and the Financial Sector', in David Lane (ed.), *The Political Economy of Russian Oil*, Rowman & Littlefield, Lanham MD, 1999, p.52.
6. Freinkman, 'Financial-industrial Groups', p.54; Hoffman, *Oligarchs*, p.46; Manfred F. R. Kets de Vries, Stanislav Shekshnia, Konstantin Korotov and Elizabeth Florent-Treacy, *The New Russian Business Leaders*, Edward Elgar, Cheltenham UK and Northampton MA, 2004, p.152.

7. Juliet Johnson, 'Russia's Emerging Financial-industrial Groups', *Post-Soviet Affairs*, vol. 13, no. 4, 1997, pp.351–2; William Tompson, 'The Present and Future of Banking Reform', in David Lane (ed.), *Russian Banking. Evolution, problems and prospects*, Edward Elgar, Cheltenham and Northampton, MA, 2002, p.130.

8. 'O merakh po usileniiu kontrolia za ispol'zovaniem sredstv federal'nogo biudzheta', presidential decree of 12 May 1997, No. 477, *Sobranie Zakonodatel'stva Rossiiskoi Federatsii*, no. 20, 1997, item 2235.

9. Hans-Henning Schröder, 'The "Oligarchs": a force to be reckoned with?', in Stefanie Harter and Gerald Easter (eds), *Shaping the Economic Space in Russia. Decision making processes, institutions and adjustment to change in the El'tsin era*, Ashgate, Aldershot, 2000, p.964.

10. Tompson, 'Present and Future', p.62.

11. Johnson, 'Russia's Emerging', p.348.

12. Igor' Bunin, 'Vlast'' i biznes v novoi Rossii', *Politcom.ru*, 11 June 2004, *http://www.politcom.ru/print.php*.

13. There is a huge literature on privatization. Two examples are J. Blasi, M. Kroumova and D. Kruse, *Kremlin Capitalism. Privatizing the Russian Economy*, Cornell University Press, Ithaca, 1996; and M. Boycko, A. Shleifer and R. Vishny, *Privatizing Russia*, MIT Press, Cambridge MA, 1995. The author has contributed the following: 'The Privatisation of Soviet Large-scale Industry', in H. Hendrischke (ed.), *Market Reform in the Changing Socialist World*, Macquarie Studies in Chinese Political Economy, Macquarie University, Sydney, July 1992; 'Privatisation of Russian Industry', *Australian Journal of Political Science*, vol. 29, no. 1, March 1994, pp.135–53; 'Privatisation of Large-scale Russian Industry', in A. Saikal and W. Maley (eds), *Russia in Search of Its Future*, Cambridge University Press, Cambridge, 1995, chapter 6; 'Privatisation, Corporate Governance and Enterprise Performance in Russia', *Russian and Euro-Asian Bulletin*, vol. 7, no. 5, May 1998, pp.1–10.

14. S. Chugaev, 'E. Gaidar predstavil deputatam pravitel'stvennuiu programmu', *Izvestiia*, 6 October 1992, p.1.

15. For a case study, see Kathryn Hendley, 'Legal Development and Privatisation in Russia: a case study', *Soviet Economy*, vol. 8, no. 2, 1992, pp.130–57.

16. For an example, see V. Sopov, 'Sibirskie predprinimateli smogut kupit' sibirskikh promyshlennikov', *Kommersant*, no. 46, 1991, p.5.

17. M. Rogozhnikov and D. Bogdanovich, 'Investory polny optimizma. No u odnikh net deneg, a u drugikh – zhelaniia ikh vkladyvat'', *Kommersant*, no. 35, 1991, p.28.

18. See the case of VAZ. S. Zhigalov, 'Volzhskii avtozavod stanovitsia aktsionernym predpriiatiem', *Izvestiia*, 24 November 1992, p.1.

19. One notorious and politically charged case was that of the company 'Kolo', within the defence sector. See M. Rogozhnikov, 'Bor'ba s "nomenklaturnoi privatizatsiei": spor o terminakh idet na milliardy', *Kommersant*, no. 9, 1992, p.1.

20. N. Kirichenko and M. Rogozhnikov, 'Ukaz o privatizatsionnykh chekakh: pochem vaucher dlia naroda?', *Kommersant*, no. 34, 1992, p.1.

21. Fortescue, 'Privatisation of Large-scale Russian Industry', p.3.

22. One source describes Alfa on this occasion as a front for bureaucratic agencies close to Grishin. Alfa is generally known, however, as a close partner of

Renova. M. Berger, 'Komu dostanetsia Vladimirskii Traktornyi Zavod?', *Izvestiia*, 11 June 1993, p.5.

23. 'The Revolution Begins', *The Economist*, 3 July 1993, p.59.
24. M. Berger, 'Vladimirskie prikliucheniia', *Izvestiia*, 2 November 1994, p.5. Bakaleinik enjoyed little more success than Grishin. He is now, in early 2006, first deputy vice-president of SUAL, the aluminium producer owned by Vekselberg. Jerry F. Hough, *The Logic of Economic Reform in Russia*, Brookings Institution Press, Washington DC, 2001, p.113.
25. 'Who Owns Russia: the ferrous-metals sector', *The Russia Journal Online*, 13 October 2001, *http://beta.russiajournal.com*, accessed on 16 October 2001.
26. Alekperov claimed in 2005 still to have only 13 per cent of the company's shares, and to be constantly buying more. 'Interv'iu: Vagit Alekperov, prezident NK "Lukoil" ', *Vedomosti*, 11 July 2005, *http://www.vedomosti.ru/newspaper/print.shtml?2005/07/11/94500*.
27. Alekperov, and Bogdanov of Surgutneftegaz, began appearing at 'oligarch' functions from 1997. Hans-Henning Schröder, 'El'tsin and the Oligarchs: the role of financial groups in Russian politics between 1993 and July 1998', *Europe-Asia Studies*, vol. 51, no. 6, 1999, p.968.
28. Kryukov and Moe, 'Banks and the Financial Sector', p.56. For another complimentary account of Alekperov's clear-headed drive to create a modern global oil company, see Peter Maass, 'The Triumph of the Quiet Tycoon', *NYTimes.com*, 1 August 2004.
29. Kryukov and Moe, 'Banks and the Financial Sector', p.57; David Lane and Iskander Seifulmulukov, 'Company profiles: LUKoil, YuKOS, Surgutneftegaz, Sidanko', in David Lane (ed.), *The Political Economy of Russian Oil*, Rowman & Littlefield, Lanham MD, 1999, pp.117–19.
30. Lane and Seifulmulukov, 'Company Profiles', p.116.
31. Kryukov and Moe, 'Banks and the Financial Sector', pp.63–4.
32. Iana Galukhina, Maksim Rubchenko, 'Podarok prezidentu', *Ekspert*, 8 December 2003, *http://www.expert.ru/expert/current/data/tema1_4.shtml*.
33. Kryukov and Moe, 'Banks and the Financial Sector', p.169.
34. Larisa Gorbatova, 'Formation of Connections between Finance and Industry in Russia: basic stages and forms', *Communist Economies and Economic Transformation*, vol. 7, no. 1, 1995, pp.29–30.
35. I. Trosnikov, ' "Menatep" poluchil bol'shinstvo v sovete direktorov AO "AVISMA" ', *Kommersant*, 26 November 1993, p.1.
36. Galina Keshiktina, 'Aktsii idut po vtoromu krugu', *Delovoi mir*, 10 August 1995, p.4.
37. 'Konflikt v "Zapolianeftegazgeologii', *Kommersant*, 30 May 1995, p.5.
38. A. Kovalev and G. Pechinina, 'Volzhskii avtozavod ulichen v neznanii arifmetiki', *Kommersant*, 26 November 1993, p.8.
39. Stephen Fortescue, 'The Russian Mining and Metals Sector: integration or disintegration?', in Vladimir Tikhomirov (ed.), *Anatomy of the 1998 Russian Crisis*, Contemporary Europe Research Centre, University of Melbourne, Melbourne, 1999, pp.218–21.
40. Julia Flynn, Patricia Krantz and Carol Matlack, 'Grabbing a Corner on Aluminum', *Business Week*, 16 September 1996.
41. Mariia Rozhkova and Petr Sapozhnikov, 'Razval rossiiskoi imperii TWG', *Kommersant*, 3 December 1997, p.9.

42. German Galkin, Dmitrii Ziabkov and Mariia Rozhkova, 'Inkombank namagnitilsia', *Kommersant*, 5 August 1997, p.7.
43. Vladimir Silant'ev, 'Tretii po poriadku partner obeshchaet stat' pervym po vazhnosti', *Kommersant*, 7 May 1996, p.9.
44. Bernard Black, Reinier Kraakman and Anna Tarassova, 'Russian Privatization and Corporate Governance: what went wrong?', *Stanford Law Review*, vol. 52, 1999–2000, p.1766.
45. Tatyana G. Dolgopyatova (ed.), *Russian Industry: institutional development*, State Unviersity Higher School of Economics, Analytical Survey Issue 1, Moscow, 2003, pp.19–21. On the difference in outsider ownership rates in strong and weak firms, see Merritt B. Fox and Michael A. Heller, 'Corporate governance lessons from Russian enterprise fiascoes', *New York University Law Review*, vol. 75, no. 6, December 2000, p.1773.
46. Freinkman, 'Financial-industrial Groups', pp.60–1.
47. Kets de Vries, *New Russian Business Leaders*, p.170.
48. Fortescue, 'Russsian Mining and Metals', pp.225–6.
49. Il'ia Kolli, 'Direktor "KrAZa" popal "pod pritsel" MVD', *Delovoi mir*, 19 June 1997, p.3; Andrew Yorke, 'Business and Politics in Krasnoyarsk *Krai*', *Europe-Asia Studies*, vol. 55, no. 2, 2003, pp.241–62.
50. Fortescue, 'Privatisation, Corporate Governance', pp.6–7.
51. Johnson, 'Russia's Emerging', p.359.
52. Stephen Fortescue, 'Ownership and Corporate Strategy in the Russian Mining and Metals Sector', *The Soviet and Post-Soviet Review*, vol. 25, no. 2, 1998, p.171.
53. *Prikhvatizatsiia* is a play on the Russian word *prikhvatit'*, meaning to grab.
54. Sometimes known as 'loans for shares'. In Russian the usual phrase is 'zalogovyi auktsion'. Tompson uses in English the direct translation of the Russian phrase, 'collateral auction'. Tompson, 'Present and Future', p.63.
55. Anders Åslund, 'Comparative Oligarchy: Russia, Ukraine and the United States', paper presented to the CASE conference, 'Europe after the Enlargement', Warsaw, 8–9 April 2005, p.13.
56. Letitia Rydjeski writes that 'loans-for-shares was probably the all-corrupting point of no return in the entire reform effort'. 'The Russian Crisis: what the Russian analysts "missed", 1990–8', in Peter Westin, *The Wild East. Negotiating the Russian financial frontier*, Reuters/Pearson Education, Harlow, 2001, p.60. Jeffrey Sachs, one of the founding fathers of shock therapy economic reform, is said to have declared at a Washington presentation that the Russian government should renationalize resource firms that had been wrongly privatized. He clearly had in mind the shares-for-credit deals. John Nellis, *Time to Rethink Privatization in Transition Economies?* International Finance Corporation Discussion Paper No. 38, World Bank, Washington DC, 1999, p.9.
57. Duncan Allan, 'Banks and the Loans-for-Shares Auctions', in David Lane (ed.), *Russian Banking. Evolution, problems and prospects*, Edward Elgar, Cheltenham and Northampton, MA, 2002, p.143.
58. Allan, 'Banks', pp.141–2.
59. Chrystia Freeland, *Sale of the Century. Russia's wild ride from communism to capitalism*, Crown, New York, 2000, pp.162–3.
60. Allan, 'Banks'.

61. Neil Robinson, 'The Myth of Equilibrium: winner power, fiscal crisis and Russian economic reform', *Communist and Post-Communist Studies*, vol. 34, no. 4, December 2001, pp.423–46.
62. Freinkman, 'Financial-industrial Groups', p.64; Johnson, 'Russia's Emerging', pp.338–9.
63. Juliet Johnson, *A Fistful of Rubles. The rise and fall of the Russian banking system*, Cornell University Press, Ithaca and London, 2000, p.8; Stephen Fortescue, *Policy-Making for Russian Industry*, Macmillan, Basingstoke and London, 1997, pp.155–8.
64. For a discussion of the desirability of bank equity holdings in industrial assets, see P. Dittus and S. Prowse, 'Corporate control in Central Europe and Russia. Should banks own shares?', in R. Frydman, C.W. Gray and A. Rapaczynski (eds), *Corporate Governance in Central Europe and Russia*, vol. 1, *Banks, Funds, and Foreign Investors*, Central European University Press, Budapest, 1996.
65. Hoffman, *Oligarchs*, pp.308–17.
66. 'Another blow', *The Economist*, 7 June 1997, pp.86–7.
67. David Lane and Iskander Seifulmulukov, 'Structure and Ownership', in David Lane (ed.), *The Political Economy of Russian Oil*, Rowman & Littlefield, Lanham MD, 1999, p.36.
68. Allan, 'Banks'.
69. Freeland, *Sale of the Century*, pp.175–6.
70. Klebnikov, *Godfather*, p.208.
71. Allan, 'Banks', pp.142–3.
72. Åslund, 'Comparative Oligarchy', p.13.
73. Fortescue, 'Privatisation, Corporate Governance', pp.6–8.
74. Black, Kraakman, Tarassova, 'Russian Privatization', pp.1772–3.
75. 'Norilsk Nickel', *Troika Dialog Research*, 24 June 1999, p.6.
76. Mikhail Seleznev, 'Norilsk Nickel: killing two birds with one stone', *Russia Metals Comment*, United Financial Group, 25 October 2001.
77. Black, Kraakman, Tarassova, 'Russian Privatization', pp.1769–70.
78. Marina Lepina, 'Svetlane Bakhminoi zachitali vosem' milliardov', *Kommersant*, 18 October 2005, http://www.kommersant.ru/doc.html?docId= 618589.
79. Black, Kraakman, Tarassova, 'Russian Privatization', pp.1769–70.
80. Black, Kraakman, Tarassova, 'Russian Privatization', pp.1772–3.
81. Kets de Vries, *New Russian Business Leaders*, p.154.
82. Yuko Iji, *Corporate Control and Governance Practices in Russia*, Centre for the Study of Economic and Social Change in Europe, School of Slavonic and East European Studies, University College London, Working Paper No. 33, June 2003, p.22.
83. 'Norilsk Nickel', *Troika Dialog Research*, 24 June 1999.
84. Vijai Maheshwari, 'Kill or cure?', *Business Central Europe*, May 1998, pp.26–7.
85. For a description of the process, see Aleksandr Volkov, Tat'iana Gurova and Viktor Titov, 'Sanitary i maroedy', *Ekspert*, 1 March 1999, pp.19–25.
86. Fortescue, 'Russian Mining and Metals Sector', pp.229–30.
87. 'Zhivilo razvodiat', *Ekspert*, 11 September 2000, p.4.
88. Andrei Lemeshko, ' "Rusal" otbilsia ot Zhivilo', *Vedomosti*, 11 May 2004, *http://www.vedomosti.ru/stories/2004/05/11–40–04.html*. Recently, in order to

settle endless court battles, Deripaska paid off Zhivilo and other old adversaries, including the Ruebens of TWG, the Chernoi brothers, and Anatolii Bykov. Mariia Rozhkova, 'Deripaska perepisyvaet istoriiu', *Vedomosti*, 30 June 2005, *http://www.vedomosti.ru/newspaper/article.shtml?2005/06/30/ 94054*.

89. Evgenyi Bagaev, 'Sud'ba Kuznetskogo metkombinata reshena', *Kommersant*, 14 August 1998, p.8.
90. Dmitrii Sivakov, 'Tainyi sovetnik gubernatora', *Ekspert*, 6 December 1999, pp.28–9.
91. Igor' Lavrenko and Dmitrii Sivakov, 'Zapsib i KMK vydut iz bankrotstva dosrochno', *Ekspert*, 23 October 2000, p.38.
92. Aleksandr Volkov, Tat'iana Gurova and Viktor Titov, 'Sanitary i maroedy', *Ekspert*, 1 March 1999, pp.19–25. For an account of typical bankruptcy battles in the copper industry, see German Galkin, ' "Karabashmed' " okazalsia bankrotom', *Kommersant*, 22 January 2002, p.5.
93. Irina Granik, 'Duma reshila bankrotit' po-novomu', *Kommersant*, 7 March 2002, p.4. On further efforts to tighten the law to prevent bankruptcy being used for the redistribution of property, see Irina Granik, 'Pravitel'stvo usovershenstvovalo bankrotstva', *Kommersant*, 21 January 2005, *http://www. kommersant.ru/doc.html?docId=540576*.
94. Kathryn Hendley, 'Temporal and Regional Patterns of Commercial Litigation in Post-Soviet Russia', *Post-Soviet Geography and Economics*, vol. 39, no. 7, September 1998, p.379.
95. James Anderson, David Bernstein and Cheryl Gray, *Judicial Systems in Transition Economies. Assessing the past, looking to the future*, World Bank, Washington DC, 2005.
96. 'Ot redaktsii: khitrye sud'i', *Vedomosti*, 23 October 2002, http:www. kapital.ru/stories/2002/10/23–47–02.html; Aleksei Nikol'skii, 'Verkhovnyi sud zashchitit biznes', *Vedomosti*, 28 September 2005, *http:www.vedomosti.ru/ newspaper/article.shtml?2005/09/28/97572*.
97. On Bykov, see Aleksei Tarasov, 'Brat'ia Chernye i drugie', *Izvestiia*, 12 July 1996, p.4.
98. 'Former Aluminium Titan and Would-be Political Refugee Returns', *RFE/RL Newsline*, vol. 4, no. 81, Part 1, 25 April 2000.
99. 'Prosecutor-general Office Pursues the Murder Case Without a Corpse', *RFE/RL Newsletter*, vol. 4, no. 200, Part 1, 16 October 2000; 'Bykov Ready to Sell Aluminum Stake', *RFE/RL Newsline*, vol. 4, no. 203, Part 1, 19 October 2000.
100. For a good extended discussion of events in Krasnoyarsk, covering both KrAZ and Norilsk Nickel, see Yorke, 'Business and Politics'.
101. Konstantin Smirnov et al., 'Imushchie otvetili vlast' imushchim', *Kommersant*, 10 July 2003, *http://www.kommersant.ru/archive/archive-materials.html? docid=394823*.
102. Joseph Stiglitz, *Globalization and Its Discontents*, Penguin, London, 2002, p.160.
103. 'Russian Organized Crime Today', Jamestown Foundation, *Prism*, vol. 3, no. 8, Part 2, 30 May 1997.
104. For an early but extensive account, see Mikhail Mikhailin, 'Proverennye', *Kommersant*, 21 October 1995, p.19.
105. Mikhail Mikhailin, 'Proverennye', *Kommersant*, 21 October 1995, p.19.
106. Sergei Topol', Aleksandr Igorev and Oleg Stulov, 'Ural'skogo magnata nakazali "kopeikoi" ', *Kommersant*, 6 May 2000, p.8.

107. Åslund, 'Comparative Oligarchy', p.8. See the comment of a middle-ranking Russian businessman, that it was 'precisely [the oligarchs] who were the "contractors" in the removal of the criminals from business.' 'Aleksei Kudriavtsev, general'nyi director Kompanii ISG', *Politcom.ru*, 17 March 2006, *http://www.politcom.ru/print.php?id=2384*.

108. Hoffman, *Oligarchs*, p.51.

109. 'Genprokuratura proverit deyatel'nost' TWG', *Kommersant*, 29 August 1998, p.5.

110. 'SATCOR Report on International Conference "Stop Money Laundering" ', London, 26 February 2002, accessed at *http://www.antimoneylaundering. ukf.net/papers/ensatcor.html* on 22 November 2005.

111. Aleksandr Voronov and Dmitrii Sidorov, 'Amerikanskii sud vzial pod zash-chitu zhurnalistov', *Kommersant*, 29 September 2005, url not available.

112. Grigorii Asmolov, 'Russkie i tyt', *Kommersant*, 9 March 2005, *http://www. kommersant.ru/doc.html?docId=552975*; Tat'iana Stanovaia, 'Oligarkhi ne otmylis", *Politcom.ru*, 14 March 2005, *http://www.politcom.ru/2005/ zloba5390.php*; 'Nachato rassledovanie skandala v Marbel'e', *Vedomosti*, 30 March 2005, http://www.kommersant.ru/doc.html?docId=624325.

113. Anfisa Voronina, Ekaterina Kudashkina and Anna Nikolaeva, 'Za Berezovskogo vzialis' opiat", *Vedomosti*, 13 May 2005, *http://www. vedomosti. ru/newspaper/print.shtml?2005/05/13/91919*.

114. Buiter, 'From Predation', p.614.

115. 'Russkie i tut', *Kommersant*, 9 March 2005, *http://www.komersant.ru/ doc.html?docId=552975*; Anfisa Voronina, Ekaterina Kudashkina and Anna Nikolaeva, 'Za Berezovskogo vzialis' opiat", *Vedomosti*, 13 May 2005, *http://www.vedomosti.ru/newspaper/print.shtml?2005/05/13/91919*.

116. Rinat Sagdiev and Elena Vinogradova, 'Podnozhka dlia konkurenta', *Vedomosti*, 13 December 2005, *http://www.vedomosti.ru/newspaper/print.shtml? 2005/12/13/100709*.

117. See the proud claim by Alekperov that every commercial document dealt with by Lukoil, particularly those related to trade, is vetted by the security department. 'Interv'iu: Alekperov', *Vedomosti*, 11 July 2005, *http://www.vedo-mosti.ru/newspaper/print.shtml?2005/07/11/94500*.

118. Nikolai Borisov, 'Advokaty poteriali Shorora', *Vedomosti*, 12 December 2005, *http://www.vedomosti.ru/newspaper/article.shtml?2005/12/12/100642*.

119. 'Mikhail Khodorkovskii: Rokfelleru bylo namnogo tiazhelee', *Kommersant*, 1 June 2005, *http://www.kommersant.ru/doc.html?docId=582013*.

120. In 2005 Evrazkholding raised $442 million for 8.3 per cent of its shares, and NLMK $609 million for 7 per cent. Both offerings were in London. Iuliia Fedorinova, 'Konsolidatsii – net', *Vedomosti*, 29 December 2005, *http://www.vedomosti.ru/newspaper/article.shtml?2005/12/29/101401*.

121. Kets de Vries, *New Russian Business Leaders*, p.159.

122. Sergei Guriev and Andrei Rachinsky, 'The Role of Oligarchs in Russian Capitalism', *Journal of Economic Perspectives*, vol. 19, no. 1, Winter 2005, p.141.

123. Roland Nash, 'Corporate Consolidation: Russia's latest lurch towards capitalism', in Peter Westin (ed.), *The Wild East. Negotiating the Russian financial frontier*, Reuters/Pearson Education, Harlow, 2001, p.109.

124. Kets de Vries, *New Russian Business Leaders*, pp.156–8.

125. 'Mikhail Khodorkovskii: Rokfelleru bylo namnogo tiazhelee', *Kommersant*, 1 June 2005, *http://www.kommersant.ru/doc.html?docId=582013*.

126. See, for example, the care with which SUAL dealt with the regionally sensitive 'social sphere': Stephen Fortescue, 'Ownership and corporate strategy in the Russian mining and metals sector', *The Soviet and Post-Soviet Review*, vol. 25, no. 2, 1998, p. 172.

127. Ol'ga Proskurnina and Anna Nikolaeva, 'Shchedrost' napokaz', *Vedomosti*, 27 November 2003, *http://www.vedomosti.ru/stories/2003/11/27-55-01.html*.

128. He actually attributed the statement to the Dean of the Harvard Business School. 'Mikhail Khodorkovskii: Rokfelleru bylo namnogo tiazhelee', *Kommersant*, 1 June 2005, *http://www.kommersant.ru/doc.html?docId=582013*.

129. In November 2003 RSPP created a new vice president for social responsibility in business, and in autumn 2004 recommended that its members use social auditing. Ol'ga Proskurnina and Anna Nikolaeva, 'Shchedrost' napokaz', *Vedomosti*, 27 November 2003, *http://www.vedomosti.ru/stories/2003/11/27-55-01.html*; Andrei Panov and Kirill Koriukin, 'Auditory uchat oligarkhov', *Vedomosti*, 18 October 2004, *http://www.vedomosti.ru/newspaper/ print.shtml? 2004/10/18/82208*.

130. Finance Minister Kudrin was most persistent in including social responsibility, as defined by the state, as a condition for a new contract with business. Tat'iana Stanovaia, 'Biznes i vlast': nachalo bol'shogo torga', *Politcom.ru*, 26 April 2004, *http://www.politcom.ru/print.php*.

131. Mariia Kravtsova, 'Ne dopustit'!', *Ekspert*, 14 November 2005, *http://www.expert.ru/expert/current/data/43-grob.shtml*.

132. 'Ot redaktsii: muzhchiny na $1 mird', *Vedomosti*, 14 March 2005, *http://www.vedomosti.ru/newspaper/print.shtml?2005/03/14/89370*.

133. Stephen Fortescue, 'The Russian Aluminum Industry in Transition', *Eurasian Geography and Economics*, vol. 47, no. 1, 2006, pp.76–94.

134. Barnes disputes the view that the period after 1998 has seen the consolidation of ownership and a consequent greater focus on increasing wealth rather than prying further assets from the state. Andrew Barnes, 'Russia's New Business Groups and State Power', *Post-Soviet Affairs*, vol. 19, no. 2, 2003, pp.154–86.

4　The Economic Performance of the Barons and Magnates

1. Raghuram Rajan and Luigi Zingales, *Saving Capitalism from the Capitalists. Unleashing the power of financial markets to create wealth and spread opportunity*, Crown, New York, 2003, p.155.

2. Vera Krasnova, 'Bez deneg i bez strategii', *Ekspert*, 15 June 1998, p.28.

3. Aleksei Golubovich, ' "Delo IuKOSa" – pokazatel'nyi protsess ili plata za oshibki?', *Ekspert*, 5 December 2005, *http://www.expert.ru/expert/current/data/ 46-yukos.shtml*.

4. Vladimir Lisin, 'Zhestkost' tekhnokratov i ekonomistov', *Ekspert*, 5 October 1998, p.8.

5. Paul Klebnikov, *Godfather of the Kremlin. Boris Berezovsky and the looting of Russia*, Harcourt, New York, 2000, p.14.

6. Klebnikov, *Godfather*, p.267.

7. Joseph Stiglitz, *Globalization and Its Discontents*, Penguin, London, 2002, p.141.

8. Fox and Heller quote a Russian car industry specialist commenting on AvtoVAZ, the company that Berezovsky was involved with: 'The company is

going to die a death by a thousand cuts. It's just going to sit there ... until someone sees the potential value in some of its assets, strips them out and creates a different franchise or does a complete management overhaul'. They go on to be critical of owners who do not sell off the assets, including land, of value-subtracting firms. Merritt B. Fox and Michael A. Heller, 'Corporate Governance Lessons from Russian Enterprise Fiascoes', *New York University Law Review*, vol. 75, no. 6, December 2000, pp.1747,1759.

9. Bernard Black, Reinier Kraakman and Anna Tarassova, 'Russian Privatization and Corporate Governance: what went wrong?', *Stanford Law Review*, vol. 52, 1999–2000, pp.1750–1.

10. R.S. Dzarasov and D.V. Novozhenov, *Krupnyi biznes i nakoplenie kapitala v sovremennoi Rossii*, URCC, Moscow, 2005, p.183.

11. Aleksandr Zaporozhnyi, 'Rozhdenie sverkhnovoi', *Ekspert-Ural*, 16 May 2005, *http://www.expert.ru/ural/current/18ubizp.shtml*.

12. D. Michael Shafer, *Winners and Losers. How sectors shape the development prospects of states*, Cornell University Press, Ithaca and London, 1994, chapter 3.

13. Rajan and Zingales, *Saving Capitalism*, p.57.

14. Black, Kraakman and Tarassova, 'Russian Privatization', p.1769.

15. Fox and Heller, 'Corporate governance lessons', pp.1721–5, 1757, 1761.

16. Sergei Guriev and Andrei Rachinsky, 'The Role of Oligarchs in Russian Capitalism', *Journal of Economic Perspectives*, vol. 19, no. 1, Winter 2005, pp.142–5. For another study that shows labour productivity in the country's ten biggest companies (all but one of which are in the resource sector) to be four times higher than the national average, see Aleksandr Dynkin, 'Krupnyi biznes: nashe nasledie', *Vedomosti*, 20 January 2004, *http://www.vedomosti.ru /newspaper/article.shtml?2004/01/20/71241*.

17. Michael Kapoor, 'Out of the Ashes', *Business Central Europe*, November 1996, pp.9–11; Juliet Johnson, 'Russia's Emerging Financial-industrial Groups', *Post-Soviet Affairs*, vol. 13, no. 4, 1997, p.360.

18. Jerry F. Hough, *The Logic of Economic Reform in Russia*, Brookings Institution Press, Washington DC, 2001, p.59.

19. Alexander S. Bim, 'Ownership and Control of Russian Enterprises and Strategies of Shareholders', *Communist Economies and Economic Transformation*, vol. 8, no. 4, 1996, pp.476–8.

20. David Hoffman, *The Oligarchs. Wealth and power in the new Russia*, Perseus, Cambridge MA, 2002, p.311.

21. Michael Burawoy and Kathryn Hendley, 'Between Perestroika and Privatisation: divided strategies and political crisis in a Soviet enterprise', *Soviet Studies*, vol. 44, no. 3, 1992, pp.371–402. See also Kathryn Hendley, 'Temporal and Regional Patterns of Commercial Litigation in Post-Soviet Russia', *Post-Soviet Geography and Economics*, vol. 39, no. 7, September 1998, pp.141–2.

22. Igor Gurkov, 'Typology of Russian Enterprises' Adaptation to New Economic Realities', International Institute for Applied Systems Analysis, Laxenburg, WP96–083, July 1996, pp.13–16.

23. Natal'ia Gotova and Petr Ivanov, 'Diversifikatsiia proizvodstva okazalas' slishkom masshtabnoi', *Kommersant*, 19 December 1995, p.9; Sergei Isaev, 'Ternistyi put' reform', *Metally Evrazii*, no. 2, 1998, pp.42–3.

24. Viktor Klochkov, 'Rabochie prodali direktora za 100 millionov', *Profil'*, 12 October 1998, p.11.

25. The importance of trading contracts can be seen in the making of such contracts binding on new owners as a 1990s Russian form of the takeover 'poison pill'. Dmitrii Sivakov, 'Dogovor dorozhe deneg', *Ekspert*, 3 December 2001, p.27.

26. Dzarasov and Novozhenov, *Krupnyi biznes*, p.279. For another analysis of the positive benefits of oligarch management, see Yuko Adachi, 'The Ambiguous Effects of Russian Corporate Governance Abuses of the 1990s', *Post-Soviet Affairs*, vol. 22, no. 1, 2006, pp.65–89.

27. 'Glavnoe delo zhizni', *Tsvetnye metally*, no. 6, 2000, pp.96–7.

28. Kirill Vishnepol'skii, 'ONEKSIMbanku na "Noril'skom nikele" – pomogut Bog i prezident', *Kommersant*, 16 May 1996, p.9.

29. Johnson, 'Russia's Emerging', p.358.

30. *Finansovye Izvestiia*, 5 December 1995; Iurii Adno, 'Svet v kontse tonnelia uzhe poiavicsia', *Metally Evrazii*, no. 6, 1997, p.38.

31. Aleksei Parshikov, 'Na vneshnii rynok – bez vnytrennei konkurentsii', *Metally Evrazii*, no. 3, 1999, p.21.

32. K.P. Zlotnikov, 'Trudnyi put' k uspekhu', *Tsvetnye metally*, no. 6, 2000, p.8.

33. Valery Kryukov and Arild Moe, 'Banks and the Financial Sector', in David Lane (ed.), *The Political Economy of Russian Oil*, Rowman & Littlefield, Lanham MD, 1999, pp.66–8. In the same source the opinion is expressed that it would have taken considerable restructuring and rigorous management of Sidanko to be able to siphon money out of it, since it had previously had a highly decentralized management structure.

34. Fedorov had worked his way through the ranks of the company, but was clearly a Menatep man, leaving his post in November 2004, when Menatep sold out. *Murmanskii telegraf. Biograficheskaia spravka, http://www. mtelegraf.ru/default.html?name=WhoisWho&pfile=18*, downloaded 1 February 2005.

35. S.G. Fedorov, 'Aktsionernoe obshchestvo "Apatit": vchera, segodnia, zavtra', *Gornyi zhurnal*, no. 9, 1999, pp.4–8.

36. Andrei Lemeshko and Aleksei Nikol'skii, 'Genprokuratura pobyvala na "Apatite" ', *Vedomosti*, 15 July 2003, *http://www.vedomosti.ru/stories/2003/07/15-40-01.html*.

37. It should be noted that Johnson cites an *Izvestiia* article of September 1996, to the effect that Menatep was able to restore the fortunes of Apatit by increasing its prices to such levels that its main customer Ammofos was bankrupted and duly taken over by Apatit. Johnson, 'Russia's Emerging', p.357.

38. Irina Malkova, ' "Apatit" igraet vdlinnuiu', *Vedomosti*, 18 January 2006, *http://www.vedomosti.ru/newspaper/print.shtml?2006/01/18/101767*.

39. Nepheline is used in the production of alumina as a substitute for bauxite, of which Russia suffers serious shortages. Anatolii Temkin, ' "Fosagro" khochet porabotat' na "Rusal" ', *Vedomosti*, 9 November 2005, *http://www.vedomosti.ru/newspaper/article.shtml?20005/11/09/99260*.

40. Rudol'f Shkol'nikov, 'Ural'skii aliuminievyi: iubilei na poroge XXI stoletiia', *Metally Evrazii*, no. 3, 1999, p.42.

41. Aleksandr Iulin, 'Strasti po krasnoi rude', *Izvestiia*, 28 October 1995, p.4.

42. A.V. Kuznetsov, 'Syr'evaia baza glinozemnogo proizvodstva na Ural'skom aliuminievom zavode', *Tsvetnye metally*, no. 8, 1999, special insert pp.23–4; Clifford G. Gaddy and Barry W. Ickes, *Russia's Virtual Economy*, Brookings Institution Press, Washington DC, 2002, p.249.

43. Aleksandr Okatov, 'Vremia Timana', *Metally Evrazii*, no. 5, 1998, p. 16; Mariia Istomina, 'Tiaga k vysokomu', *Ekspert-Ural*, 12 September 2005, *http://www.expert.ru/ural/current/34umar-ist2.shtml*.

44. Dmitrii Sivakov, 'Po lezviiu nozha', *Ekspert*, 9 October 2000, p.41.

45. A. A. Konoplianik, 'Neizbezhen li krizis v rossiiskoi neftedobyche?', *Mineral'nye resursy Rossii*, no. 1, 2001, *http://www.geoinform.ru/mrr.files/issues/articles/konol-01.html*.

46. Vitalii Ermakov, 'Prirodnaia renta: vremennyi uspekh', *Vedomosti*, 10 February 2004, *http://www.vedomosti.ru/stories/2004/02/10-47-04.html*.

47. Kryukov and Moe, 'Banks and the Financial Structure', p.56.

48. David Lane and Iskander Seifulmulukov, 'Company Profiles: LUKoil, YuKOS, Surgutneftegaz, Sidanko', in David Lane (ed.), *The Political Economy of Russian Oil*, Rowman & Littlefield, Lanham MD, 1999, p.117.

49. David Lane and Iskander Seifulmulukov, 'Structure and Ownership', in David Lane (ed.), *The Political Economy of Russian Oil*, Rowman & Littlefield, Lanham MD, 1999, p.31.

50. Manfred F.R. Kets de Vries, Stanislav Shekshnia, Konstantin Korotov and Elizabeth Florent-Treacy, *The New Russian Business Leaders*, Edward Elgar, Cheltenham UK and Northampton MA, 2004, p.156. Schlumberger cancelled the arrangement in October 2004. Irina Reznik, Iuliia Bushueva and Rodion Levinskii, ' "IuKOS" ostalsia bez nou-khau', *Vedomosti*, 25 October 2004, *http://www.vedomosti.ru/newspaper/print.shtml?2004/10/25/82557*.

51. Kets de Vries, *New Russian Business Leaders*, pp.155–61.

52. Aleksei Golubovich, ' "Delo IuKOSa" – pokazatel'nyi protsess ili plata za oshibki?', *Ekspert*, 5 December 2005, *http://www.expert.ru/expert/current/data/46-yukos.shtml*.

53. Yuko Iji, 'Corporate Control and Governance Practices in Russia', Centre for the Study of Economic and Social Change in Europe, School of Slavonic and East European Studies, University College London, Working Paper No. 33, June 2003; Andrei Shleifer and Daniel Treisman, 'A Normal Country: Russia after communism', *Journal of Economic Perspectives*, vol. 19, no. 1, Winter 2005, pp.161–2.

54. Roland Nash, 'Corporate Consolidation: Russia's latest lurch towards capitalism', in Peter Westin (ed.), *The Wild East. Negotiating the Russian financial frontier*, Reuters/Pearson Education, Harlow, 2001, p.109.

55. Peter Maass, 'The Triumph of the Quiet Tycoon', *NYTimes.com*, 1 August 2004.

56. Black, Kraakman, Tarassova, 'Russian Privatization', p.1776.

57. Aleksandr Koksharov, 'Zatianuvshiisia endshpil'', *Ekspert*, 16 August 2004, *http://www.expert.ru/expert/current/data/yukos-2_4.shtml*.

58. Vladimir Milov, 'Globalist: vinovnik nashego uspekha', *Vedomosti*, 19 May 2005, *http://www.vedomosti.ru/newspaper/print.shtml?2005/05/19/92226*.

59. In July 1995 the Russian Central Bank introduced a narrow currency corridor, with upper and lower limits on the nominal ruble:dollar exchange rate. With

ruble inflation higher than dollar inflation, the effect was an appreciation of the ruble against the dollar in real terms, reducing export revenues as they were converted into rubles.

60. Vladimir Tikhomirov, 'Capital Flight from Post-Soviet Russia', *Europe-Asia Studies*, vol. 49, no. 4, 1997, pp.591–615.
61. Pavel Arabov, ' "Noril'skii nikel' " opredelil doliu aktsionerov', *Kommersant*, 30 May 2002, p.16; Aleksandr Tutushkin and Rodion Levinskii, ' "LUKOIL" stanet shedree', *Vedomosti*, 22 February 2005, *http://www.vedomosti.ru/newspaper/print.shtml?2005/02/22/87317*; Tat'iana Egorova and Elena Mazneva, '$3,5 mlrd ot TNK-BP', *Vedomosti*, 9 February 2005, *http://www.vedomosti.ru/newspaper/print.shtml?2005/02/09/86715*.
62. 'Ot redaktsii: l'goty oligarkhov', *Vedomosti*, 8 August 2003, *http://www.vedomosti.ru/stories/2003/08/08-47-01.html*.
63. Klebnikov, *Godfather*, p.181.
64. Black, Kraakman and Tarassova, 'Russian privatization', p.1777.
65. Black, Kraakman and Tarassova, 'Russian privatization', p.1777.
66. *Kommersant*, 12 April 2001, p.8.
67. Konstantin Baskaev, 'Metallurgov SNG vydavlivaiut s rynka', *Finansovye Izvestiia*, 13 May 1997, p.2.
68. Johnson, 'Russia's Emerging', p.359.
69. 'Metallurgicheskii kompleks segodnia', *Metallosnabzhenie i sbyt*, no. 4, 1997, p.8.
70. L.N. Shevelev, 'Itogi raboty metallurgii v 1996g i zadachi na 1997g', *Chernaia metallurgiia*, nos 3–4, 1997, p.5.
71. Iurii Komratov, ' "Staryi sobol" ', novaia stat", *Metally Evrazii*, no. 4, 1998, pp.38–42; Viktor Klochkov, 'Rabochie prodali direktora za 100 millionov', *Profil'*, 12 October 1998, p.11; 'Perspektivy razvitiia NTMK', *Ekspert*, 14 May 2001, p.65.
72. A. A. Smolianinov, 'Zapsib – etapy vozrozhdeniia', *Ekspert*, 9 July 2001, p.79; Sergei Morozov and Aleksei Maslakov, 'Modernizatsiia bez investitsii', *Metally Evrazii*, no. 5, 1999, pp.50–1.
73. Valeriia Selivanova and Vera Krasnova, 'Stal'naia logika', *Ekspert*, 20 September 1999, pp.26–8.
74. In 2004 the company made $1.4 billon profit on turnover of $6.6 billon. Iuliia Fedorinova, ' "Severstal" pritormozila', *Vedomosti*, 24 October 2005, *http://www.vedomosti.ru/newspaper/article.shtml?2005/10/24/98623*.
75. Åslund, 'Comparative Oligarchy', p.27.
76. Kets de Vries, *New Russian Business Leaders*, p.156.
77. V.V. Veselkov and V.D. Lazarev, 'V novyi vek so staroi tekhnologiei?', *Tsvetnye metally*, no. 3, 1999, pp.70–1; V.M. Siziakov, 'Sostoianie i problemy razvitiia aliuminievoi promyshlennosti Rossii v usloviiakh ekonomiki perekhodnogo perioda', nos 11–12, 2000, pp.29–33.
78. Stephen Fortescue, 'The Russian Aluminum Industry in Transition', *Eurasian Geography and Economics*, vol. 47, No. 1, 2006, p.86.
79. Stephen Fortescue, 'The Mining and Metals Industry and Globalization', in Klaus Segbers (ed), *Explaining Post-Soviet Patchworks*, Ashgate, Aldershot, 2001, vol. 1, p.149.
80. 'Metallurg-info', *Metallurg*, no. 4, 2002, p.18.
81. V.F. Rashnikov, 'V novyi vek – s novymi tekhnologiiami', *Metallurg*, no. 1, 2002, pp.3–4; Mariia Rozhkova, 'Mir na Magnitke', *Vedomosti*, 3 July 2002, p.B2.
82. Fortescue, 'Russian Aluminum Industry', p.89.

5   Oligarchy and Political Power

1. See Robert W. Orttung, 'Business and Politics in the Russian Regions', *Problems of Post-Communism*, vol. 51, no. 2, March–April 2004, pp.48–60.
2. The periodization presented here is similar to that contained in Igor' Bunin, 'Vlast' i biznes v novoi Rossii', *Politcom.ru*, 11 June 2004, *http://www.politcom.ru/print.php*.
3. Hans-Henning Schröder, 'El'tsin and the Oligarchs: the role of financial groups in Russian politics between 1993 and July 1998', *Europe-Asia Studies*, vol. 51, no. 6, 1999, pp.967,985.
4. Juliet Johnson, *A Fistful of Rubles. The rise and fall of the Russian banking system*, Cornell University Press, Ithaca and London, 2000, pp.119–21; Juliet Johnson, 'Russia's Emerging Financial-industrial Groups', *Post-Soviet Affairs*, vol. 13, no. 4, 1997, pp.352–3.
5. Sergei Guriev and Andrei Rachinsky, 'The Role of Oligarchs in Russian Capitalism', *Journal of Economic Perspectives*, vol. 19, no. 1, Winter 2005, pp.145–6.
6. Bunin, 'Vlast' i biznes'.
7. In August 2005 Mikhail Khodorkovsky, writing from a prison cell, suggested that with hindsight he now believed that Russia would have been better off if Yeltsin had lost the 1996 election. In a 2002 interview, first published in June 2005, however, he expressed no regrets over his role in the 1996 election. 'Mikhail Khodorkovskii: Rokfelleru bylo namnogo tiazhelee', *Kommersant*, 1 June 2005, *http://www.kommersant.ru/doc.html?docId=582013*; Kseniia Iudaeva, 'Strannye sblizheniia: oligarkhicheskii sotsializm', *Vedomosti*, 25 May 2005, *http://www.vedomosti.ru/newspaper/print.shtml? 2005/08/25/96229*.
8. Aleksei Iu. Zudin, 'Oligarchy as a Political Problem of Russian Postcommunism', *Russian Social Science Review*, vol. 41, no. 6, November–December 2000, pp.4–33; Ia.Sh. Pappe, *"Oligarkhi". Ekonomicheskaia khronika. 1992–2000*, GU Vysshaia ekonomicheskaia shkola, Moscow, 2000.
9. One of the most important was his persuading Yelstsin to dismiss his security chief Korzhakov in the first part of 1996 and thereby leave Chubais and the oligarchs to run his presidential re-election campaign. Chrystia Freeland, *Sale of the Century. Russia's wild ride from communism to capitalism*, Crown, New York, 2000, pp.233–4
10. Bulat Stoliarov, 'Chelovek nedeli: neuviazka', *Vedomosti*, 14 July 2003, *http://www.vedomosti.ru/stories/2003/07/14-47-05.html*.
11. Bunin. 'Vlast i biznes'.
12. Hans-Henning Schröder, 'The "Oligarchs": a Force to be Reckoned With?', in Stefanie Harter and Gerald Easter (eds), *Shaping the Economic Space in Russia. Decision making processes, institutions and adjustment to change in the El'tsin era*, Ashgate, Aldershot, 2000, p.60.
13. Zudin, 'Oligarchy', pp.6–7.
14. Pappe, *'Oligarkhi'*, p.22.
15. Johnson, 'Russia's emerging', p.356.
16. Hoffman, David, *The Oligarchs. Wealth and power in the new Russia*, Perseus, Cambridge MA, 2002, pp.285–92.
17. Konstantin Smirnov *et al.*, 'Imushchie otvetili vlast' imushchim', *Kommersant*, 10 July 2003, *http://www.kommersant.ru/archive/archive-material.html?docid=394823*.

18. Tat'iana Stanovaia, 'Nalogovaia politika', *Politcom.ru*, 12 April 2005, *http://www.politcom.ru/2005/gvozd599.php*.

19. 'Business leaders complain of tax claims, uncertain property rights, judicial corruption', *RFE/RL Newsline*, vol. 9, no. 13, Part 1, 21 January 2005.

20. 'Prezident RSPP o reshenii suda po delu IuKOSa', news release, 31 May 2005, *http://www.rspp.ru/news/?nid=1751*.

21. A group of oligarchs met at a residence in the Moscow suburb of Sparrow Hills in the mid-1990s to work out rules of behaviour in their relations with each other. Berezovsky has been accused of nullifying the effort by using the meetings for commercial purposes. Hoffman, *Oligarchs*, pp 271–2. On the RSPP's efforts, see Petr Netreba, 'Predprinimateli berutsia vershit' pravosudie', *Kommersant*, 29 May 2002, p.14.

22. The point is developed in Stephen Fortescue, 'Pravit li Rossiia oligarkhiia?', *Polis*, vol. 5, 2002, pp.64–73.

23. Zudin, 'Oligarchy as a Political Problem', p.14.

24. Schröder, 'El'tsin and the Oligarchs', p.970.

25. Nikolai Vardul' and Petr Negreba, 'Chto skazhet prezident', *Kommersant*, 19 May 2004, *http://www.kommersant.ru/doc.html?docId=475553*.

26. 'Putin and Oligarchs Set to Meet Tomorrow', Jamestown Foundation, *Monitor*, vol. 6, no. 146, 27 July 2000, citing *Novaia gazeta*, 24 July 2000.

27. The Family was the popular name for the group of officials immediately around Yeltsin in the presidential administration. One, with whom Berezovsky was said to have particularly good relations, was a member of the small-f family, Yeltsin's daughter Tatyana Dyachenko.

28. Irina Nagornykh, 'Prezidenta pod zemlei dostali', *Kommersant*, 23 March 2002, p.2. Peregudov interprets *ravnoudalennost'* as the equal treatment of all sectors of the economy. S.P. Peregudov, *Korporativnyi kapital v mirovoi i rossiiskoi politike*, Institut mirovoi ekonomiki i mezhdunarodnykh otnoshenii, Moscow, 2005, p.79.

29. El'mar Murtazaev, 'Kapitalizm: Khokkei s oligarkhami', *Vedomosti*, 25 February 2003, *http://www.kapital.ru/stories/2003/02/25-47-03.html*.

30. On cheating in oligarchies, see J. Mark Ramseyer and Frances M. Rosenbluth, *The Politics of Oligarchy. Institutional choice in Imperial Japan*, Cambridge University Press, 1995, p.6.

31. Schröder, 'El'tsin and the Oligarchs', p.974.

32. One could not describe the other victim of Putin's would-be anti-oligarch campaign, Gusinsky, as a cheater. He certainly could not be accused of trying to suborn the referee. However he had made himself an outsider, by concentrating on media interests rather than following the other oligarchs into the resource sector. Using that media to attack the referee was probably seen by the oligarchy as not much less disruptive than trying to suborn him.

33. Peter Rutland, 'Putin and the Oligarchs', in Dale R. Herspring (ed.), *Putin's Russia. Past imperfect, future uncertain*, Rowman & Littlefield, Lanham MD, 2003, pp.141–2.

34. Bunin, 'Vlast' i biznes'.

35. Bunin, 'Vlast' i biznes'.

36. Mikhail Deliagin, 'Biznes i vlast': investitsionnyi pakt', *Vedomosti*, 18 November 2003, *http://www.vedomosti.ru/stories/2003/11/18-47-04.html*.

37. William Tompson, 'Putin and the "Oligarchs": a two-sided commitment problem', in Alex Pravda (ed.), *Leading Russia. Putin in perspective. Essays in honour of Archie Brown*, Oxford University Press, Oxford, 2005, p. 184.
38. Barnes, 'Russia's New Business Groups', pp.178–9.
39. For tax problems in the metals sector, see Dmitrii Butrin, Nikolai Ivanov and Sergei Tiagai, 'Prishli za Potaninym', *Kommersant*, 1 December 2000, pp.1 and 4. During 2000 Potanin was repeatedly threatened with a review of the shares-for-credit deal through which he had obtained Norilsk Nickel. 'Putin Says Law will be Observed in Norilsk Nickel Case', *RFE/RL Newsline*, vol. 4, no. 127, Part 1, 30 June 2000.
40. For example, in March 2002 the RSPP complained about the arbitrary actions of the *siloviki*. Putin took their concerns, with apparent sympathy, to Mikhail Fradkov, then head of the tax police and subsequently prime minister. The situation did not change. Petr Netreba, 'Bunt oligarkhov', *Kommersant*, 14 March 2002, p.1; Andrei Bagrov, 'Prezident uslyshal oligarkhov', *Kommersant*, 16 March 2002, p.1.
41. Kirill Rogov, 'Politekonomiia: dva mandata', *Vedomosti*, 26 February 2003, *http://www.kapital.ru/stories/2003/02/26-47-03.html*.
42. Mark Urnov, ' "Kazus IuKOSa": tri fundamental'nykh voprosa', *Politcom.ru*, 9 July 2003, *http://www.politcom.ru/print/php*.
43. 'V Rossi gotovitsia oligarkhicheskii perevorot', *Utro.ru*, 26 May 2003, *http://www.utro.ru/articles/2003/05/26/201631.shtml*.
44. Bulat Stoliarov, 'Chelovek nedeli: burevestnik', *Vedomosti*, 8 September 2003, *http://www.vedomosti.ru/newspaper/article.shtml?2003/09/08*. Pavlovsky was subsequently successfully sued for slander by Pugachev. 'Pugachev pobedil Pavlovskogo v sude', *Vedomosti*, 1 December 2003, *http://www.vedomoti.ru/newspaper/article.shtml?2003/12/01*.
45. 'Priglashenie "IuKOSa" na kazn': v roli topora – Bogdanchikov', *Novaia gazeta*, 17 July 2003, *http://2003.Novaya Gazeta.Ru/nomer/2003/51n/n51n-s00.shtml*. It should be noted that although Bogdanchikov is attributed to the *silovik* clan, his career has been entirely in the oil industry. For a biography, see *http://www.rustrana.ru/grom-article.php?nid=10648&sq=19,23,673, 1749,1751 &crypt=*.
46. Denis Skorobogat'ko, Petr Sapozhnikov and Pavel Prezhentsev, 'IuKOSu pereschitali dela', *Kommersant*, 21 July 2003, *http://www.kommersant.ru/archive-material.html?docid=397866*.

6 Taxation in the Resource Sector

1. David Lane, 'The Political Economy of Russian Oil', in Peter Rutland (ed.), *Business and State in Contemporary Russia*, Westview, Boulder, Colorado, 2001, p.115.
2. Andrei Shleifer and Daniel Treisman, *Without a Map. Political tactics and economic reform in Russia*, MIT Press, Cambridge MA, 2000, p.73.
3. Lane, 'Political Economy', p.116.
4. Lane, 'Political Economy', p.115.
5. Shleifer and Treisman, *Without a Map*, pp.77, 79.
6. Vlad Ivanenko, 'The Statutory Tax Burden and its Avoidance in Transitional Russia', *Europe-Asia Studies*, vol. 57, no. 7, November 2005, pp.1031–2.

7. Sheila A. Chapman and Marcella Mulino, 'Predicting Russia's Currency and Financial Crises', in David Lane (ed.), *Russian Banking. Evolution, problems and prospects*, Edward Elgar, Cheltenham and Northampton, MA, 2002, p.191.
8. A. Miasnikov, 'Illiuziia blagopoluchiia vnushaet trevogu', *Ekonomika i zhizn'*, no. 51, 1994, p.4; V. Savenko, 'Prokat i truby', *Metallosnabzhenie i sbyt*, no. 6, 1998, pp.8–12.
9. Petr Ledovskii, 'S novym Boosom ne soskuchish'sia', *Profil'*, 12 October 1998, p.16.
10. Sergei Aukutsionek, 'Some Characteristics of the Transition Economy', *Communist Economies and Economic Transformation*, vol. 9, no. 3, 1997, p.309.
11. Data taken from Russian Federal Tax Service, 1997.
12. Andrei Serov, 'Sviashennye korovy otdany na zaklanie', *Kommersant*, 7 September 1995, p.3. See also Petr Ledovskii, 'S novym Boosom ne soskuchish'sia', *Profil'*, 12 October 1998, p.16.
13. Petr Ledovskii, 'S novym Boosom ne soskuchish'sia', *Profil'*, 12 October 1998, p.16.
14. S.V. Kolpakov, 'Ekonomicheskie usloviia vozrozhdeniia metallurgicheskogo proizvodstva v Rossii', *Chernaia metallurgiia*, nos 7–8, 1998, p.4; 'Metallurgiia i neftegaz: poisk vzaimootnosheniia v stenakh Gosudarstvennoi Dumy', *Metallosnabzhenie i sbyt*, no. 2, 1999, p.15; Iurii Masliukov, 'Zakony – na sluzhbu industrii', *Metally Evrazii*, no. 3, 2000, p.7.
15. L.N. Shevelev, 'Itogi raboty metallurgii v 1996 g. i zadachi na 1997 g.', *Chernaia metallurgiia*, nos 3–4, 1997, p.7.
16. For other data presenting a similar picture, see Leonid Makarov, 'Neravnyi gruz', *Metally Evrazii*, no. 6, 1997, p.24; Anatolii Sysoev, 'Rossiiskaia metallurgiia: ot "monetarizma" k protektsionizmu', *Metally Evrazii*, no. 5, 1998, p.9.
17. A.A. Brodov, 'Sostoianie i problemy razvitiia chernoi metallurgii', *Chernaia metallurgiia*, nos 1–2, 2000, p.12.
18. Anatolii Sysoev, 'Rossiiskaia metallurgiia: ot "monetarizma" k protektsionizmu', *Metally Evrazii*, no. 5, 1998, p.9.
19. S.V. Kolpakov, 'Ekonomicheskie usloviia vozrozhdeniia metallurgicheskogo proizvodstva v Rossii', *Chernaia metallurgiia*, nos 7–8, 1998, p.6.
20. Viktor Titov, 'Skandal v Novosibirske', *Ekspert*, 17 May 1999, p.35; 'Ekonomika metallurgii', *Metallosnabzhenie i sbyt*, no. 4, 1997, p.10.
21. Stephen Fortescue, 'The Russian Aluminum Industry in Transition', *Eurasian Geography and Economics*, vol. 47, no. 1, 2006, p.78.
22. L.N. Shevelev, 'Itogi raboty metallurgii v 1996g. i zadachi na 1997g.', *Chernaia metallurgiia*, nos 3–4, 1997, p.6; unpublished government data.
23. A.I. Sukhoruchenkov, 'Sostoianie i problemy zhelezorudnoi podotrasli metallurgicheskoi promyshlennosti Rossii', *Gornyi zhurnal*, no. 7, 1998, p.4.
24. L.P. Makarov, 'Struktura nalogovykh dokhodov federal'noi biudzheta v 2001 godu', *Metallurg*, no. 9, 2000, p.7.
25. 'Statistical appendix', Yegor Gaidar (ed.), *The Economics of Transition*, MIT Press, Cambridge Mass., 2003, p.985. The author has averaged the monthly data presented in the original source.
26. Valery Kryukov, 'Adjustment to Change: the case of the oil and gas industry', in Stefanie Harter and Gerald Easter (eds), *Shaping the Economic Space in Russia. Decision making processes, institutions and adjustment to change in the El'tsin era*, Ashgate, Aldershot, 2000, p.104.

27. For details on lobbying in the metals sector, see Stephen Fortescue, 'Taxation in the Russian Mining and Metals Sector', *Arbeitspapiere und Materialien*, No. 27, Forschungsstelle Osteuropa, University of Bremen, July 2001.
28. Anders Åslund, 'Russia's Economic Transformation under Putin', *Eurasian Geography and Economics*, vol. 45, no. 6, 2004, pp.405–6.
29. Andrei Konoplianik, 'Otchego ukhodili – k tomu i prishli', *Rossiiskaia gazeta*, undated, downloaded from *www.rg.ru/bussines/rinky/689.shtm*, 18 June 2003. See also Maksim Korobov, 'Neftianoi sektor kremlevskogo kruga', *Ekspert*, 23 July 2001 p.34; V.D. Mel'gunov and K.V. Fonar'kov, 'O novoi sisteme platezhei pri pol'zovanii nedrami', *Mineral'nye resursy Rossii*, no. 3, 2002, *www.geoinform.ru*; Natal'ia Neimysheva and Aleksandr Bekker, 'Slishkom bogatye', *Vedomosti*, 30 January 2003, *http://www.vedomosti.ru/newspaper/ article.shtml?2003/01/30/57367*. Ever since unsuccessful attempts have been made to make the NDPI a differentiated tax.
30. Irina Rybal'chenko and Galina Lopunova, 'Aleksei Kudrin vvodit biudzhet-nuiu trekhletku', *Kommersant*, 27 February 2002, p.4. There is evidence that the government had always made it clear that these offsets would be removed. Kseniia Nechaeva, 'Deputaty khoroniat nalogovuiu reformu', *Kommersant*, 13 February 2002, p.2.
31. Nikolai Vardul' and Galina Liapunova, 'Mikhailu Kas'ianovu dolozhili o nal-ogovoi revoliutsii', *Kommersant*, 26 November 2002, *http://www.kommer-sant.ru/archive/archive-material.html?docId=352986*.
32. Natal'ia Ratnikova, 'Nalogovaia indul'gentsiia stoila Abramovichu v 3 raza deshevle "Chelsi" '. *Politcom.ru*, 18 April 2005, *http://www.politcom.ru/2005/ zloba5510.php*.
33. Alena Kornysheva, 'Neftianiki ekonomiat na nalogakh', *Kommersant*, 13 May 2003, *http://www.kommersant.ru/archive/archive-material.html?docId=381339*.
34. 'Ot redaktsii: Chukotka dlia vsekh', *Vedomosti*, 21 November 2003, *http://www.vedomosti.ru/stories/2003/11/21-47-02.html*.
35. Vadim Visloguzov, 'Takoi ofshor im ne nuzhen', *Kommersant*, 18 November 2003, *http://www.kommersant.ru/archive/archive-material.html?docId=428693*.
36. 'Ot redaktsii: Sodom i Gomorra', *Vedomosti*, 4 December 2003, *http://www.vedomosti.ru/stories/2003/12/04-47-01.html*.
37. Kirill Rogov, 'Politekonomiia: sluchai Kudrina-Nevzlina', *Vedomosti*, 19 November 2003, *http://www.vedomosti.ru/stories/2003/11/19-47-03.html*.
38. Vadim Visloguzov, 'Pravitel'stvo izvlekaet dividendy', *Kommersant*, 9 April 2004, *http://www.kommersant.ru/doc.html?docId=465164*.
39. Svetlana Ivanova, 'Na rynochnye tseny', *Vedomosti*, 24 March 2004, *http://www.vedomosti.ru/stories/2004/03/24-55-02.html*.
40. Tat'iana Stanovaia, 'Prezident protiv neftianogo lobbi', *Politcom.ru*, 24 November 2003, *http://www.politcom.ru/2003/zloba3326.php*.

7 The Yukos Affair

1. Anastasiia Onegina, Vitalii Ivanov and Dmitrii Simakov, 'Reshili ne mel'-chit", *Vedomosti*, 22 July 2003, *http://www.vedomosti.ru/stories/2003/07/22-55-01. html*. For excerpts from the letter, see Nikolai Bardul' and Sergei Tiagai, 'Voina resursov', *Kommersant*, 17 July 2003, *http://www.kommersant.ru/ archive-material.html?docid=396943*.

2. 'Ot redaktsii: bez tormoza', *Vedomosti*, 14 July 2003, *http://www.vedomosti.ru/stories/2003/07/14-47-01.html*.

3. Anastasiia Onegina, Boris Grozovskii and Mikhail Overchenko, 'Ne tsarskoe delo', *Vedomosti*, 17 July 2003, *http://www.vedomosti.ru/stories/2003/07/17-55-01.html*,

4. 'Business Leader Urges Oligarch to Obey "The Rules of the Game" ', *RFE/RL Newsline*, vol. 7, no. 134, Part 1, 17 July 2003.

5. Anastasiia Onegina, Vitalii Ivanov and Dmitrii Simakov, 'Reshili ne mel'chit", *Vedomosti*, 22 July 2003, *http://www.vedomosti.ru/stories/2003/07/22-5501.html*.

6. 'Prime Minister again Criticizes Moves against Yukos', *RFE/RL Newsletter*, vol. 7, no. 140, Part 1, 25 July 2003; 'Leading Liberal Says Prosecutors are "Humiliating Russia" ', *RFE/RL Newsletter*, vol. 7, no. 137, Part 1, 22 July 2003; Ekaterina Zapodinskaia and Nikolai Bardul', 'Genprokuratura poluchila kryshu', *Kommersant*, 10 October 2003, *http://www.kommersant.ru/archive-material.html?docid-418471*; Tat'iana Stanovaia, ' "Piterskie" protiv Iukosa', Politcom.ru, 7 July 2003, *http://www.politcom.ru/ print.php*.

7. Anfisa Voronina, 'Putin ishchet vykhod', *Vedomosti*, 31 July 2003, *http://www.vedomosti.ru/stories/2003/07/31-55-01.html*. Stories were to circulate later that Putin was telling people that he had been persuaded by the Prosecutor General Ustinov that the arrest of Khodorkovsky was necessary. Nikolai Vardul', 'Prezident prikazal vziat' IuKOS zhivym', *Kommersant*, 18 June 2004, *http://www.kommersant.ru/doc.html?docId=483698*.

8. Konstantin Smirnov, 'Imushchie otvetili vlast' imushcham', *Kommersant*, 10 July 2003, *http://www.kommersant.ru/archive-material.html?docid=394823*.

9. Vitalii Ivanov, 'Poshli na lichnosti', *Vedomosti*, 21 October 2003, *http://www.vedomosti.ru/stories/2003/10/21-67-01.html*.

10. 'As Oligarch Again Decries Campaign Against Yukos', *RFE/RL Newsletter*, vol. 7, no. 127, Part 1, 8 July 2003.

11. Vitalii Ivanov and Aleksei Nikol'skii, 'Nado sovetovat'sia', *Vedomosti*, 7 October 2003, *http://www.vedomosti.ru/stories/2003/10/07-55-02.html*.

12. Boris Grozovskii, Aleksei Nikol'skii and Vitalii Ivanov, 'Delo o l'gotakh', *Vedomosti*, 15 July, 2003, *http://www.vedomosti.ru/stories/2003/07/15-67-01.html*.

13. Vitalii Ivanov and Aleksei Nikol'skii, 'Nado sovetovat'sia', *Vedomosti*, 7 October 2003, *http://www.vedomosti.ru/stories/2003/10/07-55-02.html*.

14. Ekaterina Zapodinskaia and Nikolai Bardul', 'Genprokuratura poluchila kryshu', *Kommersant*, 10 October 2003, *http://www.kommersant.ru/archive-material.html?docid-418471*.

15. For a description of Khodorkovsky's arrest and a summary of the charges against him and Lebedev, see Marina Lepina et al., 'Sidet', *Kommersant*, 27 October 2003, *http://www.kommersant.ru/archive/archive-material. html?docid=423197*.

16. Vitalii Ivanov, Boris Grozovskii, Kirill Gorskii and Boris Safronov, 'Biznesmeny prosiat Vladimira Putina vmeshchat'sia', *Vedomosti*, 27 October 2003, *http://www.vedomosti.ru/stories/2003/10/27-55-02.html*.

17. Anastasiia Onegina, Boris Grozovskii, Ol'ga Proskurnina and Anfisa Voronina, 'Ne o chem govorit", *Vedomosti*, 28 October 2003, *http://www.vedomosti.ru/stories/2003/10/28-55-01.html*.

18. 'Dogovor okonchatel'nyi, obzhalovaniiu ne podlezhit', *Kommersant*, 24 November 2003, *http://www.kommersant.ru/k-vlast/get_page.asp? page_id-20034616-4.htm&ws=1*. Volsky later famously and surprisingly said in public that the Yukos affair was a case of 'bankruptcy to order', 'and I know well who ordered it. But I won't say. I have six grandchildren, and I am simply frightened.' Evgenyi Iasin, 'Delo "IuKOSa": seiateli strakha', *Vedomosti*, 30 July 2004, *http://www.vedomosti.ru/newspaper/print.shtml?2004/ 07/30/79031*.

19. 'Zachem sobiralis'?', *Kommersant*, 17 November 2003, *http://www.kommersant.ru/direct_speech.html*.

20. Mikhail Deliagin, 'Biznes i vlast': investitsionnyi pakt', *Vedomosti*, 18 November 2003, *http://www.vedomosti.ru/stories/2003/11/18-47-04.html*.

21. 'Zachem sobiralis'?', Kommersant, 17 November 2003, *http://www.kommersant. ru/direct–seech.html*.

22. For the comments of Fridman and Alekperov, see Aleksandr Bekker, 'Interv'iu: Mikhail Fridman, sovladelets "Al'fa-grupp" ', *Vedomosti*, 7 October 2004, *http://www.vedomosti.ru/newspaper/print.shtml?2004/10/07/81805*; Peter Maass, 'The Triumph of the Quiet Tycoon', *NYTimes.com*, 1 August 2004.

23. Stephen Fortescue, *Policy-Making for Russian Industry*, Macmillan, Basingstoke and London, 1997, p.117.

24. Boris Grozovsky and Anna Nikolaeva, 'Zhulikov bylo ne tak uzh mnogo', *Vedomosti*, 24 December 2003, *http://www.vedomosti.ru/stories/2003/12/ 24-55-01.html*.

25. 'Deputy Ministers Ignore Putin's Ban on Comments on Yukos', *RFE/RL Newsline*, vol. 7, no. 207, Part 1, 31 October 2003.

26. 'Il'ya Iuzhanov kritikuet delo IuKOSa', *Kommersant*, 25 December 2003, *http://www.kommersant.ru/lenta.html?id=74548*.

27. Iuliia Bushueva and Vladimir Karpov, '"IuKOS" ostanetsia rossiiskim', *Vedomosti*, 28 October 2003, *http://www.vedomosti.ru/stories/2003/10/ 28-55-03.html*.

28. Aleksandr Tutushkin, 'Prokuratura pomozhet Minprirody', *Vedomosti*, 29 October 2003, *http://www.vedomosti.ru/stories/2003/10/29-40-04.html*.

29. Irina Reznik and Aleksandr Tutushkin, ' "IuKOS" – ne partner', *Vedomosti*, 6 November 2003, *http://www/vedomosti.ru/stories/2003/11/06-55-01.html*.

30. 'And seeks to maintain an image of fairness', *RFE/RL Newsline*, vol. 7, no. 211, Part 1, 6 November 2003; 'Prime minister defies Purin by speaking out on Yukos', *RFL/RL Newsline*, vol. 7, no. 217, Part 1, 18 November 2003.

31. 'Another Yukos Official Jailed', *RFE/RL Newsline*, vol. 8, no. 14, Part 1, 23 January 2004.

32. Aleksei Nikol'skii and Iuliia Bushueva, 'Malin zria soglasilsia na $15 mln', *Vedomosti*, 1 March 2004, *http://www.vedomosti.ru/stories/2004/03/01-55-02. html*.

33. Dmitrii Butin, Denis Skorobogat'ko, Petr Sapozhnikov and Elena Naumova, 'Prikazano vyzhit', *Kommersant*, 15 July 2004, *http://www.kommersant.ru/ doc.html?docId=490131*.

34. For Gerashchenko's immediate reaction to Khodorkovsky's attack and his account of conflicts within Yukos, see Denis Skorobogat'ko, 'Viktor Gerashchenko nichem ne otlichilsia v IuKOSe', *Kommersant*, 19 July 2004, *http://www.kommersant.ru/doc.html?docId=490840*.

35. For just a single example, see Dmitrii Butrin, 'IuKOS gotov poiti v kabalu na tri goda', *Kommersant*, 12 July 2004, *http://www.kommersant.ru/doc.html? docId=489228.*

36. Irina Reznik and Anastasiia Onegina, ' "IuKOS" pishet pis'ma', *Vedomosti*, 12 July 2003, *http://www.vedomosti.ru/newspaper/print.shtml?2004/07/12/78271.*

37. Irina Reznik and Anastasiia Onegina, ' "IuKOS" pishet pis'ma', *Vedomosti*, 12 July 2003, *http://www.vedomosti.ru/newspaper/print.shtml?2004/07/12/78271*; Petr Sapozhnikov, Denis Skorobogat'ko and Alena Miklashevskaia, 'Nenyzhnyi IuKOS', *Kommersant*, 7 July 2004, *http://www.kommersant.ru/ doc.html?docId=488163.*

38. Ekaterina Derbilova, Iuliia Fedorinova, Irina Reznik and Sevast'ian Kozitsyn, ' "IuKOS" raskachali', *Vedomosti*, 7 July 2004, *http://www.vedomosti.ru/newspaper/ print.shtml?2004/07/07/78137.*

39. Kirill Rogov, 'Politekonomiia: preodolennyi kurs', *Vedomosti*, 8 December 2004, *http://www.vedomosti.ru/newspaper/article.shtml?2004/12/08/84480.*

40. Irina Reznik and Iuliia Bushueva, ' "IuKOS" obankrotiat', *Vedomosti*, 4 November 2004, *http://www.vedomosti.ru/newspaper/print.shtml?2004/11/04/ 83115.*

41. On the Temerko case, see Ekaterina Zapodinskaia, 'Genprokurature Rossii ponadobilsia londonskii advokat', *Kommersant*, 8 November 2005, *http://www.kommersant.ru/doc.html?docId=624325.* It is over this matter that Bogdanchikov complained to the prosecutor's office at the very beginning of the Yukos affair. The Bakhmina case will be looked at in the next chapter.

42. Irina Reznik and Iuliia Bushueva, 'Nachali s glavnogo', *Vedomosti*, 21 July 2004, *http://www.vedomosti.ru/newspaper/print.shtml?2004/07/21/78624.*

43. Tat'iana Stanovaia, 'IuKOS: nachalo kontsa', *Politcom.ru*, 26 July 2004, *http://www.politcom.ru/2004/analit156.php*; Natal'ia Ratnikova, 'Kommercheskaia taina "Rosnefti" ', *Politcom.ru*, 20 August 2004, *http://www.politcom.ru/ 2004/zloba4588.php.*

44. Denis Skorobogat'ko, 'Gosudarstvo tsenit YuKOS vse bol'she i bol'she', *Kommersant*, 2 November 2004, *http://www.kommersant.ru/doc.html? docId=521543.*

45. Yugansk's capital structure consisted of 75 per cent voting shares and 25 per cent non-voting. Only the voting shares were sold. On the debate around the proper discount for the sale of only a proportion of shares, see Irina Reznik and Ekaterina Derbilova, 'Deshevle nekuda', *Vedomosti*, 15 October 2004, *http://www.vedomosti.ru/newspaper/print.shtml?2004/10/15/ 82193.* For detail on the valuation process as a whole, see also Denis Skorobogat'ko, ' "Iuganskneftegazu" naznachali krainuiu tsenu', *Kommersant*, 15 October 2004, *http://www.kommersant.ru/doc.html?docId=515355.*

46. Denis Skorobogat'ko, Dmitrii Butrin and Nikolai Kovalev, ' "Iugansk" kupili liudi iz "Londona" ', *Kommersant*, 20 December 2004, *http://www.kommer-sant.ru/doc.html?docid=534631.*

47. Aleksandr Tutushkin, Ekaterina Derbilova and Rodion Levinskii, 'Kitai ne kho-chet rasstavat'sia s "IuKOSom" ', *Vedomosti*, 20 August 2004, *http://www.vedo-mosti.ru/newspaper/print.shtml?2004/08/20/79823*; Aleksandr Tutushkin and Rodion Levinskii, ' "IuKOS" idet ko dnu', *Vedomosti*, 30 December 2004, *http://www.vedomosti.ru/newspaper/print.shtml?2004/12/30/ 85426.*

48. Irina Reznik and Ekaterina Derbilova, 'Esli zavtra pasprodazha', *Vedomosti*, 27 September 2004, *http://www.vedomosti.ru/newspaper/print.shtml?2004/09/27/81362.*

Note that Putin is quoted as having told Western investors in the same month that 'no Rosnefts (*nikakaia Rosneft'*) can possibly buy Yukos'. Vitalii Ivanov, Svetlana Ivanova, Irina Reznik, Ekaterina Derbilova and Vasilii Kashin, 'Absoliutno legal'nyi peredel', *Vedomosti*, 24 December 2004, *http://www.vedomosti.ru/newspaper/print.shtml?2004/12/24/85155*.

49. Dmitrii Butrin, Pavel Prezhentsev and Iulii Chaikina, 'Skupka IuKOSa stala delom internatsional'nogo dolga', *Kommersant*, 8 December 2004, *http://www. kommersant.ru/doc.html?docId=531802*.

50. Dmitrii Butrin, ' "Gazprom" ostalsia bez sponsorov', *Kommersant*, 17 December 2004, *http://www.kommersant.ru/doc.html?docId=534164*.

51. Denis Skorobogat'ko, Dmitrii Butrin and Nikolai Kovalev, ' "Iugansk" kupili liudi iz "Londona" ', *Kommersant*, 20 December 2004, *http://www.kommersant. ru/ doc.html?docid=53431*.

52. Denis Skorobogat'ko, Dmitrii Butrin and Nikolai Kovalev, ' "Iugansk" kupili liudi iz "Londona" ', *Kommersant*, 20 December 2004, *http://www.kommersant.ru/doc.html?docid=534631*.

53. Ekaterina Derbilova, Irina Reznik and Svetlana Petrova, 'Pobeditel', pokhozhii na "Surgutneftegaz" ', *Vedomosti*, 21 December 2004, *http://www.vedomosti.ru/newspaper/print.shtml?2004/12/21/85020*.

54. Anna Nikolaeva, Irina Reznik, Ekaterina Derbilova and Mikhail Overchenko, 'Liudi prezidenta', *Vedomosti*, 22 December 2004, *http://www.vedomosti.ru/newspaper/print.shtml?2004/12/22/85038*.

55. Irina Reznik, Ekaterina Derbilova and Tat'iana Egorova, 'Pod kryshu "Rosneft' " ', *Vedomosti*, 24 December 2004, *http://www.vedomosti.ru/newspaper/print.shtml?2004/12/24/85154*. The identities of the *fizicheskie litsa* have, to the best of the author's knowledge, never been revealed.

56. Ekaterina Derbilova and Boris Safronov, ' "Rosneft" vyruchil vneshnii dolg', *Vedomosti*, 15 August 2005, *http://www.vedomosti.ru/newspaper/print.shtml?2005/08/15/95809*.

57. Irina Reznik, Ekaterina Derbilova and Tat'iana Egorova, 'Pod kryshu "Rosneft' " ', *Vedomosti*, 24 December 2004, *http://www.vedomosti.ru/newspaper/print.shtml?2004/12/24/85154*.

58. Ekaternia Derbilova, Irina Reznik and Aleksandr Bekker, ' "Gazpromu" nuzhen "Iugansk" ', *Vedomosti*, 28 February 2005, *http://www.vedomosti.ru/newspaper/print.shtml?2005/02/28/88006*.

59. Ekaterina Derbilova, Irina Reznik and Andrei Panov, 'Milliardy dlia "Gazproma" ', *Vedomosti*, 18 May 2005, *http://www.vedomosti.ru/newspaper/print.shtml?2005/05/18/92164*.

60. Gazprom paid around $3.20 per barrel of reserves, which compares to the $1.25 per barrel that Rosneft paid for Yugansk (and the $1.80 that BP paid for its share in TNK-BP). Catherine Belton, 'Gazprom Scoops Up Sibneft for $13Bln', *Russia Profile.org*, 29 September 2005, *http://www.russiaprofile.org/business/2005/9/29/390.wb*, accessed 6 March 2006.

61. Aleksandr Tutushkin et al., 'V "Iuganske" novyi khoziain', *Vedomosti*, 11 January 2005, *http://www.vedomosti.ru/newspaper/print.shtml?2005/01/11/85475*. At one stage Yukos's Gerashchenko tried claiming that all Yugansk's plant belonged to Yukos. Maksim Shilov, 'Bol'shoi surpriz ot Yukosa', *Politcom.ru*, 22 March 2005, *http://www.politcom.ru/2005 /gvozd584.php*.

62. Dmitrii Butrin, Elena Kiseleva and Evgenyi Khvostik, 'Gruppa isk', *Kommersant*, 14 December 2004, *http://www.kommersant.ru/doc.html?docId=533085*.

63. Irina Reznik, ' "Rosneft'" khochet bol'she', *Vedomosti*, 20 July 2005, *http://www.vedomosti.ru/newspaper/article.shtml?2005/07/20/94834*.

64. 'Chelovek-milliardik', *Kommersant*, 7 July 2005, *http://www.kommersant.ru/doc.html?docId=589303*.

65. Ekaterina Derbilova and Irina Reznik, ' "Rosneft'" prosit mir', *Vedomosti*, 14 January 2005, *http://www.vedomosti.ru/newspaper/print.shtml?2005/01/14/85663*.

66. Aleksandr Tutushkin and Nikolai Borisov, 'Novaia pobeda "Iuganska", *Vedomosti*, 11 October 2005, *http://www.vedomosti.ru/newspaper/ print.shtml? 2005/10/11/98112*.

67. Anna Skorniakova, Denis Skorobogat'ko and Alena Miklashevskaia, 'Rosnefti prostiat nalogovyi dolg IuKOSa', *Kommersant*, 25 November 2005, *http://www.kommersant.ru/doc.html?docId=629602*.

68. Ekaterina Derbilova and Irina Reznik, ' "Iugansk" priviazhet pokrepche', *Vedomosti*, 10 March 2005, *http://www.vedomosti.ru/newspaper/print.shtml?2005/03/10/89291*; Ekaterina Derbilova and Anastasiia Bokova, ' "Iugansk" malo zarabotal', *Vedomosti*, 17 November 2005, *http://www.vedomosti.ru/newspaper/print.shtml?2005/11/17/99632*.

69. Irina Reznik and Ekaterina Derbilova, 'Otvetnyi udar', *Vedomosti*, 1 June 2005, *http://www.vedomosti.ru/newspaper/print.shtml?2005/06/01/92809*; Denis Skorobogat'ko, 'IuKOS prizval k otvetu', *Kommersant*, 1 June 2005, *http://www.kommersant.ru/doc.html?docId=582036*.

70. Irina Reznik and Nikolai Borisov, 'Kreml' zovut v sud', *Vedomosti*, 26 October 2005, *http://www.vedomosti.ru/newspaper/print.shtml?2005/10/26/98775*.

71. Mikhail Khodorkovskii, 'Tiur'ma i mir: sobstvennost' i svoboda', *Vedomosti*, 28 December 2004, *http://www.vedomosti.ru/newspaper/print.shtml?2004/12/28/85295*. 'Basmannyi justice' has become the post-Soviet equivalent of the Soviet term 'telephone justice', meaning a justice system which is under the control of the poltiical authorities. The charges against Lebedev and Khodorkovsky were heard in the court of the Basmannyi district of Moscow.

72. Nikolai Borisov, ' "Iugansk" za IuKOS ne otvechaet', *Vedomosti*, 20 March 2006, *http://www.vedomosti.ru/newspaper/print.shtml?2006/03/20/104162*.

73. Ol'ga Pleshanova, 'Sud nashel upravu na IuKOS', *Kommersant*, 29 March 2006, *http://www.kommersant.ru/doc.html?docId=661633*.

74. Ol'ga Pleshanova and Denis Rebrov, 'Kreditory prigovorili IuKOS', *Kommersant*, 26 July 2006, *http://www.Kommersant.ru/doc.html?docId=692789*

75. Ekaterina Zapodinskaia, ' "Menia khot' seichas mogut zaderzhat' na 48 chasov" ', *Kommersant*, 4 April 2006, *http://www.kommersant.ru/content.html?IssueId=30059*

76. Vladislav Trifonov, 'Novyi vitse-prezident IuKOS uspel skazat', *Kommersant*, 6 April 2006, *http://www.kommersant.ru/doc.html?docId=664057*; Vladislav Trifonov, 'Genprokuratura slozhila prezidentskie polnomochiia', *Kommersant*, 7 April 2006, *http://www.komersant.ru/doc.html?docId=664463*.

77. For references to such a view, see Vladimir Shlapentokh, 'Wealth Versus Political Power: the Russian case', *Communist and Post-Communist Studies*, vol. 37, 2004, p.137.

78. It is worth recalling that in 1999 the oligarchs, or at least the Family element of the group, had been able to get rid of a Prosecutor General who had taken them on. It was Putin, as head of the FSB, who arranged for the public disgrace of the unfortunate Skuratov by having a video aired on TV showing him, or 'someone who closely resembled him', in bed with two prostitutes.

Paul Klebnikov, *Godfather of the Kremlin. Boris Berezovsky and the looting of Russia*, Harcourt, New York, 2000, p.297.

79. For example 'Ot redaktsii: poriadok v sudakh', *Vedomosti*, 28 October 2003, *http://www.vedomosti.ru/stories/2003/10/78-47-01.html*

80. Vitalii Ivanov et al., 'Absoliutno legal'nyi peredel', *Vedomosti*, 24 December 2004, *http://www.vedomosti.ru/newspaper/print.shtml?2004/12/24/85155*.

81. 'Putin says state should avoid bankrupting Yukos', *RFE/RL Newsline*, vol.8, no. 115, Part 1, 18 June 2004.

82. Another case of Putin's words not being heeded is his early statement that he did not believe that people should be held without bail on chages of economic crimes. Yukos officials continued long after those statements to be arrested without bail. The prosecutor's office might have been encouraged in doing so by Putin's defence of the holding of Lebedev without bail, despite his general opposition to the practice, because, he claimed, the Yukos executive had been hiding from the authorities in hospital. Ekaterina Zapodinskaia and Nikolai Bardul', Genprokuratura poluchila kryshu', *Kommersant*, 10 October 2003, *http://www.kommersant.ru/archive/archive-material.html? docld=418471*.

83. Khodorkovsky claims that he always gained the approval of the Kremlin for his political funding. Kirill Rogov, 'Politekonomiia: nashe mylo', *Vedomosti*, 9 July 2003, *http://www.vedomosti.ru/stories/2003/07/09-47-03.html*. He expressed it slightly differently, that he would have been prepared to withdraw funding if asked, in 'Seichas mne prikhoditsia ezdit' v Kreml' chashche, chem ia privyk', *Kommersant*, 7 July 2003, *http://www.kommersant.ru/archive/archive-material.html?docld=394029*.

84. Anders Oslund [Åslund], 'Investory i IuKOS: pora opuskat' zanaves', *Vedomosti*, 28 July 2003, *http://www.vedomosti.ru/stories/2003/07/28-47-04.html*; 'Tanets dlia dvoikh', *Ekspert*, 22 September 2003, *http://www.expert. ru/politics/2003/09/35ex-serafim*.

85. Khodorkovsky claims that Putin is not the type of person to be ruffled by vigorous debate. However the attention the matter received in the state-controlled media did put him on his guard. ' "Seichas mne prikhoditsia ezdit' v Kreml' chashche, chem ia privyk" ', *Kommersant*, 7 July 2003, *http:// www.kommersant.ru/archive/archive-material.html?docld=394029*.

86. As Mikhail Deliagin puts it: 'The annihilation of "YUKOS" is the embodiment of the immaturity of the Russian bureaucracy, which feels its inability to cooperate with business in a civilized way and cannot give up interaction on the basis of "Hey, you, come here!" '. 'Strana i neft': chernoe zoloto partii', *Vedomosti*, 16 August 2004, *http://www.vedomosti.ru/newspapers/article.shtml?2004/08/16/79618*.

87. Khodorkovsky admits to having rarely agreed with Putin, and says, seemingly with reference to all the oligarchs: 'Again, it's unlikely that we are attractive to him or arouse in him the warmest emotions'. This was said in an interview done in February 2002 but published only in June 2005. 'Mikhail Khodorkovskii: Rokfelleru bylo namnogo tiazhelee', *Kommersant*, 1 June 2005, *http://www.kommersant.ru/doc.html?docld=582013*.

88. Perhaps it was the fate of two couriers in the Kurtsin case to be described in the next chapter who were prepared to cooperate with the prosecution but nevertheless received seven-year sentences that suggested to the others that surrender would do them no good. But those sentences seem to have been a case of a judge 'overfulfilling the plan', since even the prosecutor found the

sentences harsh. Ekaterina Zapodinskaia, 'Prokuratura oprotestovala srok raskhititeliami deneg luKOSa', *Kommersant*, 16 December 2005, http://www.*Kommersant.ru/doc.html? DocID=636170&IssueId=23588*.

89. 'Ot redaktsii: Vozvrat k proshlomu', *Vedomosti*, 18 November 2003, *http://www.vedomosti.ru/stories/2003/11/18-47-02.html*.

90. Andrei Pionkovskii, 'Nashe vse', *Politcom.ru*, 14 November 2003, url not available.

91. For example, 'Ot redaktsii: nadezhda na MAP', *Vedomosti*, 6 October 2003, *http://www.vedomosti.ru/stories/2003/10/06-47-01.html*.

92. On Voloshin's hints, see Anfisa Voronina, 'Putin ishchet vykhod', *Vedomosti*, 31 July 2003, *http://www.vedomosti.ru/stories/2003/07/31-55-01.html*. For Illarionov's, see Iraida Semenova, 'Andrei Illarionov: so vremeni my uznaem bol'she', *Rossiiskaia gazeta*, 4 December 2003, *http://www.rg.ru/2003/12/04/ illarionov.html*.

93. Irina Reznik, Dmitrii Simakov and Rodion Levinskii, ' "IuKOS" razrushili troe', *Vedomosti*, 18 April 2005, *http://www.vedomosti.ru/newspaper/ print.shtml?2005/04/18/90921*. In an earlier interview Nevzlin had strongly implied that Putin was behind the whole thing, and refused to be drawn on Abramovich's role, although not hiding his distaste for the Sibneft owner. Iuliia Bushueva, 'Interv'iu: Leonid Nevzlin, osnovnoi benefitsiar Group Menatep', *Vedomosti*, 19 January 2005, *http://www.vedomosti.ru/newspaper/ print.shtml?2005/01/19/85829*.

94. Tat'iana Stanovaia, 'Kamchatka stanet Chukotkoi', *Politcom.ru*, 10 August 2005, *http://www.politcom.ru/2005/gvozd680.php*.

95. 'Priglashenie "IuKOSa" na kazn': v roli topora – Bogdanchikov', *Novaia gazeta*, 17 July 2003, *http://2003.NovayaGazeta.Ru/nomer/2003/51n/n51n-s00.shtml*.

96. [Kris Uifer] Chris Weafer, 'Geroi Dostoevskogo: Putin i Khodorkovskii', *Vedomosti*, 23 May 2005, *http://www.vedomosti.ru/newspaper/print.shtml?2005/ 05/23/92362*.

97. Olga Kryshtanovskaya and Stephen White, 'Inside the Putin court: a research note', *Europe-Asia Studies*, vol. 57, no. 7, November 2005, p. 1072.

98. Kryshtanovskaya and White, 'Inside the Putin Court', p.1072.

99. Andrei Kozenko, 'Biznes-plan russkogo antiglobalizma', *Kommersant*, 6 December 2005, *http://www.kommersant.ru/doc.html?docId=632741*.

100. 'Putin Says Business Climate being Made More Orderly', *RFE/RL Newsline*, vol. 4, no. 134, Part 1, 14 July 2000.

101. Svetlana Ivanova, Anna Nikolaeva and Anastasiia Onegina, ' "IuKOS" – ne poslednii', *Vedomosti*, 29 October 2004, *http://www.vedomosti.ru/newspaper/ print.shtml?2004/10/29/82786*. In a comment on the suggestion that Khodorkovsky could avoid prosecution by offering to pay off his tax debts, Putin had declared that such an approach was unacceptable and obtained the required legislation in November 2003. (Lukoil had been allowed to pay as advised by Shuvalov in the Baikonur case). Vitalii Ivanov, 'Duma raskaialas", *Vedomosti*, 24 November 2003, *http://www.vedomosti.ru/stories/ 2003/11/24-55-02.html*.

102. 'Tax Collections Rise following Yukos Case', *RFE/RL Newsline*, vol. 9, no. 149, Part 1, 9 August 2005.

103. Boris Grozovskii, Tat'iana Egorova and Svetlana Ivanova, 'Pochti Gollandiia', *Vedomosti*, 22 March 2005. *http://www.vedomosti.ru/newspaper/print. shtml?2005/03/22/89730*.

104. Irina Reznik, 'Preobrazhenie', *Vedomosti*, 17 May 2005, *http://www.vedomosti. ru/ newspaper/print.shtml?2005/05/17/92138*.
105. Boris Grozovskii, ' "IuKOS" ne odin', *Vedomosti*, 10 October 2005, *http://www.vedomosti.ru/newspaper/print.shtml?2005/10/10/98041*.
106. Svetlana Ivanova, 'Kas'ianov opredelil sverkhpribyl'', *Vedomosti*, 26 December 2003, *http://www.vedomosti.ru/stories/2003/12/26-68-01.html*.
107. Maksim Shilov, 'Sobrat' nalogi pomog "effekt Iukosa" ', *Politcom.ru*, 8 August 2005, *http://www.politcom.ru/2005/zloba5885.php*.
108. 'Ot redaktsii: peredelai oligarkha', *Vedomosti*, 10 October 2005, *http://www.vedomosti.ru/newspaper/print.shtml?2005/10/10/98032*.
109. 'A Survey of Russia', *The Economist*, 22 May 2004, p.5.
110. Anastasiia Onegina, Vitalii Ivanov and Dmitrii Simakov, 'Reshili ne mel'chit', *Vedomosti*, 22 July 2003, *http://www/vedomosti.ru/stories/2003/07/ 22-55-01.html*.
111. 'Kudrin – eto Lenin segodnia', *Ekspert*, 26 April 2004, *http://www.expert.ru/ expert/current/data/redak.shtml*; Tat'iana Stanovaia, 'Biznes i vlast': nachalo bol'shogo torga', *Politcom.ru*, 26 April 2004, *http://www.politcom.ru/ print.php*.
112. Tat'iana Stanovaia, 'Smena skhem', *Politcom.ru*, 7 June 2004, *http:// www.politcom.ru/2004/zloba4262.php*; Ol'ga Proskurnina and Igor' Fediukin, 'Deripaska predosteregaet', *Vedomosti*, 11 February 2004, *http://www. vedomosti.ru/stories/2004/02/11-68-02.html*.

8   The Aftermath of Yukos

1. Bernard Black, Reiner Kraakman and Anna Tarassova, 'Russian Privatization and Corporate Governance: what went wrong?', *Stanford Law Review*, vol. 52, 1999–2000, pp. 1799–1801.
2. Pol Khlebnikov (Paul Klebnikov), 'Delo "IuKOSa": vekha na puti k zakonnosti', *Vedomosti*, 18 November 2003, *http://www.vedomosti.ru/stories/2003/ 11/18–47–05.html*.
3. Sergei Guriev and Andrei Rachinsky, 'The Role of Oligarchs in Russian Capitalism', *Journal of Economic Perspectives*, vol. 19, no. 1, Winter 2005, p.147.
4. Willem Buiter, 'From Predation to Accumulation? The second transition decade in Russia', *Economics of Transition*, vol. 8, no. 3, 2000, p.607.
5. Marshall I. Goldman, 'Anders in Wonderland: comments on Russia's economic transformation under Putin', *Eurasian Geography and Economics*, vol. 45, no. 6, 2004, p.434.
6. One group of critics, in calling for some exemplary justice, suggest that aid to Russia should be made conditional on 'putting a respectable number of corrupt officials and kleptocrats in jail.' Whether they believe the numbers arrested since mid-2003 to be 'respectable' is not known. Black, Kraakman and Tarassova, 'Russian privatization', pp. 1799, 1801.
7. Svetlana Ivanova and Anastasia Onegina, 'Neftianiki nastupaiut', *Vedomosti*, 10 February 2004, *http://www.vedomosti.ru/stories/2004/02/10–68-01.html*.
8. Igor' Nikolaev, 'Ekonomicheskii rost: sviazannye odnoi dogmoi', *Vedomosti*, 24 March 2005, *http://www.vedomosti.ru/newspaper/print.shtml?2005/03/24/ 89846*; Aleksandr Bekker, Boris Grozovskii and Mikhail Overchenko, 'Velel prostit', *Vedomosti*, 26 April 2005, *http://www.vedomosti.ru/newspaper/print. shtml?2005/04/26/91281*.

9. Aleksei Shapovalov, 'Aleksei Kudrin nagovoril s tri goda', *Kommersant*, 7 December 2005, *http://www.kommersant.ru/doc.html?docid=633106*.
10. For some details on domestic and investments abroad in the metals sector, see Iuliia Fedorinova, 'Konsolidatsii – net', *Vedomosti*, 29 December 2005, *http://www.vedomosti.ru/newspaper/article.shtml?2005/12/29/101401*; Iuliia Fedorinova, 'Pokhod na Zapad', 2 June 2005, *http://www.vedomosti.ru/newspaper/print.shtml?2005/06/02/92886*.
11. Stephen Fortescue, 'The Russian Aluminum Industry in Transition', *Eurasian Geography and Economics*, vol. 47, no. 1, 2006, p.89.
12. Tat'iana Gurova, 'Ne ochen' dlinnaia pauza', *Ekspert*, 17 November 2003, *http://www.expert.ru/expert/current/data/tema-2.shtml*.
13. Conrad de Aenlle, 'Russia's Oil Industry Caught in a Tug of War', *NYTimes.com*, 9 November 2003.
14. Natal'ia Ratnikova, 'Vtorogo Iukosa S&P ne vyderzhit', *Politcom.ru*, 26 April 2005, *http://www.politcom.ru/2005/zloba5536.php*.
15. In a letter to Putin the US investment funds wrote: 'If the minorities lose their investments, that places in doubt the protection of private property rights and the rights of investors in Russia. And ordinary Russians will see that the state in the pursuit of its own ends will not stop even at the manipulation of the courts'. 'Cherez dvoinuiu sploshnuiu', *Ekspert*, 12 July 2004, *http://www.expert.ru/expert/current/data/titan__2.shtml*.
16. 'Interv'iu: Vagit Alekperov, president NK "LUKOIL" ', *Vedomosti*, 11 July 2005, *http://www.vedomosti.ru/newspaper/print.shtml?2005/07/11/94500*.
17. 'TNK-BP Officials Continue Assault on Government at London Forum', *RFE/RL Newsline*, vol. 9, no. 69, Part 1, 13 April 2005.
18. *Komu prinadlezhit Rossiia*, Vagrius, Moscow, 2003, pp.199–203.
19. 'President Calls for Tax Increases on Oil Sector's "Super Profits" ', *RFE/RL Newsline*, vol. 7, no. 238, Part 1, 19 December 2003.
20. 'Vopros dnia: ch'e bremia tiazhelee?', *Vedomosti*, 4 February 2004, *www.vedomosti.ru/stories/2004/02/04–08–01.html*.
21. Aleksandr Bekker, 'Nalogovaia reforma vernetsia v ianvare', *Vedomosti*, 6 December 2002, *http://www.kapital.ru/stories/2002/12/06–68–01.html*.
22. Aleksandr Bekker, 'Nalogovaia reforma ne dlia vsekh', *Vedomosti*, 31 January 2003, *http://www.kapital.ru/stories/2003/01/31–55–02.html*; Svetlana Ivanova, 'Kas'ianov opredelil sverkhpribyl", *Vedomosti*, 26 December 2003, *http://www.vedomosti.ru/stories/2003/12/26–68–01.html*.
23. Svetlana Ivanova and Anastasiia Onegina, 'Neftianiki nastupaiut', *Vedomosti*, 10 February 2004, *http://www.vedomosti.ru/stories/2004/02/10–68–01.html*; Boris Grozovskii, 'Nalogi vmeste investitsii', *Vedomosti*, 3 November 2004, *http://www.vedomosti.ru/newspaper/print.shtml?2004/11/03/83019*.
24. Aleksandr Bekker, 'Predpriiatiiam dobavili $20 mlrd', *Vedomosti*, 27 May 2003, available at *http://www.vedomosti.ru/stories/2003/05/27–68–01.html*.
25. One notes that Alfa has quickly turned into cash the BP equity it gained in the TNK-BP joint venture. This, though, might have been as much to shore up its shaky banking assets or to finance a strategic diversification into telecommunications as the cash-hungry greed of the individuals involved. Tat'iana Egorova, Aleksandr Bekker and Anastasiia Onegina, 'Rasprodazha na $2 mlrd', *Vedomosti*, 15 December 2004, *http://www.vedomosti.ru/newspaper/article.shtml?2004/12/15/84773*.

26. 'Vopros dnia: ch'e bremia tiazhelee?', *Vedomosti*, 4 February 2004, *www. vedomosti.ru/stories/2004/02/04-08-01.html*.

27. Anastasiia Onegina, 'Pora schitat' poteri', *Vedomosti*, 24 December 2003, *http://www.vedomosti.ru/stories/2003/12/24-68-01.html*.

28. 'Slushalis'. Postanovili', *Kommersant*, 20 March 2004, *http://www. kommersant. ru/doc.html?docId=459274*.

29. Vadim Visloguzov and Alena Kornysheva, 'Pravitel'stvo zavershilo predstar-tovuiu podgotovku nalogovoi reformy', *Kommersant*, 8 April 2004, *http://www. kommersant.ru/doc.html?docId=464685*.

30. Aleksandr Bekker and Aleksandra Petrachkova, 'Nalogovye kanikuly', *Vedomosti*, 12 September 2005, *http://www.vedomosti.ru/newspaper/article. shtml?2005/09/12/96889*; 'As Energy Minister Asks Putin for Tax Relief for Oil Producers', *RFE/RL Newsline*, vol. 9, no. 179, Part 1, 21 September 2005.

31. Aleksandra Petrachkova and Ekaterina Derbilova, 'Putin pomog nef-tianikam', *Vedomosti*, 17 January 2006, *http://www.vedomosti.ru/newspaper/ print.shtml?2006/01/17/101693*.

32. Aleksandra Petrachkova, 'Neftianoi nalog sniziat', *Vedomosti*, 11 October 2005, *http://www.vedomosti.ru/newspaper/print.shtml?2005/10/11/98081*.

33. In April 2005 the Minister for Economic Development and Trade German Gref declared that tax rates in the metals sector had been neglected in all the debate around the oil industry, and that his ministry was considering ways of shifting some of the tax burden from oil to metals. He admitted that he was reacting to proposals from oil companies. Svetlana Ivanova, 'K Grefu prishel apetit', *Vedomosti*, 7 April 2005, *http://www.vedomosti.ru/newspaper/print. shtml?2005/04/07/90497*.

34. 'Ot redaktsii: partiia "IuKOSa"', *Vedomosti*, 1 March 2004, *http://www. vedomosti.ru/stories/2004/03/01–47–01.html*; Ekaterina Zapodinskaia, 'Advokaty otstavili protokol', *Kommersant*, 24 August 2004, *http://www.kommersant.ru/ doc.html?docId=499924*.

35. Natal'ia Neimysheva, 'Prokurory na zashchite biznesa', *Vedomosti*, 4 April 2003, *http://www.vedomosti.ru/stories/2003/04/04–55–01.html*.

36. Dmitrii Butrin and Vadim Visloguzov, 'Otdat', *Kommersant*, 27 May 2004, *http://www.kommersant.ru/doc.html?docId=477998*.

37. 'Ot redaktsii: Sodom i Gomorra' *Vedomosti*, 4 December 2003, *http://www. vedomosti.ru/stories/2003/12/04–47–01.html*.

38. Dmitrii Butrin, 'V "Sibnefti" proshel den' doznanii', *Kommersant*, 14 October 2003, *http://www.kommersant.ru/archive/archive-material.html?docid=419309*.

39. Marina Lepina, ' "V dele otsutstvuiut dannye o protivopravnykh deistviiakh Platona Lebedeva" ', *Kommersant*, 26 January 2005, *http://www.kommersant.ru/ doc.html?docId=541949*.

40. The government's VAT claims are highly contentious in themselves. The issue of the liability of exporters to VAT is immensely complicated and undoubtedly involves some very dubious behaviour by 'false exporters'. But a company as public as Yukos would have good grounds to believe that the VAT claims are spurious. In the Yukos case they are based on the technicality that Yukos itself did not sign the VAT documentation, but rather the front companies through which Yukos conducted its operations. One of the con-tentious issues in the case against Yukos was its liability for the actions of these companies. It seems that their signing VAT documentation was the one

thing which was not taken as being carried out on Yukos's behalf. Boris Grozovsky, 'Luchshe podgotovilis', *Vedomosti*, 30 July 2004, *http://www.vedomosti.ru/newspaper/print.shtml?2004/07/79025*; Boris Grozovskii, ' "IuKOS" vyzyvaet k logike', *Vedomosti*, 26 August 2004, *http://www.vedomosti.ru/newspaper/print.shtml?2004/08/26/80070*.

41. Svetlana Ivanova, 'Udarniki iz FNS', *Vedomosti*, 3 November 2004, *http://www.vedomosti.ru/newspaper/print.shtml?2004/11/03/83008*. 'Ot redaktsii: nikogda ne pozdno', *Vedomosti*, 21 April 2005, *http://www/vedomosti.ru/ newspaper/article.shtml?2005/04/21/91100*.

42. Ekaterina Zapodinskaia, 'Prezumptsiia podchinennosti', *Kommersant*, 11 December 2004, *http://www.kommersant.ru/doc.html?docId=532860*.

43. Marina Lepina, 'Advokat rastsenil dokhody Svetlany Bakhminoi', *Kommersant*, 4 April 2006, *http://www.kommersant.ru/doc.html?DocID= 663521&IssueId=30059*; Marina, Lepina, 'Advokaty vstupilis' za detei iurista IuKOSa', *Kommersant*, 5 April: 2006, *http://www.kommersant.ru/doc.html? DocID=663927&IssueId=30060*; Anastasiia Kornia, 'Sem' let za ispolnenie ukazanii', *Vedomosti*, 20 April 2006, *http://www.vedomosti.ru/newspaper/ article.shtml?2006/04/20/105558*.

44. Ekaterina Zapodinskaia, 'Prokuratura oprotestovala srok raskhititeliami deneg IuKOSa', *Kommersant*, 16 December 2005, *http://www.kommersant.ru/doc.html?DocID=636170&issueId=23588*. It appears that the custodial sentences for the couriers were confirmed on appeal. Aleksandr Turov, 'Sazhat' vopreki vsemu i vsia', *Vedomosti*, 28 April 2006, *http://www.vedomosti.ru/newspaper/article.shtml?2006/04/28/105991*.

45. Ekaterina Zapodinskaia, 'Prezumptsiia podchinennosti', *Kommersant*, 11 December 2004, *http://www.kommersant.ru/doc.html?docId=532860*.

46. In a March 2005 meeting with business Putin stated: 'The tax authorities do not have the right to terrorise business. They must work steadily ... paying the greatest attention to audits of the current year'. They cannot ignore violations of the law, but should find ways of allowing the paying off of tax arrears that 'do not destroy the economy and drive business into a deadend'. Anna Nikolaeva and Boris Grozovskii, 'Prostranstvo dlia biznesa', *Vedomosti*, 26 April 2005, *http://www.vedomosti.ru/newspaper/print.shtml?2005/04/ 26/91295*.

47. 'Ot redaksii: vospitanie chuvstv', *Vedomosti*, 30 March 2005, *http://www.vedomosti.ru/newspaper/print.shtml?2005/03/30/90162*.

48. 'Ot redaktsii: posle pravosudiia', *Vedomosti*, 1 June 2005, *http://www.vedomosti.ru/newspaper/print.shtml?2005/06/01/92788*.

49. It should be noted that Kostina herself has no doubt that Nevzlin was responsible. 'Prosecutor-General's Office Brings New Murder Charges Against Yukos Security Official', *RFE/RL Newsline*, vol. 9, no. 128, Part 1, 11 July 2005.

50. Aleksandr Zheglov, 'Chisto oligarkhicheskoe ubiistvo', *Kommersant*, 27 July 2004, *http://www.kommersant.ru/doc.html?docId=492832*; Aleksei Nikol'skii, 'Pichuginu dali 20 let', *Vedomosti*, 31 March 2005, *http://www.vedomosti.ru/ newspaper/print.shtml?2005/03/31/90176*.

51. Aleksei Nikol'skii and Anfisa Voronina, 'Nevzlinu dobavili obvinenie', *Vedomosti*, 6 July 2005, *http://www.vedomosti.ru/newspaper/print. shtml?2005/07/06/94321*.

52. Larisa Rychkova, 'Nefteiugansk zaiavil o sebe pokusheniem', *Kommersant*, 21 September 2005, *http://www.kommersant.ru/doc.html?docId=610684*;

'Prosecutors investigate death of local official', *RFE/RL Newsline*, vol. 10,no. 4, Part 1, 10 January 2006.

53. On other murder and attempted murder charges against Pichugin, see Vladislav Trifonov, 'Podel'niki Alekseia Pichugina meniaiut zashchitu', *Kommersant*, 4 April 2006, *http://www.kommersant.ru/doc.html?DocId=663255& IssueId=30059.*

54. 'Ot redaktsii: nalogovaia zagadka', *Vedomosti*, 2 February 2005, *http://www. vedomosti.ru/newspaper/print.shtml?2005/02/02/86401*; Svetlana Ivanova and Arina Sharipova, 'Nalogovikov – v tiur'mu', *Vedomosti*, 28 December 2005, *http://www.vedomosti.ru/newspaper/article.shtml?2005/12/ 28/101317.*

55. Galina Liashenko, 'Razgovor dorozhe deneg', *Kommersant*, 21 April 2005, *http://www.kommersant.ru/doc.html?docId=572283*; Mariia Tikhomirova, 'Ne khochu delit'sia', *Ekspert*, 26 September 2005, *http://www.expert.ru/expert/ current/data/36-tishk.shtml.*

56. Boris Grozovskii, 'Kak "podvesti chertu" ', *Vedomosti*, 20 December 2004, *http://www.vedomosti.ru/newspaper/print.shtml?2004/12/20/84967.*

57. On this particular approach to 'paying' tax, see William Tompson, 'Nothing Learned, Nothing Forgotten: restructuring without reform in Russia's banking sector', in Stefanie Harter and Gerald Easter (eds), *Shaping the Economic Space in Russia. Decision making processes, institutions and adjustment to change in the El'tsin era*, Ashgate, Aldershot, 2000, pp.78–9.

58. 'Ot redaktsii: slovotvorchestvo', *Vedomosti*, 9 June 2004, *http://www. vedomosti.ru/newspaper/print.shtml?2004/06/09/76902.*

59. Dmitrii Butrin, 'Sroki davnosti bol'she ne deistvuiut', *Kommersant*, 18 March 2005, *http://www.kommersant.ru/doc.html?docId=555663.*

60. ' "IuKOSu my vsego lish' nachali vydvygat' pretenzii" ', *Kommersant*, 5 May 2004, *http://www.kommersant.ru/doc.html?docId=471931*. When asked what those precedents might be, Kudrin referred to the Lukoil-Baikonur case. That case was settled out of court before the legal process was exhausted.

61. Boris Grozovskii, 'Uroki "IuKOSa" ', *Vedomosti*, 8 June 2004, *http://www. vedomosti.ru/newspaper/print.shtml?2004/06/08/76821.*

62. Aleksandr Tutushkin and Natalia Neimysheva, 'Baikonur Comes Back to Bite "Lukoil" ', *OILUA.com nefteportal*, 16 August 2002, *http://www.oilua.com/ show.php?id=1356*, downloaded 11 August 2004.

63. Vadim Visloguzov, 'Nalogi perekhodiat na lichnosti', *Kommersant*, 2 June 2005, *http://www.kommersant.ru/doc.html?docId=582465.*

64. Svetlana Ivanova and Boris Grozovsky, 'Po zapakhu', *Vedomosti*, 9 July 2004, *http://www.vedomosti.ru/newspaper/print.shtml?2004/07/09/78246.*

65. Natal'ia Ratnikova, 'Zaplatiat vse', *Politcom.ru*, 28 October 2004, *http://www.politcom.ru/2004/zloba4871.php.*

66. 'Ot redaktsii: peresmotr prava', *Vedomosti*, 27 February 2004, *http://www. vedomosti.ru/stories/2004/02/27-47-01.html.*

67. Vadim Visloguzov, 'Uklonenie ot nalogov mozhno otlichit' ot optimizatsii', *Kommersant*, 2 June 2005, *http://www.kommersant.ru/doc.html?docId=582556*; Svetlana Ivanova, 'Zakon o "khoroshikh" skhemakh', *Vedomosti*, 22 September 2004, *http://www.vedomosti.ru/newspaper/print.shtml?2004/09/22/81196.*

68. Svetlana Ivanova, 'Sud priznal, chto "IuKOS" meshal nalogovikam', *Vedomosti*, 5 October 2005, *http://www.vedomosti.ru/newspaper/print.shtml?2005/10/05/ 97881.*

69. There has been much discussion of what many see as the removal of the presumption of innocence in tax cases. This is based on Ministry of Finance proposals that the tax office have the right to levy fines without, as is currently required, a court order. But the fines being talked of are small, and so it is not an issue directly applicable to oligarch tax affairs. Boris Grozovskii, 'Sud ne nuzhen', *Vedomosti*, 24 January 2005, *http://www.vedomosti.ru/newspaper/print.shtml?2005/01/24/85993.*

70. Boris Grozovskii, 'RSPP protiv nalogovikov', *Vedomosti*, 1 February 2005, *http://www.vedomosti.ru/newspaper/print.shtml?2005/02/01/86338.*

71. Galina Liashenko, 'Proverki na doroge', *Kommersant*, 31 March 2005, *http://www.kommersant.ru/doc.html?docId=559216.*

72. Anna Nikolaeva and Boris Grozovskii, 'Prostranstvo dlia biznesa', *Vedomosti*, 26 April 2005, *http://www.vedomosti.ru/newspaper/print.shtml?2005/04/26/91295.*

73. 'Putin Proposes Lowering Statute of Limitations on Property Deals', *RFE/RL Newsline*, vol. 9, no. 57, Part 1, 25 March 2005.

74. Galina Liashenko, 'Alekseia Kudrina podvergli vstrechnoi proverke', *Kommersant*, 14 April 2005, *http://www.kommersant.ru/doc.html?docId= 570015.*

75. Vadim Visloguzov, 'Proverochnaia rabota', *Kommersant*, 28 April 2005, *http://www.kommersant.ru/doc.html?docId=574149.*

76. Boris Grozovskii and Svetlana Ivanova, 'Bochka degtia', *Vedomosti*, 4 May 2005, *http://www.vedomosti.ru/newspaper/print.shtml?2005/05/04/91607.*

77. Galina Liashenko, 'Naezdnaia model', *Kommersant*, 10 October 2005, *http://www.kommersant.ru/doc.html?docId=616099.*

78. Irina Granik, Gosduma Otnimaet u nalogovogo terrora zakonodatel'nuiu baza', *Kommersant*, 1 July 2006, *http://www.komersent.ru/doc.html?DocID= 686954&IssueID=30135.*

79. Mikhail Yurev, a businessman with long-standing links with the Kremlin, included in a long list of 'enemies', 'anyone who says it is unnecessary to imprison the billionaires who have seized power because it is bad for the investment climate'. After the publication of that statement in the *silovik* house organ, *Komsomolsakaya Pravda*, Yurev was invited to the Kremlin for a long chat with Putin. Ol'ga Kryshtanovskaya and Stephen White, 'Inside the Putin Court: a research note', *Europe-Asia Studies*, vol. 57, no. 7, November 2005, p.1074.

80. For a good introduction to tax state theory, see Mick Moore, 'Revenues, State Formation, and the Quality of Governance in Developing Countries', *International Political Science Review*, vol. 25, no. 3, 2004, pp.297–319.

81. Petr Netreba, 'Bunt oligarkhov', *Kommersant*, 14 March 2002, p.1; Konstantin Smirnov, 'Kremlevskie pokhody oligarkhov', *Kommersant*, 23 May 2002, p.13. On support for the oligarchs from 'liberal' members of the government, see Konstantin Smirnov, 'Genprokuraturu obviniat vo vreditel'stve', *Kommersant*, 20 May 2002, pp.1 and 14.

82. Some have seen this new pact in the presidential 'State of the Union' address to the legislature in May 2005 and subsequent meetings with business representatives. In the address he referred to the impermissibility of the use of 'terror' by the tax authorities. S.P. Peregudov, *Korporativnyi kapital v mirovoi i rossiikoi politike*, Institut mirovoi ekonomiki i mezhdunarodnykh otnoshenii, Moscow, 2005, p. 89.

83. Pappe claims that the current business strategy is to combine 'political disarmament with the active lobbying of specific economic issues'. 'Iakov Pappe: "Oligarkhicheskii period zakonchen. Zabud'te" ', *Politcom.ru*, 7 October 2005, *http://www.politcom.ru/2005/business8.php*.

84. Peregudov, *Korporativnyi kapital*, pp. 88–9.

85. In nineteenth century Britain Gladstone famously created a new political culture in which the payment of tax was a signal of citizenship to be welcomed by those who became subject to it. Martin Daunton, *Trusting Leviathan. The politics of taxation in Britain, 1799–1914*, Cambridge University Press, Cambridge, 2001.

86. Ella Paneiakh, 'Pravila igry: te, kto platit', *Vedomosti*, 16 December 2003, *http://www.vedomosti.ru/stories/2003/12/16-47-03.html*.

9 Conclusion

1. For the Latin American parallel, see Aleksei Bessudnov, 'Konets illiuzii', *Ekspert Severo-Zapad*, 21 July 2003, *http://www.expert.ru/server/current/sotred.shtml*.

2. Michael L. Ross, 'The Political Economy of the Resource Curse', *World Politics*, vol. 51, no. 2, January 1999, pp.297–322. For an application of the concept of the resource curse to Russia, see *Transition Report 2001. Energy in transition*, European Bank for Reconstruction and Development, London, 2001, esp. chapter 4; Pauline Jones Luong and Erika Weinthal, 'Prelude to the Resource Curse. Explaining oil and gas development strategies in the Soviet successor states and beyond', *Comparative Political Studies*, vol. 34, no. 4, May 2000, pp.367–99.

3. Anders Åslund, 'Comparative Oligarchy: Russia, Ukraine and the United States', paper presented to the CASE conference, 'Europe after the Enlargement', Warsaw, 8–9 April 2005, pp.28–9; Marshall Goldman, 'The Rule of Outlaws is Over', *Transition*, vol. 14/15, nos 10 & 1, December 2003/April 2004, p.25. The Yabloko party has come out in favour of such a policy. 'Yavlinskii Proposes "Road Map" for Russian Reform', *RFE/RL Newsletter*, vol. 9, no. 123, Part 1, 29 June 2005. Stiglitz calls for a special capital gains tax that could be paid in shares. Maksim Rubchenko, 'Domostroi dlia biznesmena', *Ekspert*, 26 April 2004, *http://www.expert.ru/expert/current/data/tema__2.shtml*.

4. The dilemma is set out in Boris Grozovskii and Anna Nikolaeva, 'Oligarkhi "ispravilis" ', *Vedomosti*, 14 January 2004, *http://www.vedomsti.ru/newspaper/article.shtml?2004/01/14/71033*.

5. 'Zachem vam v VTO?', *Kommersant*, 14 February 2002, p.16; Robert Cottrell and Stefan Wagstyl, 'Putin's Bid to Join WTO Splits Business', *Financial Times*, 27 March 2002, p.5.

6. Sergei Guriev and Andrei Rachinsky, 'The Role of Oligarchs in Russian Capitalism', *Journal of Economic Perspectives*, vol. 19, no. 1, Winter 2005, pp.140–1; Anastasiia Dagaeva and Polina Mikhaleva, 'Dolzhnosti peredaiutsia po nasledstvu', *Vedomosti*, 9 August 2005, *http://www.vedomosti.ru/newspaper/article.shtml?2005/08/09/95590*.

7. Guriev and Rachinsky, 'Role of Oligarchs', pp.140–1.

8. 'Anatolii Karachinskii, prezident gruppy kompanii IBS: "Rossiiskii biznes razvivaetsia ot krizisa k krizisu" ', *Politcom.ru*, 20 October 2005, *http://www.politcom.ru/2005/business10.php*.

Bibliography

Allan, Duncan, 'Banks and the Loans-for-Shares Auctions', in David Lane (ed.), *Russian Banking. Evolution, problems and prospects*, Edward Elgar, Cheltenham and Northampton, MA, 2002, chapter 6.

Amirov, Anvar and Pribylovskii, Vladimir, *Rossiiskie biznesmeny i menedzhery. Biograficheskii spravochnik*, Informatsionno-ekspertnaia gruppa 'Panorama', Moscow, February 1997.

Anderson, James, Bernstein, David and Gray, Cheryl, *Judicial Systems in Transition Economies. Assessing the past, looking to the future*, World Bank, Washington DC, 2005.

Åslund, Anders, 'Russia's Economic Transformation under Putin', *Eurasian Geography and Economics*, vol.45, no.6, 2004, pp.397–420.

Åslund, Anders, 'Comparative Oligarchy: Russia, Ukraine and the United States', paper presented to the CASE conference, 'Europe after the Enlargement', Warsaw, 8–9 April 2005.

Aukutsionek, Sergei, 'Some Characteristics of the Transition Economy', *Communist Economies and Economic Transformation*, vol.9, no.3, 1997, pp.289–336.

Balzer, Harley, 'Managed Pluralism: Vladimir Putin's emerging regime', *Post-Soviet Affairs*, vol.19, no.3, 2003, pp.189–227.

Barnes, Andrew, 'Comparative Theft: context and choice in the Hungarian, Czech and Russian transformations, 1989–2000', *East European Politics and Societies*, vol.17, no.3, 2003, pp.533–65.

Barnes, Andrew, 'Russia's New Business Groups and State Power', *Post-Soviet Affairs*, vol.19, no.2, 2003, pp.154–86.

Bim, Alexander S., 'Ownership and Control of Russian Enterprises and Strategies of Shareholders', *Communist Economies and Economic Transformation*, vol.8, no.4, 1996, pp.471–500.

Biznesmeny Rossii. 40 istorii uspekha, 'OKO', Moscow, 1994.

Black, Bernard, Kraakman, Reinier and Tarassova, Anna, 'Russian Privatization and Corporate Governance: what went wrong?', *Stanford Law Review*, vol.52, 1999–2000, pp.1731–1808.

Blasi, J., Kroumova, M. and Kruse, D., *Kremlin Capitalism. Privatizing the Russian Economy*, Cornell University Press, Ithaca, 1996.

Boycko, M., Shleifer, A. and Vishny, R., *Privatizing Russia*, MIT Press, Cambridge MA, 1995.

Brzezinski, Matthew, *Casino Moscow. A tale of greed and adventure on capitalism's wildest frontier*, Free, New York, 2002.

Buiter, Willem, 'From Predation to Accumulation? The second transition decade in Russia', *Economics of Transition*, vol.8, no.3, 2000, pp.603–22.

Bunin, Igor, 'Vlast' i biznes v novoi Rossii', *Politcom.ru*, 11 June 2004, http://www.politcom.ru/print.php.

Burawoy, Michael and Hendley, Kathryn, 'Between *Perestroika* and Privatisation: divided strategies and political crisis in a Soviet enterprise', *Soviet Studies*, vol.44, no.3, 1992, pp.371–402.

Chapman, Sheila A. and Mulino, Marcella, 'Predicting Russia's Currency and Financial Crises', in David Lane (ed.), *Russian Banking. Evolution, problems and prospects*, Edward Elgar, Cheltenham and Northampton, MA, 2002, chapter 8.

Daunton, Martin, *Trusting Leviathan. The politics of taxation in Britain, 1799–1914*, Cambridge University Press, Cambridge, 2001.

Dolgopyatova, Tatyana G. (ed.), *Russian Industry: institutional development*, State Unviersity Higher School of Economics, Analytical Survey Issue 1, Moscow, 2003.

Dosal, Paul J., *Power in Transition. The rise of Guatemala's industrial oligarchy, 1871–1994*, Praeger, New York, 1995.

Dzarasov, R.S. and Novozhenov, D.V., *Krupnyi biznes i nakoplenie kapitala v sovremennoi Rossii*, URCC, Moscow, 2005.

Easter, Gerald, 'Institutional Legacy of the Old Regime as a Constraint to Reform: the case of fiscal policy', in Stefanie Harter and Gerald Easter (eds), *Shaping the Economic Space in Russia. Decision making processes, institutions and adjustment to change in the El'tsin era*, Ashgate, Aldershot, 2000, chapter 14.

Edel, Abraham (ed.), *Aristotle*, Dell, New York, 1967.

Fortescue, Stephen, 'The Mining and Metals Industry and Globalization', in Klaus Segbers (ed.), *Explaining Post-Soviet Patchworks*, Ashgage, Aldershot, 2001, vol.1, chapter 7.

Fortescue, Stephen, 'Ownership and Corporate Strategy in the Russian Mining and Metals Sector', *The Soviet and Post-Soviet Review*, vol.25, no.2, 1998, pp.163–80.

Fortescue, Stephen, 'Privatisation, Corporate Governance and Enterprise Performance in Russia', *Russian and Euro-Asian Bulletin*, vol.7, no.5, May 1998, pp.1–10.

Fortescue, Stephen, 'Privatisation of Large-scale Russian Industry', in A. Saikal and W. Maley (eds), *Russia in Search of Its Future*, Cambridge University Press, Cambridge, 1995, chapter 6.

Fortescue, Stephen, 'Privatisation of Russian Industry', *Australian Journal of Political Science*, vol.29, no.1, March 1994, pp.135–53.

Fortescue, Stephen, 'The Privatisation of Soviet Large-scale Industry', in H. Hendrischke (ed.), *Market Reform in the Changing Socialist World*, Macquarie Studies in Chinese Political Economy, Macquarie University, Sydney, July 1992.

Fortescue, Stephen, 'The Russian Aluminum Industry in Transition', *Eurasian Geography and Economics*, vol. 47, no.1, 2006, pp. 76–94.

Fortescue, Stephen, 'The Russian Mining and Metals Sector: integration or disintegration?', in Vladimir Tikhomirov (ed.), *Anatomy of the 1998 Russian Crisis*, Contemporary Europe Research Centre, University of Melbourne, Melbourne, 1999.

Fortescue, Stephen, 'Taxation in the Russian Mining and Metals Sector', *Arbeitspapiere und Materialien*, no.27, Forschungsstelle Osteuropa, University of Bremen, July 2001.

[Fortesk'iu, Stiven] Fortescue, Stephen, 'Pravit li Rossiia oligarkhiia?', *Polis*, vol.5, 2002, pp.64–73.

Fox, Merritt B. and Heller, Michael A., 'Corporate Governance Lessons from Russian Enterprise Fiascoes', *New York University Law Review*, vol.75, no.6, December 2000, pp.1720–80.

Freeland, Chrystia, *Sale of the Century. Russia's wild ride from communism to capitalism*, Crown, New York, 2000.

Freinkman, Lev, 'Financial-industrial Groups in Russia: emergence of large diversified private companies', *Communist Economies and Economic Transformation*, vol.7, no.1, 1995, pp.51–66.

From Transition to Development. A country economic memorandum for the Russian Federation, World Bank, Washington DC, Report No.32308-RU, March 2005.

Frye, Timothy, 'Capture or Exchange? Business lobbying in Russia', *Europe-Asia Studies*, vol.54, no.7, 2002, pp.1017–36.

Gaddy, Clifford G. and Ickes, Barry W., *Russia's Virtual Economy*, Brookings Institution Press, Washington DC, 2002.

Gaidar, Yegar (ed.), *The Economics of Transition*, MIT Press, Cambridge MA and London, 2003.

Goldman, Marshall I., 'Anders in Wonderland: comments on Russia's economic transformation under Putin', *Eurasian Geography and Economics*, vol.45, no.6, 2004, pp.429–34.

Gorbatova, Larisa, 'Formation of Connections between Finance and Industry in Russia: basic stages and forms', *Communist Economies and Economic Transformation*, vol.7, no.1, 1995, pp.21–34.

Guriev, Sergei and Rachinsky, Andrei, 'The Role of Oligarchs in Russian Capitalism', *Journal of Economic Perspectives*, vol.19, no.1, Winter 2005, pp.130–150.

Gurkov, Igor, 'Typology of Russian Enterprises' Adaptation to New Economic Realities', International Institute for Applied Systems Analysis, Laxenburg, WP96–083, July 1996.

Gustafson, Thane, *Capitalism Russian Style*, Cambridge University Press, Cambridge, 1994.

Harter, Stefanie and Easter, Gerald (eds), *Shaping the Economic Space in Russia. Decision making processes, institutions and adjustment to change in the El'tsin era*, Ashgate, Aldershot, 2000.

Hendley, Kathryn, 'Temporal and Regional Patterns of Commercial Litigation in Post-Soviet Russia', *Post-Soviet Geography and Economics*, vol.39, no.7, September 1998, pp.379–98.

Hendrischke, H. (ed.), *Market Reform in the Changing Socialist World*, Macquarie Studies in Chinese Political Economy, Macquarie University, Sydney, July 1992.

Herspring, Dale R. (ed.), *Putin's Russia. Past imperfect, future uncertain*, Rowman & Littlefield, Lanham MD, 2003.

Hoffman, David, *The Oligarchs. Wealth and power in the new Russia*, Perseus, Cambridge MA, 2002.

Hough, Jerry F., *The Logic of Economic Reform in Russia*, Brookings Institution Press, Washington DC, 2001.

Ivanenko, Vlad, 'The Statutory Tax Burden and its Avoidance in Transitional Russia', *Europe-Asia Studies*, vol.57, no.7, November 2005, pp.1021–45.

Jensen, Donald N., 'How Russia is Ruled', in Peter Rutland (ed.), *Business and the State in Contemporary Russia*, Westview, Boulder, 2001.

Johnson, Juliet, *A Fistful of Rubles. The rise and fall of the Russian banking system*, Cornell University Press, Ithaca and London, 2000.

Johnson, Juliet, 'Russia's Emerging Financial-industrial Groups', *Post-Soviet Affairs*, vol.13, no.4, 1997, pp.333–65.

Kets de Vries, Manfred F.R., Shekshnia, Stanislav, Korotov, Konstantin and Florent-Treacy, Elizabeth, *The New Russian Business Leaders*, Edward Elgar, Cheltenham UK and Northampton MA, 2004.

Klebnikov, Paul, *Godfather of the Kremlin. Boris Berezovsky and the looting of Russia*, Harcourt, New York, 2000.

Komu prinadlezhit Rossiia, Vagrius, Moscow, 2003.

Kryshtanovskaya, Ol'ga and White, Stephen, 'Inside the Putin Court: a research note', *Europe-Asia Studies*, vol.57, no.7, November 2005, pp.1065–75.

Kryshtanovskaya, O. and White, S., 'The Rise of the Russian Business Elite', *Communist and Post-Communist Studies*, vol.38, 2005, pp.293–307.

Kryukov, Valery, 'Adjustment to Change: the case of the oil and gas industry', in Stefanie Harter and Gerald Easter (eds), *Shaping the Economic Space in Russia. Decision making processes, institutions and adjustment to change in the El'tsin era*, Ashgate, Aldershot, 2000, chapter 5.

Kryukov, Valery and Moe, Arild, 'Banks and the Financial Sector', in David Lane (ed.), *The Political Economy of Russian Oil*, Rowman & Littlefield, Lanham MD, 1999, chapter 2.

Lane, David (ed.), *The Political Economy of Russian Oil*, Rowman & Littlefield, Lanham MD, 1999.

Lane, David, 'Introduction', in David Lane (ed.), *The Political Economy of Russian Oil*, Rowman & Littlefield, Lanham MD, 1999.

Lane, David, 'The Political Economy of Russian Oil', in Peter Rutland (ed.), *Business and State in Contemporary Russia*, Westview, Boulder, Colorado, 2001.

Lane, David (ed.), *Russian Banking. Evolution, problems and prospects*, Edward Elgar, Cheltenham and Northampton, MA, 2002, chapter 4.

Lane, David, 'The Russian Oil Elite: background and outlook', in David Lane (ed.), *The Political Economy of Russian Oil*, Rowman & Littlefield, Lanham MD, 1999, chapter 3.

Lane, David and Seifulmulukov, Iskander, 'Company Profiles: LUKoil, YuKOS, Surgutneftegaz, Sidanko', in David Lane (ed.), *The Political Economy of Russian Oil*, Rowman & Littlefield, Lanham MD, 1999, Appendix.

Lane, David and Seifulmulukov, Iskander, 'Structure and Ownership', in David Lane (ed.), *The Political Economy of Russian Oil*, Rowman & Littlefield, Lanham MD, 1999, chapter 1.

Lapina, N.Iu., *Formirovanie sovremennoi rossiiskoi elity (Problemy perekhodnogo perioda)*, Institut nauchnoi informatsii po obshchestvennym naukam, Moscow, 1995.

Luong, Pauline Jones and Weinthal, Erika, 'Prelude to the Resource Curse. Explaining oil and gas development strategies in the Soviet successor states and beyond', *Comparative Political Studies*, vol.34, no.4, May 2000, pp.367–99.

Moore, Mick 'Revenues, State Formation, and the Quality of Governance in Developing Countries', *International Political Science Review*, vol.25, no.3, 2004, pp.297–319.

Nash, Roland, 'Corporate Consolidation: Russia's latest lurch towards capitalism', in Peter Westin (ed.), *The Wild East. Negotiating the Russian financial frontier*, Reuters/Pearson Education, Harlow, 2001, chapter 9.

Orttung, Robert W., 'Business and Politics in the Russian Regions', *Problems of Post-Communism*, vol.51, no.2, March-April 2004, pp.48–60.

Pappe, Ia.Sh., *'Oligarkhi'. Ekonomicheskaia khronika. 1992–2000*, GU Vysshaia ekonomicheskaia shkola, Moscow, 2000.

Pappe, Ia.Sh., 'Rossiiskii krupnyi biznes kak ekonomicheskii fenomen: osoben-nosti stanovleniia i sovremennogo etapa razvitiia', *Problemy prognozirovaniia*, no.1, 2002, pp.29–46.

Pleines, Heiko, 'Corruption and Crime in the Russian Oil Industry', in David Lane (ed.), *The Political Economy of Russian Oil*, Rowman & Littlefield, Lanham MD, 1999, chapter 4.

Rajan, Raghuram and Zingales, Luigi, *Saving Capitalism from the Capitalists. Unleashing the power of financial markets to create wealth and spread opportunity*, Crown, New York, 2003.

Ramseyer, J. Mark and Rosenbluth, Frances M., *The Politics of Oligarchy. Institutional choice in Imperial Japan*, Cambridge University Press, Cambridge, 1995.

Robinson, Neil, 'The Myth of Equilibrium: winner power, fiscal crisis and Russian economic reform', *Communist and Post-Communist Studies*, vol.34, no.4, December 2001, pp.423–46.

Ross, Michael L., 'The Political Economy of the Resource Curse', *World Politics*, vol.51, no.2, January 1999, pp.297–322.

Rueschmeyer, Dietrich, Stephens, Evelyne Huber and Stephens, John D., *Capitalist Development and Democracy*, University of Chicago Press, Chicago, 1992.

Rutland, Peter (ed.), *Business and the State in Contemporary Russia*, Westview, Boulder, Colorado, 2001.

Rutland, Peter, 'Introduction: business and the state in Russia', in Peter Rutland (ed.), *Business and State in Contemporary Russia*, Westview, Boulder, Colorado, 2001.

Rutland, Peter, 'Putin and the Oligarchs', in Dale R. Herspring (ed.), *Putin's Russia. Past imperfect, future uncertain*, Rowman & Littlefield, Lanham MD, 2003, chapter 7.

Rydjeski, Letitia, 'The Russian Crisis: what the Russian analysts "missed", 1990–8', in Peter Westin, *The Wild East. Negotiating the Russian financial frontier*, Reuters/Pearson Education, Harlow, 2001.

Saikal, A. and Maley, W. (eds), *Russia in Search of Its Future*, Cambridge University Press, Cambridge, 1995.

Satter, David, *Darkness at Dawn. The rise of the Russian criminal state*, Yale University Press, 2003.

Schröder, Hans-Henning, 'El'tsin and the Oligarchs: the role of financial groups in Russian politics between 1993 and July 1998', *Europe-Asia Studies*, vol.51, no.6, 1999, pp.957–88.

Schröder, Hans-Henning, 'The "Oligarchs": a force to be reckoned with?', in Stefanie Harter and Gerald Easter (eds), *Shaping the Economic Space in Russia. Decision making processes, institutions and adjustment to change in the El'tsin era*, Ashgate, Aldershot, 2000, chapter 3.

Shlapentokh, Vladimir, 'Wealth versus Political Power: the Russian case', *Communist and Post-Communist Studies*, vol.37, 2004, pp.135–60.

Shleifer, Andrei and Treisman, Daniel, 'A Normal Country: Russia after communism', *Journal of Economic Perspectives*, vol.19, no.1, Winter 2005, pp.151–74.

Shleifer, Andrei and Treisman, Daniel, *Without a Map. Political tactics and economic reform in Russia*, MIT Press, Cambridge MA, 2000.

Solnick, Steven L., *Stealing the State. Control and collapse in Soviet institutions*, Harvard University Press, Cambridge MA, 1998.

Starodubrovskaya, Irina, 'Financial-industrial Groups: illusions and reality', *Communist Economies and Economic Transformation*, vol.7, no.1, March 1995, pp.5–19.

'Statistical appendix', in Yegor Gaidar (ed.), *The Economics of Transition*, MIT Press, Cambridge MA, 2003.

Stiglitz, Joseph, *Globalization and Its Discontents*, Penguin, London, 2002.

Strategy for the Russian Federation, European Bank for Reconstruction and Development, London, 16 November 2004.

Tikhomirov, Vladimir, 'Capital Flight from Post-Soviet Russia', *Europe-Asia Studies*, vol.49, no.4, 1997, pp.591–615.

Tompson, William, 'Nothing Learned, Nothing Forgotten: restructuring without reform in Russia's banking sector', in Stefanie Harter and Gerald Easter (eds), *Shaping the Economic Space in Russia. Decision making processes, institutions and adjustment to change in the El'tsin era*, Ashgate, Aldershot, 2000, chapter 4.

Tompson, William, 'The Present and Future of Banking Reform', in David Lane (ed.), *Russian Banking. Evolution, problems and prospects*, Edward Elgar, Cheltenham and Northampton, MA, 2002, chapter 3.

Tompson, William, 'Putin and the "Oligarchs": a two-sided commitment problem', in Alex Pravda (ed.), *Leading Russia. Putin in perspective. Essays in honour of Archie Brown*, Oxford University Press, Oxford, 2005, Chapter 10.

Transition Report 2001. Energy in transition, European Bank for Reconstruction and Development, London, 2001.

Useem, Michael, *The Inner Circle. Large corporations and the rise of business political activity*, Oxford University Press, Oxford, 1984.

Vernadsky, George, *A History of Russia*, Yale University Press, New Haven, 1961.

Vozrozhdennaia elita rossiiskogo biznesa, Institut izucheniia reformy, Moscow, 1994.

Ward, Chris (ed.), *The Stalin Years. A reader*, Palgrave, Basingstoke, 2003.

Westin, Peter (ed.), *The Wild East. Negotiating the Russian financial frontier*, Reuters/Pearson Education, Harlow, 2001.

Yorke, Andrew, 'Business and Politics in Krasnoyarsk *Krai*', *Europe-Asia Studies*, vol.55, no.2, 2003, pp.241–62.

Zudin, Aleksei Iu., 'Oligarchy as a Political Problem of Russian Postcommunism', *Russian Social Science Review*, vol.41, no.6, November-December 2000, pp.4–33.

Zudin, A. 'Punish but Don't Destroy. The oligarchs and the state in public opinion', 2002, unpublished paper.

Zudin, Aleksei, *Rezhim Vladimira Putina: kontury novoi politicheskoi sistemy*, Moskovskii tsentr Karnegi, Moscow, April 2002.

Index

Abramov, Aleksandr Grigorevich
(1959–)
  biography, 33
  reaction to arrest of Khodorkovsky,
    124
  see also Evrazkholding
Abramovich, Roman Arkadevich
(1966–)
  and Chukotka, 118
  and European Bank for
    Reconstruction and
    Development, 183
  and Slavneft, 108
  and Yukos affair, 141–2, 212
  biography, 31, 33–4
  buying into Evrazkholding, 23
  relations with Berezovsky, 34, 49
  sale of assets, 23, 143, 178
  see also Sibneft
Achinsk Alumina Combine, 65
Alekperov, Vagit Iusufovich (1950–)
  beginnings in business, 44, 47–8
  biography, 31, 32, 36
  on foreign investment in
    Lukoil, 154
  on Yukos affair, 154
  relations with *siloviki*, 144
  see also Lukoil
Alfa Bank, 47, 65, 214
  accusations of criminal activity
    against, 69
  and shares-for-credit, 55
  involvement in TNK, 49, 214
  links with Renova, 33, 49, 190–1
  see also Fridman
Anisimov, Vasilii Vasilevich,
    23, 89
Anti-Semitism, 25, 26, 144
Apatit
  and Yukos affair, 94, 110, 121,
    127, 158
  Menatep purchase of, 50, 87
  performance, 88, 198

Asset stripping, 13, 14, 19, 39, 78–85,
    91, 173, 174, 196–7
  and investment, 93–4

Baikal Finance Group, 132–3, 143
Bakhmina, Svetlana Petrovna, 62, 129,
    160–1
Bankruptcy, 63–5, 194
'Basmannyi justice', 105, 210
Belkovsky, Stanislav Aleksandrovich,
    110
Berezovsky, Boris Abramovich
(1946–)
  and media interests, 22
  biography, 25, 29–30, 182, 187
  claimed criminal links, 67, 69
  exile, 9, 22, 104–5, 108
  Fund for Civil Freedom, 74
  relations with Abramovich,
    34, 49
  relations with Gusinsky, 104
  relations with Yeltsin, 106, 107
Blackmarket
  definition of, 24
  oligarch origins in, 24, 26,
    27, 29, 31, 35, 37, 41,
    186, 187
  under Gorbachev, 8, 12, 24, 189
Blavatnik, Lev, 33, 47, 185
Bogdanchikov, Sergei Mikhailovich
  and Yukos, 23, 110, 142, 208
  background, 203
  Gazprom–Rosneft merger, 134
  Neftegazprom, 131
  Slavneft, 108
Bogdanov, Vladimir Leonidovich
(1951–)
  biography, 31, 32, 37
  beginnings in business, 44, 47–9
  relations with *siloviki*, 144
  see also Surgutneftegaz
Browder, William, 17, 184
Bykov, Anatolii Petrovich, 66–7, 68

Capital flight, 69, 92, 153
Centre for the Scientific-Technical
    Creativity of Youth (NTTM), 27
Chamber of Trade and Industry, 124
Chernoi, Lev Semenovich, 51, 68, 69
Chernoi, Mikhail Semenovich, 34,
    68, 69
Chernomyrdin, Viktor Stepanovich,
    113
Chubais, Anatolii Borisovich, 30, 75,
    102, 151
    attitude towards oligarchs, 10, 57–8,
        102, 105–6, 174, 201
    privatization, 59, 189
    reaction to arrest of Khodorkovsky,
        124
Communist Party of the Soviet Union
    funds, 27
Competition issues, 14–15, 19, 41,
    75, 176
Cooperative movement
    and spontaneous privatization, 44
    effect on corporate management,
        84–5
    oligarch involvement, 26, 33, 35, 102
Corporate governance
    abuse of minorities, 61, 63, 71, 82–3
    centralized management, 91, 161
    decentralized management, 84–6
    dividend policy, 93, 117, 119
    oligarch abuse of, 19, 54
    reform of, 19, 61, 71–3
    share dilution, 53, 61–2
    share register abuse, 53, 61
    shareholder meeting abuse, 53, 61
    transparency, 73, 118, 124
    value transfer, 62–3, 82–3
Corporate performance, 77–8
    measurement of, 72, 81–3
    profitability, 92–3, 94, 112
Courts
    commercial, 65–6, 71
    criminal, 66–7, 71

Dart, Kenneth, 63
Deripaska, Oleg Vladimirovich
    (1968–)
    and Krasnoyarsk Aluminium
        Plant, 66

and Novokuznetsk Aluminium
    Plant, 64
and Potanin, 106
and TWG, 53, 64
biography, 31, 34–5, 188
claimed criminal links, 68
diversification, 177–8, 188
investment by, 153
links with Melnichenko, 35
personality, 103
social responsibility, 148
Dubov, Vladimir Matveevich, 119,
    122–3, 127, 140
Duma
    and tax state theory, 170, 172
    oligarch lobbying in, 109, 119, 140–1
    reversing legislation, 156
    tax administration reform, 168
    taxation sub-committee, 119

EBRD, *see* European Bank for
    Reconstruction and Development
European Bank for Reconstruction
    and Development
    on oligarchs, 14–17, 183
    on taxation, 16–17
Evrazkholding
    and Abramovich, 23
    and Kuznetsk Metal Combine, 64–5
    and Nizhnii Tagil Metal Combine,
        85–6, 95
    see also Abramov
Exchange rate, 41
    foreign currency speculation, 42
    ruble corridor, 92–3, 102, 112,
        199–200

Fedorov, Boris Grigorevich, 10, 30,
    101, 125, 181
FIGs, *see* Financial-industrial groups
Financial sector
    agency banks, 28, 42
    and oligarchy, 4, 8, 22, 38, 41–3, 100
    August 1998 crisis, 9, 13, 21, 22, 43,
        104, 107
    'bank war', 105
    foreign currency speculation, 42
    'pocket' banks, 42
    pyramid schemes, 43

Financial-industrial groups, 11, 52, 57, 104
Foreign investment
    effect of Yukos affair on, 126, 141–2, 154, 184, 214
    government attitudes to, 100–1, 109, 174
    in shares-for-credit, 58
    oligarch attitudes to, 58, 100
Fradkov, Mikhail Efimovich, 156, 167, 203
Fridman, Mikhail Maratovich (1964–)
    beginnings in business, 42
    biography, 25, 26, 28
    claimed criminal links, 69
    threats against, 104
    see also Alfa Bank

G7, *see* 'Gang of Seven'
Gaidar, Egor Timurovich, 30, 44, 100, 151
'Gang of Seven', 25–30, 38–9, 184–5, 188
Gazprom, 23, 36, 144
    and Yugaskneftegaz sale, 130, 131, 132, 143, 144–5
    merger with Rosneft, 131, 133–4
Gazprominvestkholding, 23
Gerashchenko, Viktor Vladimirovich, 127–8, 207
GKO, *see* Government bond market
Gorbachev, Mikhail Sergeevich, 8, 27, 37
Government bond market, 43, 102
Gref, German Oskarovich, 122, 126
Gusinsky, Vladimir Aleksandrovich (1952–)
    and Berezovsky, 104
    biography, 25–6, 28
    claimed criminal links, 69
    exile, 9, 104–5, 108
    involvement in politics, 100
    media interests, 22, 202
    see also Most Bank

Inflation, 42, 102
Inkombank, 28, 42, 51, 186
    and shares-for-credit, 54
    see also Vinogradov

International Monetary Fund, 15
Investment
    by oligarchs, 72–3, 94–7, 117–18
    effect of Yukos affair on, 152–4, 218
    in metals sector, 95
Ivanov, Viktor Petrovich, 110, 143

Justice
    and Yukos affair, 152, 157–63, 183
    exemplary, 13, 150–1, 161–2, 213
    selective, 161–2
    tax law, 163–8

Kasyanov, Mikhail Mikhailovich, 108, 122, 127, 156
Khodorkovsky, Mikhail Borisovich (1963–)
    arrest, 22, 123–4, 136, 206
    biography, 25, 27–8, 186
    commitment to transparency, 71
    conflict with Putin, 110, 123, 139–40, 169, 211
    early business model, 27, 41
    involvement in politics, 100, 139, 147
    oligarchs' attitude to, 125
    popular attitudes to, 12
    reaction to arrest of Lebedev, 122
    social responsibility, 74
    see also Menatep Bank, Yukos
Kirienko, Sergei Vladilenovich, 10, 101, 104
Komsomol, 24, 27, 28, 186, 188
Krasnoyarsk Aluminium Plant (KrAZ)
    and Achinsk Alumina Combine, 65
    privatization, 50–1
    struggle for control of, 53, 66–7
Kudrin, Aleksei Leonidovich, 128, 147, 165
Kurtsin, Aleksei, 129, 161

Lebedev, Platon Leonidovich, 50, 121, 211
Lisin, Vladimir Sergeevich (1956–), 23, 32, 78
    see also Novolipetsk Metal Combine

Lukoil, 23, 142, 154
  formation, 48
  performance, 49, 90–2
  shares-for-credit, 56
  taxation, 146, 165, 212
  see also Alekperov

MADAM, 34
Mafia, 2, 14, 18, 180
Magnitogorsk Metal Combine, 23,
    51, 97
  see also Rashnikov
Makhmudov, Iskander
    Kakhramonovich (1963–), 23,
    31, 34
MDM-Bank, 23, 34, 35
  see also Melnichenko
Mechel, 23, 56
Medvedev, Dmitrii Anatolevich, 143
Melnichenko, Andrei Igorevich (1972–)
  beginnings in business, 42, 52
  biography, 31, 34
  links with Deripaska, 35
  see also MDM-Bank
Menatep Bank, 27–8, 42
  Apatit, 121, 158
  corporate governance, 53
  investment, 94
  involvement in privatization, 50, 52
  shares-for-credit, 54–6, 62–3
  see also Khodorkovsky
Metals sector, xiii, 9, 185
  aluminium, 35, 75, 96, 153
  and banks, 51
  ferrous, 23–4, 97
  investment, 94–7
  lobbying, 205
  privatization, 49–51
  profitability, 94, 114
  structure, 60, 75
  taxation, 113–16, 203, 215
  trading firms, 50–1, 198
Mordashov, Aleksei Aleksandrovich
    (1965–)
  beginnings in business, 47
  biography, 31, 32–3, 187
  on arrest of Khodorkovsky, 124–5
  on 'Basmannyi justice', 105
  relations with *siloviki*, 144
  see also Severstal

MOST-Bank, 26, 42, 70
  see also Gusinsky
Muravlenko, Sergei Viktorovich, 49

Nalog na dobychu poleznykh
    ispokaemykh (NDPI), *see* Taxation,
    resource extraction tax
Nemtsov, Boris Efimovich, 10, 101
Nevzlin, Leonid Borisovich
  arrest warrant for, 127, 129–30
  claimed criminal links, 69
  murder charges against, 162–3
  on Abramovich, 141–2, 212
'New oligarchs', 22, 30–5, 38–9
  proletarian origins, 31, 39, 188
'New Russians', 12, 21, 30, 35
  definition, 25
Nizhnii Tagil Metal Combine,
    85–6, 95
NLMK, *see* Novolipetsk Metal
    Combine
Nomenklatura, 2, 3, 12, 14, 18, 21, 27,
    29, 31, 36, 180, 182, 187
  definition, 24
  privatization, 46
Norilsk Nickel
  and minorities, 61, 63
  investment, 63
  performance, 86–7
  privatization, 86
  restructuring, 61
  shares-for-credit, 55–6
  social responsibility, 74
  see also Potanin
North Urals Bauxite Mine (SUBR),
    88–9
Novokuznetsk Aluminium Plant,
    51, 64
Novolipetsk Metal Combine
  investment, 97
  shares-for-credit, 56
  see also Lisin

Oil sector
  and second *peredel*, 60–1
  oligarchs in, 9
  performance, 63, 83–4, 90
  privatization, 49
  taxation, 16, 112–13, 117,
    146, 155

Oligarchs
    age, 25, 30–1
    and investment, 93–7, 153
    attitude towards foreign
        investment, 58
    background, 12, 24–5, 68, 173,
        182, 188
    criminal activity, 25, 26, 34, 67–71,
        162–3, 195
    diversification, 153, 155, 177–8
    personality, 6, 7, 18, 38, 39,
        80, 103
    privatization, 52, 54
    relational capital, 25, 37–8,
        173–4, 187
    social responsibility, 73–5, 105,
        147–8, 174–5, 196
    see also Oligarchy
Oligarchy
    and formal office, xi, 7, 174
    asset stripping, 13, 14, 19, 39,
        78–85, 91, 173, 174, 196–7
    attitudes towards, 10–18, 150, 171,
        174–5, 182
    collective action, 2, 6, 7, 100,
        102–7, 174
    contract with state, 122, 147–8, 151,
        169, 170, 175
    coup, 110
    definition, xi–xiii, 1–2, 3, 5,
        147, 180
    economic performance, 2, 18–19,
        77–81, 174
    financial crisis, 1998, 107
    Gang of Seven, 22
    generational change, 6–7, 178
    in financial sector, 8–9
    in history, 2–5, 8–9, 40, 169
    involvement in politics, 100, 102
    lobbying, 117, 148, 205, 219
    membership, 2, 185
    'new', 14
    shares-for-credit, 54–9
    state harassment, 109, 159,
        169, 203
    state support, 28, 29, 35, 37, 42,
        57, 174
    use of term, xi–xiii, 99
    see also Oligarchs

ONEKSIMbank, 29, 42, 187
    and Norilsk Nickel, 86–7
    shares-for-credit, 54–6
    see also Potanin

Pavlovsky, Gleb Olegovich, 110,
    144, 203
Pichugin, Aleksei Vladimirovich, 70,
    110, 162–3
Populism, 77, 171–2, 175–6, 178
    and dispossession, 8, 40, 105,
        171–2, 175–6
Potanin, Vladimir Olegovich
    (1961–)
    and Deripaska, 106
    biography, 25, 28–9, 186
    on foreign investment, 58
    reaction to arrest of Khodorkovsky,
        124
    relations with *siloviki*, 144
    shares-for-credit, 54–8, 203
    social responsibility, 74, 148
    see also Norilsk Nickel,
        ONEKSIMbank
Primakov, Evgenyi Maksimovich,
    107, 125
Privatization, 43–52
    and Red Directors, 45–6, 49–50
    attitudes towards, 14, 189
    investment tenders, 50
    spontaneous, 44–5
    management, 44, 45–7, 52
    mass, 45–52, 85
    nomenklatura, 46, 54
    reversal of, 125–6, 144–5, 148,
        150–1, 171, 177, 192
    workforce ownership, 45
Property rights, xii, 5
    legitimacy of, 40, 59, 77, 150,
        173, 176
    security of, 80, 151
Prosecutor's office, 110, 122, 128, 161,
    206, 210
Public opinion
    foreign investment, 58
    oligarchs, 12, 40, 41, 43, 75, 77
Pugachev, Sergei Viktorovich,
    108, 110
Pukhov, Anatolii Pavlovich, 85

Putin, Vladimir Vladimirovich
  as populist, 11, 77, 171–2,
      175–6, 178
  as referee, 105, 108, 109
  as *silovik*, 11, 107
  attitude towards foreign
      investment, 109, 141, 145, 154,
      171, 175
  attitude towards nationalization,
      145, 171, 175
  attitude towards oligarchs, 1, 11,
      105, 109, 175, 203
  election to presidency, 9
  on arrest of Khodorkovsky,
      124, 212
  on arrest of Lebedev, 121
  on rule of law, 125, 145
  on tax reform, 161, 167–8
  Yukos affair, 137–9, 145, 208–9, 211

Rashnikov, Viktor Fillipovich (1948–),
      23, 30, 31–2
  see also Magnitogorsk Metal
      Combine
Ravnoudalennost', 105, 106
'Real economy', 8–9, 38–9, 102,
      107, 193
Red Directors, 21, 30, 57, 85, 100
  and corporate governance, 53
  and privatization, 45–6
  as asset strippers, 84
  as oligarchs, 31–3, 36–7
  definition, 24–5
Renova, 33, 47, 49, 52
Resource sector
  oligarchs in, 5, 8, 9, 22
  performance, 91
  resource curse, 6, 18, 176, 177
  taxation, 15
  see also Metals sector, Oil sector
Robber Barons, 3, 13, 74, 80, 173, 176
Rosneft
  and Yuganskneftegaz, 130, 133–6
  and Yukos, 126–7, 138, 143, 208–9
  merger with Gazprom, 131, 133–4
  see also Bogdanchikov, Sechin
Rossiiskii Kredit, 52, 53, 55
RSPP, *see* Russian Union of
      Industrialists and Entrepreneurs

Rusal, 23, 97, 153
  see also Deripaska
Russian Union of Industrialists and
      Entrepreneurs, 103, 105
  call for social contract, 122
  oligarch membership, xi
  on Berezovsky, 106
  reaction to arrest of Khodorkovsky,
      124
  reaction to arrest of Lebedev, 121–2
  social responsibility, 74, 108–9, 196
  see also Volsky

Sayanogorsk Aluminium Plant, 35, 51,
      53, 64
Sechin, Igor Ivanovich, 110, 133,
      134, 143
Second *peredel*, 60, 61, 63–5
Semibankirshchina, see 'Gang of Seven'
Severstal
  investment, 95–6
  privatization of, 47, 187
  social responsibility, 74
  tax claims, 116
  see also Mordashov
Shares-for-credit
  attitudes towards, 54, 192
  explanations of, 55–9, 101
  foreign involvement, 58
  history, 54–5
  oligarchs left out, 22, 185
Shashlychnoe soglashenie, 108, 109, 170
Shatalov, Sergei Dmitrievich, 165–6
Sheindlin, Aleksandr Efimovich,
      27, 33
Shuvalov, Igor Ivanovich, 146, 148,
      162, 166
Sibneft
  and Yukos, 126, 141–2
  corporate governance, 61
  formation, 49
  performance, 59
  sale of, 23, 34
  shares-for-credit, 56
  taxation, 146
  see also Abramovich
Siloviki
  and Slavneft, 108
  and Yukos affair, 137, 138, 142–4

Siloviki – continued
  coup, 110
  definition, 181
  increasing power of, 109, 148
  on nationalization, 143–4, 175
  relations with oligarchs, 144
Smolensky, Aleksandr Pavlovich
    (1954–)
  as *tolkach*, 26, 182
  beginnings in business, 42, 52
  biography, 25, 26, 28
  claimed criminal links, 68
  collapse of business, 22
Soskovets, Oleg Nikolaevich, 32, 35
Sparrow Hills, 105, 202
Stalin, Iosif Vissarionovich, 1, 125,
    161, 169
SUAL, 23, 33, 97, 153, 191, 196
  tax claims, 116
  see also Vekselberg
Surgutneftegaz
  and Yuganskneftegaz, 131, 133, 142
  performance, 49, 90
  privatization of, 48–9
  shares-for-credit, 56
  tax payments, 146
  see also Bogdanov
Svyazinvest, 103–4, 105

Tax state theory, 4, 168–72, 176–7, 181
Taxation
  and Yukos, 110, 111, 135,
    145–6, 148
  arrears, 112–14, 135
  attitudes to, 15–16
  audits, 159, 163–4
  dobrosovestnyi, 164–8
  'domestic offshore zones', 118–19,
    129, 145, 165
  levels of, 93, 117, 146, 155–6
  minimization schemes, 68, 74, 118,
    119–20, 147, 159, 161, 166–7
  of resource sector, 15–16, 117
  reform of administration of, 156–7,
    163–8
  resource extraction tax (NDPI), 117,
    156–7, 205
  tax terror, 161, 167–8, 216, 218
  virtual economy, 113–14

Theede, Steven, 127, 129
TNK (Tiumen Oil Company)
  deal with BP, 109, 154
  formation, 49
  tax arrears, 154
Tolkach, 12, 26, 182
Tolling, 51, 69, 116
TPP, *see* Chamber of Commerce and
    Industry
Transfer pricing, 62, 92
Tulachermet, 85
Turushchev, Mikhail, 50, 53
TWG (TransWorld Group), 32, 68
  at Krasnoyarsk Aluminium Plant,
    51, 53, 66
  at Sayanogorsk Aluminium Plant,
    35, 64
  tolling, 69, 116

Usmanov, Alisher Burkhanovich, 23

Vekselberg, Viktor Feliksovich (1957–),
    23, 33
  see also SUAL, Renova, TNK
Vinogradov, Vladimir Viktorovich
    (1955–)
  beginnings in business, 42
  biography, 25, 28
  collapse of business, 22, 185
  involvement in politics, 100
  see also Inkombank
Voloshin, Aleksandr Stalevich, 108,
    122, 126, 143
Volsky, Arkadii Ivanovich, xi,
    44, 105
  on arrest of Khodorkovsky, 122,
    124, 207
  on arrest of Lebedev, 121
  see also Russian Union of
      Industrialists and Entrepreneurs

World Bank, 14–17, 183

Yeltsin, Boris Nikolaevich
  as referee, 105, 107
  attitude towards oligarchs, 10, 11
  Family, 106, 107, 108, 122, 202, 210
  links with Berezovsky, 34
  re-election, 8, 104, 105, 201

Young Communist League, *see*
    Komsomol
Yuganskneftegaz, 49
  payment for, 133
  price for, 130–1
  sale of, 130–6
Yukos
  and minorities, 61–3
  and Sibneft, 126, 141–2
  arrests of executives, 127, 129, 136,
    140, 160
  bankruptcy, 129, 136
  formation, 48–9
  internal conflict, 128
  investment in, 126, 141–2
  investment by, 96
  lobbying, 140–1
  negotiations with government, 128
  performance, 49, 59, 63, 89–91
  sale of Yuganskneftegaz, 134
  searches of, 122–3

  shares-for-credit, 56
  tax claims, 127, 128–9
  threat to licences, 126–7
  transfer pricing, 62–3
  value transfer, 62, 160
  see also Khodorkovsky,
    Yukos affair
Yukos affair
  and 'rule of law', 152
  and social responsibility, 74
  attitudes towards, 13, 17
  consequences of, 149–55, 218
  explanations of, 136–48
  initiator of, 104, 137, 141–2
  reactions to, 126
  Rosneft, 23
'Yukos amendment', 119

Zavlab (*zaveduiushchii laboratoriei*),
  29–30, 33, 35
Zhivilo, Mikhail Iurevich, 64–5